READING THE RENAISSANCE

GARLAND STUDIES IN THE RENAISSANCE
VOLUME 4
GARLAND REFERENCE LIBRARY OF THE HUMANITIES
VOLUME 1986

Garland Studies in the Renaissance
Raymond B. Waddington, *Series Editor*

READING THE RENAISSANCE
CULTURE, POETICS, AND DRAMA

EDITED BY
JONATHAN HART

GARLAND PUBLISHING, INC.
NEW YORK AND LONDON
1996

Library of Congress Cataloging-in-Publication Data

Reading the Renaissance : culture, poetics, and drama / [edited by] Jonathan
Hart.
      p.   cm. — (Garland reference library of the humanities ; vol.
1986. Garland studies in the Renaissance ; vol. 4)
   Includes bibliographical references and index.
   Contents: Reading the Renaissance : an introduction / Jonathan Hart
— Ritual and text in the Renaissance / Thomas M. Greene — Reading in the
French Renaissance / Steven Rendall — Reading Ultima verba : Montaigne
and commemoration / Lisa Neal — Gender ideologies, women writers, and
the problem of patronage in early modern Italy and France / Carla Freccero
— Female transvestism and male self-fashioning in As you like it and La vida
es sueño / Katy Emck — The ends of Renaissance comedy / Jonathan Hart
— Troilus and Cressida / Robert Rawdon Wilson and Edward Milowicki —
Two tents on Bosworth Field / Harry Levin — As they did in the golden
world : romantic rapture and semantic rupture in As you like it / Keir Elam
— Noble deeds and secret singularity : Hamlet and Phèdre / Paul Morrison
— Narrative and theatre : from Manuel Puig to Lope de Vega / Richard A.
Young.
   ISBN 0-8153-2355-7 (alk. paper)
   1. European literature—Renaissance, 1450–1600—History and criti-
cism. 2. Renaissance.   I. Hart, Jonathan Locke, 1956– . II. Series:
Garland reference library of the humanities ; vol. 1986. III. Series: Garland
reference library of the humanities. Garland studies in the Renaissance ;
vol. 4.
PN603.R38   1996
809'.894'09031—dc20

                                                       95–25955
                                                          CIP

Printed on acid-free, 250-year-life paper
Manufactured in the United States of America

For G. Blakemore Evans

ACKNOWLEDGEMENTS

Reading the Renaissance has taken shape over a number of years. Robert Rawdon Wilson was instrumental in encouraging the idea for the volume and Milan Dimić in its execution. The contributors have been a pleasure to work with and have exercised the kind of patience that only those who have contributed to books know all too well. Such a volume is a collective and cooperative undertaking. This book began to take shape at Harvard and started to come together as part of my experience at the School of Criticism and Theory at Dartmouth College. The connection with Harvard forms part of the dedication. One of the contributors, Harry Levin, died before the book could appear in print. Its appearance is also to remember him. More formally, I would like to dedicate the volume to Gwynne Evans, who has been generous in his encouragement of my work in Shakespeare and the Renaissance.

My thanks also to the University of Alberta, especially to the offices of the Vice-Presidents, Academic and Research, for supplying support for the preparation of the manuscript. Lynn Penrod, then Associate Vice-President (Academic), deserves particular thanks. Steven Tötösy has kindly acted as a consultant on manuscript preparation on this and other projects. Roumiana Deltcheva has brought her considerable skills to preparing the manuscript, including the index. Besides these colleagues, I want to thank the anonymous readers and editors who read the manuscript with scrupulous attention. Above all, my thanks to Raymond Waddington, Series Editor, Garland Studies in the Renaissance, whose skill and efficiency matched his good nature. M.V. Dimić, who has also included this collection of the Bibliothèque de la *Revue Canadienne de Littérature Comparée* / Library of the *Canadian Review of Comparative Literature*, has granted us some associated permissions. Phyllis Korper, Senior Editor at Garland, warrants special mention for her prompt and imaginative plan for the publication of the volume. I thank friends, family, and colleagues for encouraging my research. Finally, to my wife, Mary, and to my children, James and Julia, my gratitude for their support.

CONTENTS

JONATHAN HART

Reading the Renaissance: An Introduction

The "Renaissance," or early modern period, is an important term practically but is difficult to defend theoretically on all counts. A gap exists between historical events and the names contemporaries and later writers and historians give to them. Such a slippage between event and interpretation occurs with the Renaissance. It is a shifting signifier that travels from Italy to other countries and that, depending on the estimate, begins in the fourteenth century and ends in the late seventeenth century, although on the Continent, the Baroque subsumes much of what is generally taken in the English-speaking world to be the late Renaissance. There is now a penchant for disposing of the word "Renaissance," which has suffered from fatigue, changing usage, and vagueness as many important words do; but to replace it with "early modern" also has its difficulties. One of these problems is that the modern has been proclaimed for so long now that we have had to devise the prefixed subdivisions of "early" and "post" to extend the celebration of our modernity as if embarrassed at the length of the party and as if to hold on to the notion of ourselves as subsequent in the most modern of modern periods in order to deflect attention from our songs of ourselves or our ignorance and trembling at what comes next.

The Renaissance, which extends from about 1300 to 1700 depending on the country, was originally a rebirth of letters and arts but has come in the last two centuries to apply to wider cultural change in the face of modernization. Even in England, the Renaissance is said to begin in 1485 or 1500 or 1509 or at other times, so that to speak of Western Europe generally is an even more precarious activity. The title of this collection signals that even if the word "Renaissance" is problematic, it will be maintained. One of its virtues is that those living at the time thought they were involved in such a rebirth in the arts and used the word. The term "early modern," for all its sensitivity to the triumphal and celebratory uses of the label "Renaissance" to whip those dark and ignorant Middle Ages caught between two enlightened ages, might seem a little insulting for its assumption that Rabelais, Veronica Franco, Cervantes, and Mary Sidney all considered themselves as harbingers of a truly modern age. Being early can mean canonical priority and coming before, but it can also be construed as leading to

1

2 / Jonathan Hart

something else that is more developed or fully achieved. Although I mostly use the term "Renaissance," I occasionally will deploy the alternate "early modern," perhaps to suggest that, while the one is preferable, both have their drawbacks and neither is adequate. It did not take the late twentieth century to observe the hubris of the Renaissance: in 1603 Samuel Daniel disapproved of the habit amongst humanists of speaking of other ages or peoples as barbarous because to be human implied some worth wherever and whenever (see Norbrook xxii, xxiii-xxvi; Ferguson, Quilligan, and Vickers xvii). Although *Reading the Renaissance: Culture, Poetics, and Drama* does not focus on periodization, it assumes an overlap between the Middle Ages and the Renaissance at the beginning of the period and between the Renaissance and the Enlightenment at the end. Literary history, like history itself, is full of uneven developments, where a medieval idea or practice can coincide with a humanist one during the Renaissance or early modern period.

What is important is for this and other studies to expand our notion of the literary production and reception of the period from about 1485 to 1660. The plurality of voices and readers needs to be heard as more manuscripts are discovered and different kinds of texts come to be valued. The Renaissance is an expanding discipline in which successive generations bring new but related concerns to an archive that is coming more and more to light. The most distinctive contribution of this volume to Renaissance studies is that it is a collection of essays by a group of international scholars who have in common an interest in a comparative study of the Renaissance. Most often, scholars examine the national literatures of the Renaissance in isolation (see Ferguson *et al.* for a notable exception to this rule). This volume is a reminder of the importance of the comparative nature of the Renaissance, that national literatures are not enough by themselves. Comparative Literature, Comparative European Studies, and World Literature attempt to redress the isolationism that grows around languages. It is imperative to remember the central role of language in culture because its obviousness often obscures that centrality. Even in a few of the essays that are apparently about a single author, the contributors draw crucial comparisons between past and present and set out a wider cultural context. The essays relate to one another on many levels but most closely according to four categories, which constitute the first four parts. The relation between the text and the reader defines the rhetorical and historical dimensions of public and private selves.

The essays represent a plural Renaissance and explore the boundaries between genre and gender, languages and literatures, reading and criticism, the Renaissance and the medieval, the early modern and the postmodern, world and theatre. There is also a plurality of methods that is fitting for the variety of topics and the richness of the Renaissance. Without trying to fit the essays into a term, the contiguity of interests and the openness of the collection might well suggest a way of looking at the Renaissance and at literature and history generally — cultural pluralism.

Cultural pluralism involves an awareness of past and present. It takes into account the increasingly pluralistic nature of Western society without discounting the work of earlier scholars with different models and interests, working in different contexts. The best that has been thought and said here moves beyond Arnold's classless society, but includes it as a utopian figure in a new historical situation. Modernism and postmodernism can oppose each other but coexist. For instance, from earlier scholars interested in modernism, scholars can learn about the nature of metaphor and its putative unity, while others concerned with postmodernism and poststructuralism can discuss the alienation or ideology behind that religious and ritual impulse. It is quite conceivable that a critic or theorist could perform both operations in the same essay. The deductive nature of some propositional theory can check and be checked by close reading. Within each method and interest — and feminism is particularly striking here — there is great variety and change over time, so that part of historical reading of the Renaissance has to take into account as much the current theoretical context as the one being studied in the early modern period. The subjects of study, history and literature, are so complex that an understanding of the relation between past and present requires a multifold practice and theory. If each method, and the variants within, allows us to see text and world in a new and illuminating way, then readers, students, and scholars observe more. One theory is not enough.

There is no programmatic *parti pris* for a certain kind of Renaissance in these essays, rather a creative identity and friction. This study does not argue for erasing all differences, but, paradoxically, acknowledges difference as a means of creating an open-ended community, where continuity and change both play a part. Cultural pluralism includes the differences between current feminist views of Renaissance women and those in that period because not to know about this area lessens our understanding of the subject.[1] The European encounter with the Americas also makes an appearance in this volume, but as part of other discussions.[2] Cultural pluralism, while explaining the coherent but diverse contributions in this collection, is the result of collecting the essays, and not the goal. No appeal was made for essays on cultural pluralism. The essays engage different theories and practices. In the dance of culture there is more than one spin.

This collection represents a cultural pluralism implying that the study of literature should be related to its cultural context in many ways and that studying one country and its literature is enriched by an examination of other literatures. In this view, Comparative Literature includes or is allied with Cultural Studies. A wide definition of Comparative Literature extends to comparisons between literary texts and theories of different cultures; and takes philosophy into account as much as history, anthropology as much as sociology; but in its discussion of rhetoric, linguistics, semantics, and semiotics, maintains an interest in poetics and its possible and fictional worlds.[3]

Reading the Renaissance is organized along the lines of a double movement. The first is between the Middle Ages and the postmodern age as mediated through the Renaissance. The second movement involves four parts but the general theme is a definition of self or subject, as reader or as a man or woman, in history or as a foreshadowing of the future. Who is the reader and what is his or her relation to the text and how continuous or discontinuous is that text with the past or the future are the principal concerns of the collection.

The coherence of the collection depends on the relation of text to context and the way the Renaissance relates to the classical past and the modernity and postmodernity it anticipates. The first section discusses general theoretical concerns such as the nature of the literary text, the status of the reader, and the constitution of the self. Thomas M. Greene opens the collection with a discussion of the literary text as a fall from the sacred into the secular. The memory of a lost unity or the desire for the recovering of unity is the subject of the remaining essays. Can the reader reform the meaning of the text? Must a movement from medieval community to Renaissance self be paradoxical? The second part is on genre and gender. Carla Freccero begins the section with an examination of the role of women within the ideology of patronage. Katy Emck's essay also explores the relation between male and female in the construction of genre. In the third section there is an examination of the continuities and discontinuities between the Renaissance and the classical past. My essay, which begins this part, looks at the conflict between the desire to emulate within the context of new social pressures the order of classical comedy and Renaissance theatrical innovations. Three case studies examine Shakespeare in the context of what persists and desists in the production and reproduction of culture. The fourth section is about how the Renaissance anticipates modernity and postmodernity. Paul Morrison's essay opens with an examination of how Shakespeare looks ahead to Racine and how they both foreshadow different aspects of modernity. Richard A. Young's essay also discusses how innovative Renaissance writers challenge past conventions to such an extent that in some cases they can tell us something about contemporary theory or postmodernism. From the memories of the classical past to an anticipation of the modern and postmodern worlds, *Reading the Renaissance* explores the exciting and volatile world of the text and the self, as played out in a drama between writer and reader, dramatist and audience. The Renaissance looks back and ahead but through its own presence. We look back to and through the Renaissance and anticipate the future in ways that reproduce and reproach this past, believing that to ignore our Renaissance past is to be ignorant of our present.

"The Text, the Reader, and the Self" addresses questions that have been controversial in literary studies for nearly thirty years. Where we once had works, we now have texts; where we once had the author, we now have the reader; where we once had the individual, we now have the self. And the self has been yielding to the subject. In this ground of subjectivity in the Renaissance we are perhaps more likely to hear about Freud, Foucault, and Lacan than we are Luther, Calvin, and Francis Bacon. This twentieth-century interest in the modern personality is not necessarily narcissistic — and here I allude to Freud quite consciously — because we view the Renaissance through our eyes. As Peter Gay notes, "Freud's terminology and his essential ideas pervade contemporary ways of thinking about human feelings and conduct" (*Freud Reader*, xiii). When present meets past, as it must in any kind of interpretation, including literary and historical hermeneutics, it is impossible to escape the present. What can be done is to contrast the present and the past as well as to compare them, so that estrangement reminds us that Freud's interpretations of Da Vinci or Michelangelo, or our own, are not how they or their contemporaries would have seen themselves, even if there are homologies between the myths Freud drew on to analyze human personality and those it created.[4] The estrangement of historical imagination and analysis helps to create a critical distance that allows us to see the historical text, reader, or self more clearly or at least with more understanding. This return to the past, no matter how repressed it is, requires a close investigation of Renaissance texts and history. It also suggests new hypotheses about the period. A shift from the psychological or psychoanalytical to the material conditions of book production and reading during the Renaissance can also be instructive. The essays in this section pay close attention to Renaissance texts in defining problems surrounding interpretation and the relation of private and public selves. Through the printing press and the subsequent dissemination of books by means of mechanical reproduction, the Renaissance is partly responsible for subverting a more fluid medieval notion of the text, based in part on orality and memory. The Renaissance reader was becoming a solitary figure before a more controlled and fixed book. The very reproduction and wide circulation of a book gives the illusion of a fixity of meaning. The solitary self, less dependent on an audience, begins to mark the Renaissance reader. This is a simple narrative and an abstract and chronicle of our times, at least the way the Renaissance selfhood and subjectivity is too often constructed at conferences devoted to Renaissance literature. There is, of course, some truth to this construction, but the Renaissance maintains some of the orality it inherits from the Middle Ages while it disseminates printed books. But these volumes were not available to all, so that the duality of oral and print culture applied most explicitly and widely to the literate. Oral culture still dominated the illiterate. It took until the late nineteenth and into this century (not that the process is yet complete) to produce cheap books and have public education. One problem with creating too much of a break between the Middle Ages and the Renaissance based on print is that the Renaissance is also unabashedly oral. Plays and sermons are essential to the period. But then so are pageants and paintings and other visual arts. The Bible is just one of the "little books" that cause so much controversy in the period, which is also highly literate. The Church disintegrated into churches while many countries in Western Europe began to centralize, although Italy (1861) and Germany (1871) are exceptions that almost deny the rule. Rather than insist on a schematic view of this complexity, the essays in "The Text, the Reader, and the Self" explore the fault lines. Whose text, what reader, and whose self have recently become pressing questions in the field.

In this section, Thomas M. Greene's essay dramatizes the absence of a discipline — "historical semiotics" — and discusses ritual in narrative terms. He argues that the shifting status of the ritual or ceremonial sign in society also affects the literary imagination. Greene implies that the shift from the referential to relational bears on the representation and narrativization of ceremony and ritual across genres. Ritual occurs in public ceremonies, which Greene examines in terms of the new power of the centralizing monarchy and as socially symbolic acts with their own theatrics and narratives. The movement from magical semiotics in the Middle Ages to an increasingly disjunctive semiotics during the Renaissance is reflected in literary representations. Writers incorporate ceremonies into their narratives and plays, and these ceremonies appear more vulnerable in Renaissance texts than medieval ones. In early modern texts, however, there remains a vestigial hope in the power of ceremony. Paradoxically, the questioning of ceremony during the Renaissance allows a space to play with ceremonial symbols (see Waswo 3-83). Greene asks how these narratives incorporate into themselves the crisis in ritual and signification in which there is an emptying out of the sign. In "Reading in the French Renaissance: Textual Communities, Boredom, Privacy," Steven Rendall discusses the relation between public and private in the changing practice of reading from the Middle Ages to the Renaissance. Storytelling chases away idleness in the texts by Boccaccio and Marguerite. During the Renaissance, public readings required patient listeners, even if only parts of Honoré D'Urfé's huge pastoral novel, *L'Astrée* (1607, 1635) were being read. In all these works the pastoral settings of the country allow for the leisure to tell and listen properly. For the modern audience, time is to be saved and not, as for the Renaissance audience, to be spent, so that D'Urfé's novel often appears boring now. It also shows signs of anxiety over the possibility that its tales might produce boredom. In Boileau's *L'Art poétique* (pub. 1674) the stylistic failure imagined is one that leads to a bored reader or listener. A cultural shift that concentrates more and more attention on the individual and private life seems to occur in the seventeenth century. Rendall suggests that the models of reading in Renaissance texts like the *Heptaméron* can help us to understand reading practices, to remember group and public aspects in our age of silent and private reading. In "Reading *Ultima Verba:* Commemoration and Friendship in Montaigne's Writing," Lisa Neal also examines models of reading. Two views of language enable two opposing paradigms of reading in Montaigne's *Essais:* meaning depends on reading, which is a kind of rewriting; readers reproduce unequivocal meaning that they perceive in the discourse. Death scenes, as they reveal the character of the dying, provide an illustration of the second model. Both models co-exist in the tradition of last words and in Montaigne. But he would like to die on horseback — alone. Neal gives several reasons for Montaigne's attempt to break with the tradition of last words and friendship in his own death. Montaigne ended up commemorating in advance his own death, which was in bed, but his friend, Pierre de Brach, also reported the end in a way that Montaigne could not have done, given his aphasia before death.

Feminism and gender studies have brought vast changes to the study of the Renaissance. One aspect of selfhood and subjectivity, gender needs to be as much understood as class, race, and ideology when seeking a greater comprehension of Renaissance culture and literature. The role of women in literature is something that literary theorists have been exploring increasingly. Historians also have responded to exhortations to study gender by scholars as prominent as Natalie Zemon Davis ("'Women's History' in Transition" 90). The debate is lively and informative, but inconclusive. Ruth Kelso and Joan Kelly have both argued that medieval aristocratic women were freer in social and sexual relations than their counterparts in the Renaissance, which constitutes an opposite view to the sexual equality thesis set out by writers as different as Jacob Burckhardt and Simone de Beauvoir (see Kelso; Kelly 22, 33, 39-47; Maclean 7-8, 24-26; Hart, *Theater and World* 263-70, 324-26). There is some controversy over whether the

Renaissance helped to subject or liberate women. If we are to assume that the roles of women were changing in the early modern period, but not always in ways that moved women closer to equality with men, then it is fruitful to observe how gender ideologies prevented or permitted women room to manoeuvre, how female writers represented women and how cross-dressing and female transvestism defined the boundaries in gender roles between men and women. The controversy over the role of women we observe in feminism and gender studies of the past few decades focuses in part on the Renaissance controversy over women but differs from that debate (see Bornstein; Ferguson *et al.*; Angerman; Jones, *Currency of Eros*; Jordan; Davis and Farge). The contributors to this section, "Gender and Genre," explore the complexities of gender through the different kinds of writing that male and female writers choose. They come up with different conclusions; but they agree that gender is a principal relation in the production and reception of Renaissance texts. Texts, readers, and selves are not gender neutral. The construction of gender and its manifestations in the representation and regulation of the body is something that changes from classical times through the Renaissance to the present (see Laqueur, *Making Sex*).

Carla Freccero relates the question of identity to women and ideology in her essay, "Gender Ideologies, Women Writers, and the Problem of Patronage in Early Modern Italy and France: Issues and Frameworks." She surveys the ideologies governing the relation between "woman" and speech or writing in order to understand what it might have meant, for the woman and the society, to be a woman writing in early modern Europe. The relation between patronage and absence for women writers is another concern for Freccero, who supplements previous work in psychoanalysis, feminism, and new historicism on gender and the body. Freccero sets out some of the discourses that define woman in early modern Italy and France: the woman who speaks as a danger; the sinful seductress; woman as property. During this period, class conflict and political instability also meet in the discourse on woman. In early modern Italy and France, women had to negotiate their unruly desires through these ideological territories: they defended their public role. How did women enter the public sphere? She discusses the cases of Christine de Pisan, Marguerite de Navarre, Veronica Franco, Tullia d'Aragona, Pernette du Guillet and Louise Labé (see Cooper 21; Ford 118, 133; Charpentier 182; Gabe 201).[5] Freccero concentrates on the relations between male patrons and female writers because, although noblewomen in early modern Europe also acted as patrons, this role did not challenge the gender ideologies of the time. She observes a complex relation between culture and politics, so that even when female patronage and writers are breaking new ground, women themselves can be exploited socially, politically, and economically. In Katy Emck's "Female Transvestism and Male Self-Fashioning in *As You Like It* and *La vida es sueño*," the emphasis also is on the boundaries of gender. She thinks that female transvestism during the Renaissance is allied to male identity and sets out to demonstrate how the motif of female power, deception, and insurgency becomes a resonant symbol for the construction of male identities. The transvestism of the heroines, Rosaura and Rosalind, is a basis for the development of autonomous male subjects at the centre of the two plays: Segismundo and Orlando. In both dramas, the female transvestite functions as trace and form of anxiety over self-fashioned male identity. Female transvestism figures the transgressing ambition of the heroes, their problematic relation to patriarchy and social mobility in a transition that threatens categories of identity even while transforming them into forms of stability. The hero's triumph of selfhood depends on the female transgression of role. Emck illustrates this point beyond the two plays by relating the attacks on women in the theatre in Spain with the transgression of sumptuary laws by men and women in England: class and gender come into play here. Dependency on the patriarch connects women with men who are not head of the household.

"Continuities and Discontinuities," the third section of the collection, is comprised of essays that examine the affiliations and breaks among Renaissance national literatures and between them and their classical past. During this period, there were a great number of translations of both classical and modern literary works. This comparison between the classical and the contemporary pervades the culture. In George Puttenham's rhetoric, *The Arte of English Poesie* (1589), he attributes the rebirth of learning in culture and the arts to the time of Charlemagne and does not view the Renaissance as a light after a dark age: "till after many yeares that the peace of Italie and of th' Empire Occidentall reuiued new clerkes, who recouering and perusing the bookes and studies of the ciuiler ages, restored all maner of arts, and that of the Greeke and Latine Poesie withall into their former puritie and netnes" (11, see 12). For Puttenham, rhyme was a barbarous addition that not even this revival in learning could purge from the European courts. The classical past is never far from Puttenham's mind. He says that poetry means making as much in English as in Greek: the poet is a maker and a counterfeiter or imitator as can be seen in the way Homer, a private man, can represent a great public world (3-4). The image of Troy, which stood before poets throughout Europe during the Renaissance, is a trope for that history and the great epic about it. The source of classical European culture is in that siege. Plato's critique of Homer is part of Puttenham's discussion of poetry. Puttenham's categories of genre depend on classical writers, for instance his citation of Menander and Aristophanes as comical poets, who recreated in plays the life, manners, and speech of "priuate persons, and such as were the meaner sort of men," a view not unlike that in Aristotle's *Poetics* (25). Both English and European, Puttenham praises where praise in cultural transmission is due and condemns where it is not. He notes the fine imitation of Petrarch by Surrey and Wyatt (62) but criticizes an English translator for not crediting Ronsard's fine translation of Greek lyrics by Pindar and others and for failing to translate the French at all in places (252-53). Puttenham shows anxiety over improper loan words in English then as some cultures demonstrate in the face of English now. Generic conventions and translation, the image of Troy, Aristotelian imitation and temporal estrangement, the golden age, and the fallen world all figure in the continuities between literatures in Renaissance Europe and in their recovery and reconstitution of the classical past. Each contributor in this section examines an aspect of the reproduction of classical culture and the break with it. What is in Puttenham is in their essays in a different form. In comedy, epic, history, and tragedy the rapture of the past often meets the rupture of the present. The continuities and discontinuities between the classical past and the Renaissance also extend into the present. Contemporary theory and criticism refracts the relation between Greece, Rome, and Renaissance Europe.

"Continuities and Discontinuities" begins with my essay, "The Ends of Renaissance Comedy," which argues that, while there is no denying the order brought to bear at the end of most Renaissance comedies and that criticism has often emphasized the happy ending of comedy and the movement from order through disorder to order, this assumption of an orderly happy ending needs qualification. My essay points out that in Italian, Spanish, English, and French comedies of the early modern period, the very structure of the plays, the way they end, involves disjunction, stress, and rupture. The ends of comedy represent a return to order, but a restoration with loose ends. They are often asymmetrical and leave doubt in and with the audience. Here the exception while not proving the rule complicates it, and the comedies are not simply apologies for utopian hope or the existing social and political order. There should be a recognition of recognition in Renaissance comedy. The narrative of Troy in Shakespeare is a central concern for Robert Rawdon Wilson and Edward Milowicki. In "*Troilus and Cressida*: Voices in the Darkness of Troy," they examine the mixing of genres, notably the epic rhetoric of honour with the romance rhetoric of love. The Renaissance seems to have found in Troy, especially in Hecuba, a figure of sorrow. In redefining the relation between love and honour in this play, Shakespeare is especially innovative, although Chrétien in *Yvain* and Chaucer in the *Franklin's Tale* are unconventional in their views of love and honour.

Shakespeare seems to have taken off from Ovid's representation of the heroic in the *Metamorphoses* and to have known about the re-casting of the Trojan War during the Middle Ages following the inspiration of Ovid and Virgil. Shakespeare uses many Ovidian conventions for creating character: all belong to the repertory of Medieval and Renaissance literature. The one convention that *Troilus* employs most is self-consciousness resulting in ironic undercutting. Drama has various classical and modern contexts, such as culture, poetics, and narrative, that can be refracted through a reading of Renaissance texts. Shakespeare's history plays, which give a shape to the flow of time, present a good opportunity in observing such continuities and discontinuities. A tension exists in these histories between the classical epic inheritance and the native chronicle play. Shakespeare innovates while he inherits. In "Two Tents on Bosworth Field: *Richard III* V.iii, iv, v," Harry Levin examines these scenes from the final act of Shakespeare's history play as theatrical text and in historical context. Levin says that in Tudor England, which was consolidating patriotism within a national ideology, chronicle and play conflated into the English history play, which might be considered as a kind of dramatic narrative or narrative drama. Keir Elam, too, uses Shakespeare's drama to relate the classical world to our present through the Renaissance. The reproduction of romance is, appropriately, never ending no matter how many happy ends. "As They Did in the Golden World: Romantic Rapture and Semantic Rupture in *As You Like It*" argues that Shakespeare's play lifts its *fabula* or story material and much of its plot from its source, Thomas Lodge's *Rosalynde*, which in turn borrows its *fabula* from its medieval source, *Gamelyn*, while shifting focus from events to their setting, ordering, and language. Pastoral tells a story of a nostalgic golden world: Theocritus, Tasso, and Sidney represent such a world. Romance has magical properties. In *As You Like It*, Shakespeare opposes semantic rupture to the romantic rapture of pastoral. This opposition transforms the iconic to the ironic and thus works against pastoral nostalgia. The idea that nature manifests itself as a language to the uninitiated belongs to the philosophical Platonism and pastoral drama of Renaissance Italy and its imitations in England.

"Anticipations" includes essays most concerned with specific foreshadowings of later texts in Renaissance texts. This intertextuality can be as close in time as Shakespeare and Racine, a classic instance of the early bilateral French model of Comparative Literature, to an exploration of the modern and postmodern in the early modern. Each of the essays in this part looks at the incipient modern in Renaissance texts. But even in comparing Racine and Shakespeare, there is a comparison with Goethe and the makers of the modern novel. This is not surprising considering Brian McHale's observation in *Postmodernist Fiction* that this most recent imaginative writing depends in part on heterocosm, a classical theme in poetics — the alterity or otherness of fictional worlds, something he finds in Sidney's discussion of the poet's wit and invention in his *Defense* (27-29). In an essay in *Postmodernism Across the Ages*, Bennet Schaber returns to Giotto in Boccaccio's *Decameron* to find a postmodern moment, "a moment in the history of representation when its essence as a history of deceptions, of errors, is exposed, but only insofar as that exposure itself becomes liable to the deceptions inherent in all representation" (60). Schaber is arguing for a recognition of otherness which might involve deception. Stephen Knight has used the term "postmodern medievalism" in his discussion of Chaucer (3). In *Voice Terminal Echo* Jonathan Goldberg discusses the relation between postmodernism and texts from Renaissance England, arguing that textuality always existed and that there was not a naive and romantic body before "the opening of the modern abyss" (ix-x). Like Auerbach, Lyotard sees modernity as a mode, not an epoch, that begins with Augustine's *Confessions*, a kind of paratactic attack on the syntactical shape of classical discourse, something encountered in Rabelais, Montaigne, Shakespeare, Sterne, Joyce, and Stein (Lyotard 24, 43). For Lyotard, the "post" of postmodernism does not mean repetition but a procedure of analysis, anagogy, anamnesis, and anamorphosis that makes us face the responsibility for modernity, especially for its dark side. Postmodernism does not let us get away with our initial forgetting, just as psychoanalysis will not allow the patient to forget that initial amnesia (79-80). Whether we agree with Lyotard, he raises some crucial points about how modernity and postmodernity relate. Does one anticipate the other historically and technically? As we move to a section, "Anticipations," in which the early modern anticipates the modern and postmodern, it is fruitful to think about Lyotard's assertion: "It seems to me that the essay (Montaigne) is postmodern, and the fragment (the *Athenaeum*) is modern" (15). If the postmodern is a technique found in Rabelais, Montaigne, Shakespeare, and Cervantes as well as in twentieth-century writers, then the only anticipation would be the temporal succession within a mode or technique. There is, then, a difference between technical and temporal anticipation.

The first essay of "Anticipations," "Noble Deeds and the Secret Singularity: *Hamlet* and *Phèdre*," emphasizes the differences between Shakespeare and us. Paul Morrison discusses these two plays through "generic dispensation" and Michel Foucault's view of the history of literary forms and of the social construction of subjectivity. The novel has displaced the drama from the centre of our literary culture because of form and subjectivity. Whereas *Hamlet* resists this displacement, *Phèdre* anticipates it. Hamlet searches for a genre and anticipates a novelistic or discursive subjectivity; but *Hamlet*, which is a

Renaissance play and not a proto-novel, will not grant him this untheatrical interiority and subjectivity. Hamlet identifies himself with theatre, although he speaks with an anti-theatrical prejudice, and identifies the body with the theatre. *Phèdre* does not fill up the stage with dead bodies as does *Hamlet* (see Barthes 24). Morrison's essay examines the resistance to, and anticipation of, the modern novel in these two influential Renaissance plays. Even the title of Richard A. Young's essay, "Narrative and Theatre: From Manuel Puig to Lope de Vega," makes apparent a focus on one of the central concerns of this part of the collection — the relation between the early modern and the modern and postmodern. Building on the postmodernist observation that art is now less about life than about how art represents it, Young suggests that metatheatre and metafiction are products of postmodernism that muddy the distinctions between literary genres. The Aristotelian principle for separating genres is based on the means of delivery and not on the type of discourse. The exploitation of the conventions or modes of discourse partly has led to the hybrids, theatrical novels and narrative theatre. Young wonders whether there is any difference between the general theatrical convention that Lope practises in one of his *comedias* and the metafictional device in Puig's novel where figures in a tale in which they participate tell tales while telling the tale in which they participate.

What emerges from these essays is a Renaissance that involves ruptures, shifting signs, a world of contesting identities, of flexible selves and subjectivity, a patronage network that used women as they used it, texts with plural voices, opposing ways of reading, cultural shifts, transgression, alienation, traces of ritual in ideology, mixing genres and genders, stress, crisis, and a challenge to the postmodern to come to terms with the pre or early modern. Even as this Renaissance is transgressive, it also represents a tension between the feudal and the bourgeois. The traces of this conflict are still with us. The question of identity hounds us still. If there is still a light in Troy, we cannot be sure whether it beckons us backwards or forwards or both. In reading the Renaissance we continue to read ourselves even when we think we have moved on, or especially when we think we have.

The Text, the Reader, and the Self

THOMAS M. GREENE

Ritual and Text in the Renaissance

The subject of this essay is the changing status of a certain kind of sign, and the effects of this change on literary texts, during that period we have come to call the Renaissance.[1] The changing sign is the symbolic act employed in ceremonial and ritual performances.[2] The symbolic act, the sign performed on repeated, formal, communal occasions, still exists in our contemporary society in various guises, but it no longer plays the dominant central role it plays in virtually all the traditional and archaic societies known to us. It no longer plays the role it played through most of the history of western civilization. The very word "ritual" today has acquired a clinical meaning; psychotherapists refer to certain neurotic compulsive habits as "private rituals." We are divided from most of human history by the waning of the ceremonial sign, and it is that incipient, massive, slow, uneven, almost invisible process of waning that deserves our attention. To discuss this process adequately would require the labour of a lifetime, or better, of a school. The brief historical notes that follow are not intended to demonstrate a thesis, but simply to state it.

The discomfort or indifference elicited by ritual in many modern men and women can be contrasted to the decisive role it played during the Middle Ages. It would be wrong, of course, to sentimentalize or oversimplify this role. Medieval ritual was itself subject to transmutation and debate and doubtless intermittent indifference. Nonetheless, the fabric of each medieval life was woven out of symbolic occasions. Each lifetime was punctuated by innumerable ceremonial observances, just as the organization of each year depended on a ceremonial calendar. The repeated, symbolic, communal, formal, efficacious act not only focused and defined the life of the church but also the life of the court, the city, the guild, the confraternity, the law court, the university, the aristocratic house and manor, the rustic countryside. The individual knew who he or she was, found his/her place in time and society, through this fabric of symbolic occasions. It is not too much to speak of each medieval individual as endowed with a ceremonial identity.

17

In the acquisition of this identity, ecclesiastical liturgy had a primary function. When Peter Lombard in the twelfth century fixed the number of sacraments at seven, he codified the great over-arching punctuation marks in every Christian life. In the sacraments and lesser rituals was grounded the certainty of one's status as Christian. Keith Thomas remarks that "The Church was important to [a medieval peasant] not because of its formalized code of belief, but because its rites were an essential accompaniment to the important events of his own life.... Religion was a ritual method of living, not a set of dogmas" (76-77). One is only tempted to question whether this view was limited to the peasant. Jean Daniélou has written that during the patristic era "les sacrements apparaissent comme les évènements essentials de l'existence chrétienne et de l'existence tout court, comme le prolongement des grandes oeuvres de Dieu, dans l'Ancient Testament et dans le Nouveau" (26). Something of this prestige still remained during the high Middle Ages and indeed in many pockets of European society far later. Daniélou shows that the symbolism of the sacraments was saturated in the history and ceremonial of the Old Testament. This ceremonial, in turn, had its roots in the archaic, nomadic, pre-Mosaic era of Jewish history. From the rites of that archaic society to the rituals of the medieval church there is much transformation but no rupture. The basic elements of the sacraments — sacrifice, purification, commensality, initiation, death and resurrection, union with the divine — are basic elements of rituals throughout the world. The particular Christian symbolic action links the worshipper indirectly with an immemorial universal action.

This weight of shared experience takes on a special drama when the ritual act is placed radically in question, as it was most visibly and articulately during the sixteenth century. It is true that this *mise en question* had anticipations throughout western history. The sacraments alone had provoked plenty of debate over the centuries, arguably beginning with the New Testament itself. There do at least appear to be divergences among the sacramental conceptions of Matthew, John, and Paul. The Scholastics debated the precise modality of the sacramental symbol's efficacity, the precise manner in which the sign instills grace. The Joachimite heresy of the thirteenth century was essentially anti-ritualist. The Twelve Conclusions of the Lollards (1395) included the affirmation "that exorcisms and hallowings, made in the Church, of wine, bread, and wax, water, salt and oil and incense, the stone of the altar, upon vestments, mitre, cross, and pilgrims' staves, be the very practice of necromancy, rather than of the holy theology" (Thomas 51). During the fifteenth century, a questioning of the *centrality* of ritual emerges both in the Hussite movement and the *devotio moderna*; gestural symbolism now begins to appear as external, empty, inessential. To find this attitude in Savonarola is perhaps not surprising, but we also hear something like it at the opening of the sixteenth century from the general of the Dominicans, the distinguished theologian Cajetan, who wrote after the sack of Rome that prelates of the Roman church had decayed until they were good for nothing beyond outward ceremonials (Hughes 474). Egidio da Viterbo, prior general of the Augustinian order under popes Julius II and Leo X, wrote repeatedly that the eucharist, performed without proper love and devotion, was a "*vanum opus*" (O'Malley, *Giles of Viterbo* 119).[3] This opinion was not of course heterodox, but its recurrence in Egidio's writing suggests a fear that the eucharist *had* become a mere formality. Thus the Roman sacraments were by no means untouched by ecclesiastical concern when the Reform called them into question. But it was the reformers who levelled most vigorously against sacraments and ceremonies the charge of externality and hollowness. With Luther, and earlier with Erasmus, we begin to find antitheses of inside and outside, an inner core of spiritual feeling contrasting with the outer pomp and magical hocus-pocus of the sign-in-itself. Erasmus, as Michael Screech has demonstrated, believed in the spiritual power of the sacrament but expressed scorn for ecclesiastical "*ceremoniolae*," rendered by Screech as "trivial little ritual nonsenses" (119). In Luther's *Babylonian Captivity of the Church*, at least two sacraments are retained (baptism and eucharist), but the repeated, symbolic act performed by the priest yields its determinant importance to the original, unique promise of Christ, a verbal act which the two remaining sacraments perpetuate. It is worth noting however that neither Luther nor Calvin nor Hooker at the end of the century could quite bring themselves to deny unambiguously *any* efficacious power to the sacraments retained. Calvin's thought seems to waver slightly, far more subtle and complex than the sweeping rejections of Zwingli and other Swiss reformers. One can trace even in the greatest of the revolutionaries a reluctance to dismiss the performative, efficacious sign.

If one moves beyond the sacraments, one encounters the curious destiny of the word "ceremony" and its cognates both in Latin and the continental vernaculars during the Renaissance. We have already met its slighting distortion in Erasmus. The historical dictionaries of the modern languages all record negative usages of this word beginning to appear for the first time a little before or after the turn of the sixteenth century. The *OED* gives the sub-definition for the word "ceremony": "a rite or observance regarded as merely formal or external; an empty form"; the first usage is dated 1533. In Italy there are analogous usages by Savonarola and Guicciardini, and in France by Commynes. In an ecclesiastical context, the term "ceremonies" came increasingly to designate the sensuous trappings of worship such as incense and vestments. In secular contexts, "ceremony" began to designate an excessive formality and overelaborate courtesy in social intercourse. Della Casa writes that he sees little difference between ceremonies, falsehoods, and dreams, when measured in terms of their insubstantiality (*vanità*) (della Casa and Castiglione 579). Du Bellay, appalled by the decadence of the mid-century papal court, wrote: "Je n'y trouve ... qu'une cerimonie" (1966; Sonnet 80). Montaigne, impatient with social formalities, wrote acidly: "Nous ne sommes que ceremonie" (*Essai* 2: 17).[4] Archbishop Cranmer, addressing Edward VI at his coronation in 1547, must have bewildered the boy by telling him that a king is God's anointed through divine election and that "the oil, if added, is but a ceremony" (Kantorowicz 318). Later John Donne would remark in a sermon "I have seen the state of Princes, and all that is but a ceremony, and I would be loath to put a Master of ceremonies to define ceremony, and tell me what it is" (382).[5] Robert Burton dismisses gentle birth as "a mere flash, a ceremony, a toy, a thing of nought" (*Anatomy of Melancholy* 501).

Usages like these and others suggest that a kind of crisis confronted the communal, performative sign. They do not, of course, signal any decline in the *frequency* of ceremonies, however the word is defined, except in Protestant worship. Arguably, in statistical terms, the sixteenth century provided more ritual and ceremonial occasions than any other century. It is also certain that large sectors of the population in every country were untouched by any ambivalence. Among the folk, the great popular festivities of Carnival, Midsummer Night, Yuletide, among others, seem to have continued unaltered. The newly powerful, centralized monarchies of the sixteenth century learned how to use ceremonial occasions brilliantly in order to aggrandize their own prestige. The medieval solemnity of the royal entry into a city received a new éclat; chivalric contests like the tilt and the joust were perpetuated; *mascarades, ballets de cours*, and court masques celebrated monarch and court with lavish splendour. But these brilliant fêtes heightened a manipulative element which had doubtless always been present. Despite their brilliance, we can no longer speak of the society of 1600 as we could in 1200 as a basically ceremonial society. In a growing sector of this society, we can no longer speak of ceremonial identity. During the religious wars in France, partisan mobs used ceremonial forms for their own brutal purposes, in what Natalie Davis has called "rites of violence." The traditional performative sign was called into question, and in the long run, as we in our own century can bear witness, it would enter a long decline. We may or may not regret the decline, but we are compelled to recognize in this slow, massive, uneven process a profound reversal in human techniques of signification. This shift may possibly have produced feelings of liberation, but it would be surprising if it did not also produce feelings of anxiety.

It would also be surprising if this shift did not affect the literary imagination. In fact of course it did, both directly and indirectly, and I want to turn now to a series of literary texts where the shifting status of the ritual or ceremonial sign is most clearly reflected. The choice of texts will necessarily be arbitrary and short. In some respects, as we shall see, literary history anticipated social and institutional history. We shall also see that with the decline of ceremonial force, writers felt freer to extemporize *ad hoc* ceremonies of their own.

A useful point of departure is the *Purgatorio* of Dante, surely the canticle of the *Commedia* which is most open to ritual action, from the symbolic girding of the pilgrim with the reed of humility in canto 1 to the magnificent and solemn procession of canto 29. A useful brief example can be found in the ninth canto, where Dante the pilgrim is permitted to enter Purgatory proper from the ante-Purgatory. Virgil and his companion come upon a small opening in the mountainside containing three steps, each of a different colour, topped by a gate guarded by an angel holding a sword and dressed in an ash-coloured garment. Dante throws himself before the angel's feet, strikes himself three times upon the breast, and formally requests that the gate be opened to him:

> Divoto mi gittai a' santi piedi;
>   misericordia chiesi e ch'el m'aprisse,
>   ma tre volte nel petto pria mi diedi.
> Sette *P* ne la fronte me descrisse
>   col punton de la spada, e "Fa che lavi,
>   quando se' dentro, queste piaghe" disse. (IX: 109-114)

The angel traces on the poet's forehead the letter *P* (for *peccato*) seven times, and tells him to wash away these wounds after he has entered. The angel then turns two keys, one silver and one gold, instructs Dante not to look behind him once inside, and opens the gate with a mighty roar. As the gate closes, the poet hears confusedly the sound of a "Te Deum," traditionally sung when an individual takes holy orders, although first sung spontaneously, according to an old story, by saints Ambrose and Augustine when the latter was baptised (Singleton 194). Marked as he is by his seven P's, the pilgrim hears the hymn dimly; its words blur with the sound of the gate closing behind him. Only later, in the twelfth canto, as Dante is about to leave the first terrace, does he discover that he has lost one of the letters graven on his forehead, as he will lose the rest, one by one, ascending from terrace to terrace to the earthly paradise.

Jacques Le Goff has shown how gradually and how late the conception of Purgatory acquired firm outlines during the Middle Ages and how important a role Dante played in fleshing out this conception. The little scene at the gate of Purgatory was invented without prior authority, while harmonizing flawlessly with the doctrinal and liturgical elements already available. The three colours of the three steps correspond to the three stages of penance. The ashen colour of the angel's vestment represents humility. The gold and silver keys have their own allegorical meaning. The "Te Deum" as we have seen recalls the sacrament of holy orders. But what is most arresting is the engraving of the seven P's upon the pilgrim's forehead.

Singleton interprets these as symbols of sinful inclinations to be progressively removed as Dante climbs the mountain, his ascent corresponding to that satisfaction by works which is the third stage of penance. Whether or not this is the precise meaning, it is important to recognize, as few commentators have, that the engraving recalls but reverses a symbolic gesture in the sacrament of baptism. A climactic element in that ritual is the *sphragis*, the marking of the catechumen's forehead with the sign of the cross by the officiating priest. The *sphragis* was the invisible but indelible seal of Christ which marked the newly baptised Christian as a soldier in God's army. In antiquity, a *sphragis* was a tattoo worn by a soldier or a slave to identify respectively his captain or his master, and in the slave's case the tattoo was placed on the forehead. A *sphragis* was also a brand marking sheep; it was probably the mark of Cain, placed on his forehead to protect him; it appears to refer to the *Tau* of Ezekiel 9 placed by God on the foreheads of those to be spared from the destruction of Jerusalem; in this case it should also refer to the saints of Apocalypse 7 marked with the sign of the lamb (an episode which itself echoes Ezekiel).[6] Dante the poet alludes to this Biblical and sacramental symbol but he also transforms it, from the T of the cross to the P of sin, from the indelible mark of Christian commitment to the delible symbol of sin overcome. Thus, in this dense evocation of a rite of passage, Dante mingles elements from at least three sacraments — penance most visibly but also holy orders and baptism. He invents a syncretic ritual, heavy with allegorical symbolism, reweaving and reconceptualizing the millennial forms of the existing sacraments. His adaptation of the *sphragis* even leaves ritual open to a touch of humour when, in the twelfth canto, the pilgrim has to grope with his hand on his forehead to discover his loss of the first letter while Virgil smiles. The privileged role Dante will give in the *Paradiso* to the Florentine baptistery with its fount, the "fonte del mio battesmo" (IX: 8-9) — the site of his fantasized future laureation — underscores his own ceremonial identity. But his freedom in improvising a solemn, efficacious symbol suggests an open space for ritual invention toward the end of the Middle Ages in Italy. His invented ritual does not leave the impression, as subsequent analogues will, of an insecure grounding.

One other feature of this scene is worth noting, a feature that looks backward to the traditional sacraments and indeed to most ritual performance everywhere, but also anticipates the invented rituals we will encounter in Renaissance texts. This element might most properly be called "magic," if that term is understood to denote the use of signs, words, gestures, objects, and images to represent that which they attempt to bring into being. Magic for our purposes can be described as that art which uses representation to effect an end. By this very broad definition, a sacrament is magical because it depends on efficacious representation. According to the Council of Trent, it is "the symbol of a sacred thing, having the power of sanctifying" (*symbolum rei sacrae ... sanctificandi vim habens*). Thus the imposition and removal of the seven P's are also magical, as is the symbolic opening of the massive gate of Purgatory. Without the element of magic, the rite of passage could not properly be termed a ritual at all. One need only add that Dante's use of performative liturgical magic accords perfectly with that of the ecclesiastical tradition.

The space for ritual invention which opens more than once in the *Commedia* reopens in a less solemn context on the pages of Boccaccio's *Decameron*. When, at the opening of that book, the city of Florence is stricken with plague, its civic and ecclesiastical institutions break down. The number of the dead overwhelms the ceremonial disposition of their bodies and turns the funeral service into a mockery. It is after attendance at mass that the ten young men and women, gathered in Santa Maria Novella, decide to flee together to a villa outside the city. Once they have arrived, Dioneo, the most aggressive of the men, makes a speech in favour of self-indulgence and hedonist freedom. The leader of the women, Pampinea, responds by expressing her own hope for a pleasurable life together, moderated by reason, and to ensure the highest and most orderly pleasure, proposes that each member of the group take his or her turn as king or queen for a day. When this happens, another young woman runs to a nearby laurel tree, breaks off a few sprigs, fashions a garland, and places it upon the head of Pampinea, elected the first queen.

Queste parole sommamente piacquero e ad una voce lei per reina del primo giorno elessero: e Filomena, corsa prestamente ad uno alloro, per ciò che assai volte aveva udito ragionare di quanto onore le frondi di quello eran degne e quanto degno d'honore facevano chi n'era meritamente incoronato, di quello alcuni rami colti, ne le fece una ghirlanda onorevole e apparente; la quale,

> messale sopra la testa, fu poi mentre durò la lor compagnia manifesto segno
> a ciascuno altro della real signoria e maggioranza. (Boccaccio 40-41)

This little improvised ceremony is interesting because, unlike many other historical and literary laureations, it has no precedent and thus no determinate meaning. There exists no precedent because the community itself has none. It will remain for the future, as the crown is passed from monarch to monarch, it will remain for the contest of wills between the sexes and between individuals to define the precise power of the king or queen and thus the meaning of the laureation.

This instance of ceremonial play can be contrasted with an episode from an earlier, youthful work by Boccaccio, the prose romance *Filocolo*. In a section of that work, still essentially medieval, a group of young people recite the case histories of lovers and debate their rights and wrongs. But before debating these *questioni*, questions of lovers' conduct, a young woman, Fiammetta, is chosen as "queen," and a coronet of laurel is placed upon her pretty head. The queen thus becomes the arbitress in a court of love, a familiar institution both in medieval society and literature. The scene of *her* laureation is charming but not surprising, and her prerogatives are well-defined by tradition. She becomes queen through a kind of ludic magic. Fiammetta's position is not open-ended; it lacks the improvisatory and experimental character of its counterpart in the *Decameron*. In the shift from the youthful work to the mature one, from one kind of play to another, we can observe Boccaccio entering that civilization we have come to call the Renaissance. In comparison with Dante's improvised ceremony, this one involves a greater degree of uncertainty; its meaning remains to be specified and the duration of its power is circumscribed ("mentre durò la lor compagnia"). The causal relation between gesture and effect is thin. The actual effect, that is to say the relative authority of king or queen, has to be worked out though communal interplay. The authority is not empty, since it includes the power to determine the theme of a given day's stories and thus the day's moral tone. Nonetheless, this authority is never allowed to exceed certain limits. At the end, as we know, the *brigata* will not try to maintain its tenuous order beyond a certain point and will choose to return to the city. The greater degree of ceremonial freedom is matched by a greater degree of imprecision and fragility.

These changes are traceable in a large number of texts composed during the following two centuries, texts which in other respects have little in common. To glance briefly at a work by the third of the *tre corone*, Petrarch's *Secretum* displaces the Christian examination of conscience away from its traditional ecclesiastical context to a private conversation between the writer or his surrogate and his spiritual master, Saint Augustine. The conversation has a makeshift ceremonial aspect, since it supposedly takes place in the presence of an allegorical figure, Veritas, who sits "as a silent judge" presiding over the discussion. But the presence of an allegorized Truth comes to appear ironic, since the *Secretum*, for all its brilliance of local insight, achieves no stable clarification or serenity, no final truth either for the reader or the tormented writer. It produces no efficacious symbolism, which is to say no magic. Analogously, a representative text of Florentine civic humanism, Leonardo Bruni's *Dialoghi ad Paulum Petrum*, stages a formal debate within the informal setting of a private house, a debate explicitly compared to the quintessential academic ceremony, the *disputatio*. The text thus calls attention to its deliberate ceremonial displacement. Despite the radical differences of Petrarch's and Bruni's works, they have as I read them one element in common: neither can be said to reach a definitive or unambiguous conclusion. The *Dialoghi* leaves readers wondering where the author, and his principal speaker, Niccoli, really stand on the issues under debate, just as the *Secretum* leaves the human subject deeply divided by two voices. Each debate has been displaced and each fails to resolve effectively two opposing positions. One might argue that in these cases the space for creative improvisation has permitted a blurred closure which seldom affects established ceremony.

An apparently firmer closure marks the *Convivium religiosum* of Erasmus, one of the most fully developed of the improvised rituals the Renaissance has left us. This gathering of cheerful and devout friends at a small villa to share dinner and scriptural reflection receives an explicit ritual interpretation from the host Eusebius. Anthropologists inform us that commensality, the sharing of a festive meal at a single board on a sacred occasion, is a familiar ceremonial symbol of communal harmony throughout the world. Eusebius alludes to the ecumenical character of commensality and underscores its particular meaning for the Christian: "Etenim si ethnicis quoque religiosa erat mensa, quanto magis oportet esse sacram Christianis, quibus habet imaginem quandam illius sacrosancti convivii, quod Dominus Iesus postremum egit cum suis discipulis" (*Cinq Banquets* 76). Eusebius's word "convivii," applied to the last supper, echoes the title of Erasmus's colloquy. As though to underscore the occasion's ceremonial function, Eusebius proposes a ritual of purification. He invites his guests to wash their hands before dinner in order, he says, "that we may approach the table with hands and hearts both clean" (*Colloquies* 55) (ut puris manibus et animis ad mensam accedamus) (*Cinq Banquets* 76). Since any Christian meal is holy, the custom of washing the hands has grown up, he says, "in order that if perchance any hatred, envy or shamefulness dwell in one's mind, one may get rid of it before coming to eat" (*Colloquies* 55) (ut si quid odii, livoris aut turpitudinis alicui forsitan resideat in animo, id eiiciat antequan accedat ad cibum capiendum) (*Cinq Banquets* 76). The dinner's ritual function will further be dramatized by the chanting of a hymn at the beginning and the end. Thus Erasmus invites the reader to view the entire action of his colloquy, and most particularly the central scene at the table, as a kind of informal sacrament, a sacrament which will be open to humour, to pagan philosophy, and to the pleasures of the senses, but sanctified by the spirit of Christ. The self-consciousness of the author in thus recreating a sacramental community appears in the frequent repudiations of Jewish law, here assimilated to the hollow ceremonialism of church liturgy. Though one of the speakers refers to ecclesiastical ceremonies, he states that "there are ... other, more interior means of helping us to depart from this life with cheerfulness and Christian trust" (*Colloquies* 69) (sunt alia quaedam reconditiora, quae nobis hoc praestant, ut cum alacritate spiritus, ut cum Christiana fiducia migremus hinc) (*Cinq Banquets* 88).[7]

The means employed specifically at the feast is the communal interpretation of passages from Proverbs, 1 Corinthians, and Matthew, passages which elicit a range of interpretations offered with humble demurrals and amicable fraternity. Here in this sharing of complementary hermeneutic insight, we seem to reach the high point of sacred communion, and we remember Erasmus's insistence in the "Paraclesis" that the profit derived from Christ's words by his readers is superior to the profit derived from his physical presence by his disciples. The improvised sacrament of the *Convivium religiosum* rests upon the propriety and nourishment of shared interpretation by laymen. Erasmus's confidence is moving but it is also ironic in the light of what we know of sixteenth century doctrinal history. The fraternal hermeneutic differences of this banquet would widen, grow embittered, produce bloodshed and chaos. They would scar the century as they were soon to scar Erasmus himself. Again, the grounding of the ritual improvisation emerges as precarious.

An anthropologist, Roy Rappaport, has contrasted the effects of ritual with the effects of language. He writes,

> The distinctions of language cut the world into bits — into categories, classes, oppositions, and contrasts. It is in the nature of language to search out all differences and to turn them into distinctions which then provide bases for boundaries and barriers. It is, on the other hand, in the nature of liturgical orders to unite, or reunite, the psychic, social, natural, and cosmic orders which language and the exigencies of life pull apart. (206)

Whether or not words always divide, as Rappaport would have it, they *did* divide in the sixteenth century, and the sacred word most of all. Erasmus's colloquy rests on the fragile hope that the scriptural word will induce ritual union. In the *Purgatorio*, the *Decameron*, the *Convivium religiosum* — three radically different texts — one finds an element that may be common to all ritual, the acquisition of a privilege or a power. In these three cases, despite their disparity, the privilege is a right of entry, an entry quite literal in Dante's case, and in Boccaccio and Erasmus an entry into a community which is only slightly less literal. Petrarch's *Secretum* dramatizes a blocked entry or conversion. Not all rituals are rites of initiation or passage, but in every case, in and out of the literary text, one can ask what privilege or power the participants acquire or want to acquire. Also, we can discern in the rewriting of ritual, the improvisations of ritual, a kind of nostalgia for the power which ritual tends to invoke. In Erasmus, one could even speak of a nostalgia for magic, in the broad sense of the word I have suggested. Calvin was doubtless not the first of the reformers to accuse the Roman sacrament as it had developed of implying a belief in magic. But one need not be a partisan like Calvin to recognize in the mystery of the sacrament (Greek *mysterion*), in the miraculous relation between symbol and efficacity, a link with more primitive beliefs that we commonly call magical (the magical core of most, perhaps all, rituals explains why speech-act theory as it has developed in the last decades is inadequate to the semiotics of ritual). There is nostalgia, for example, in the hope that washing the hands will cleanse the heart. The broad appeal of magic and the occult during the sixteenth century, of what Cornelius Agrippa called "ceremonial magic," doubtless owes something to this nostalgia. It stems from a reluctance to surrender the access to spiritual power that ritual had provided and that was now becoming less available.

One can trace the conflict between demystification and nostalgia clearly in the work of Rabelais. There is demystification in the great scene of the *Gargantua* (Chapter 27) which brings the soldiers of Picrochole's invading army swarming over the wall to pillage the vineyard of the abbey of Seuillé. The consternation of Frère Jean is famous as he watches the year's vintage disappearing before his eyes while his fellow monks retire to their chapel to form a solemn procession, "une belle porcession, renforcée de beaulx preschans, et letanies *contra hostium insidias*, et beaulx responds *pro pace* (Rabelais 1: 107). In the sarcasm of the repeated adjective *beaulx*, one can measure the author's scorn for liturgical futility. While the others mumble their chant "*Ini nim, pe, ne, ne, ne, ne, ne, ne, tum, ne, num, num, ini ...,*" Frère Jean will dispatch the invaders by crunching their bones with his staff (1: 107 ff.). The point lies in the impotence of the litany as against the efficacy of a sorb-apple shaft swung by vigorous arms. The formulas chanted by the monks lack any effective magical capacity to repel the invaders. The apotropaic language is cut off or irrelevant to the actual *hostes*. In place of a magical semiotics emerges what I call a disjunctive semiotics, an implicit denial of any metaphysical or miraculous relation between (verbal) representation and referent.

Against this demystification one can set the banquet aboard ship toward the close of the *Quart Livre* (chapters 64-65), a banquet that includes "divers cantiques à la louange du treshault Dieu des Cieulx." The communal meal raises the spirits of the becalmed company as it literally (magically?) raises a wind to fill their sails. There is a hint of a eucharistic miracle in Panurge's interpretation:

> Sans poinct de faulte nous doibvons bien louer le bon Dieu nostre createur, servateur, conservateur, qui par ce bon pain, par ce bon vin et frays, par ces bonnes viandes nous guerist de telles perturbations, tant du corps come de l'ame. (Rabelais 2: 239)

This improvised communion is vulnerable to the negative elements surrounding it that Terence Cave has rightly pointed out (*Cornucopian Text* 215-22), and I would want to insist on that vulnerability. But Professor Cave would not deny, I think, an *aspiration* toward a ritual power of healing. Toward the close of the *Cinquième Livre*, whoever wrote it, demystification and affirmation seem to come together as the priestess of the oracle subjects Panurge to a parodic super-ritual, more ceremonies, says the narrator, than had ever been invented (chapter 43), before Panurge receives the solace and release he has been seeking, the admission into a new life. Rabelais's book can be said to betray the ambivalence of the century that produced it, impatient as it is with *ceremoniolae*, but not without a felt need for ritual participation.

It is unclear just how seriously the reader is to take Ronsard's "Dithyrambes à la pompe du bouc de Jodelle," a poem that alludes to an actual event, a festivity and banquet honouring the success of a tragedy composed by the poet's friend Etienne Jodelle. It would appear that there really was a *bouc*, a he-goat, garlanded with ivy, which was led in a kind of Bacchic procession through the village of Arcueil and around the banqueting hall. The poem evokes the procession dimly through the rapturous haze of a Bacchic trance, and it implies an immolation of the goat which apparently did not in fact take place. One can imagine the high spirits enlivening the band of tipsy young humanists, drawing on their Hellenic learning to organize a rowdy parade. But the poem itself, almost 499 lines long, is an altogether different thing. It draws on Marullus and other Latin poets, ancient and modern, in order to chant a genuine paean to Bacchus. The "Dithyrambes" correspond to something profound in Ronsard, his intuition of an overpowering cosmic energy animating both the natural universe and his own creative gift. The poem is really about the privilege of access to that divine energy, which was at the same time access to his own private poetic *fureur*. In the Bacchic ritual lies an entry into possession:

> Par toy chargés de ton Nectar,
> Rempans avec toy dans ton char,
> Nous concevons des cieux
> Les segrés precieux,
> Et bien que ne soyons qu'hommes,
> Par toy Demidieux nous sommes.
> Iach iach Evoé,
> Evoé iach iach ...
> Dextre vien à ceux
> Qui ne sont point paresseux
> De renouveler tes mysteres.... (Ronsard 5: 75)

But the cult of Bacchus was also archaeological; it could only be revived, as at Arcueil, with a kind of self-conscious laughter, and the poem itself does not lack a certain faint self-mockery. The poetic procession and immolation translate youthful make-believe, humanist nostalgia, and hope for inspired poetic power. The mock-ceremony seems to have been needed to release the fury truly desired. Like the coronation of the *Filocolo*, Ronsard's Bacchic procession could be called ludic. But Ronsard's almost transparent irony is tinged with modern pathos; he knows at heart what he wants to deny, that the ceremony in itself can only briefly and tangentially generate the *furor poeticus*.

The texts that have been cited here suggest that the questioning of ceremony during the Renaissance left open a space for creative play with ceremonial symbols. This play could be exhilarating, but the improvised ceremonial symbols were shallowly and precariously grounded as Dante's were not. The Middle Ages had of course produced marvellous ceremonial parody, beginning with the Feast of Fools, and the sixteenth century would perpetuate medieval traditions in forms like the *sotie* and the *sermon joyeux*. But in the writers I have been discussing, after Dante, the power aimed at and the right of access desired cannot properly be called medieval. In these writers, ceremonial forms are involved as means to a particular, early modern goal which the text itself defines. Dante wanted access to salvation, but the goal of an autonomous community in the *Decameron* is an altogether different motivation, as are the genial lay spirituality of the *Convivium religiosum*, the Rabelaisian brotherhood in freedom and Ronsard's creative participation in cosmic dynamism. The uncertain status of the ceremony partly masks a vestigial hope in ceremonial power. But the grounding of this power remains shallow because the ceremony is patched together, extemporized, *bricolé*. The plays of Shakespeare are rich in experimentation with ceremonial symbolism and parody; their study might well occupy a volume. A few notes will have to suffice here. Perhaps the grimmest instance of parody is the scene in *3 Henry VI* (I.iv), where the captured duke of York has a paper crown placed on his head by his Lancastrian enemies, who do mock-obeisance to him before he is stabbed to death. This is a scene Shakespeare found in Holinshed, who pointed to the Christological parallel. Readers will also remember the mock-trial in the fourth act of *King Lear*, but I for one find equally disturbing the haunting description of Lear by Cordelia, "As mad as the ract sea singing aloud, / Crownd with ranke femiter and furrow weedes" (the *Quarto* text 18.2-3). That image flashes by so quickly in the panorama of horror that we scarcely have occasion to reflect on the twisted symbolism of Lear's auto-coronation.

The uncertain status of a ceremony is nowhere more powerfully and self-consciously dramatized than in the tetralogy running from *Richard II* to *Henry V*. Here again the ceremony at issue is a coronation, which in theory accords the right of access to sovereign power. The treacherous, fatal ambiguity of the crown, the blurred meaning of a coronation, underlie the conflict of *Richard II*. King Richard falls through too blind a faith in symbols alone, through a kind of formalist heresy. He believes, or intermittently believes, that the anointment of his head makes him magically untouchable. At the moment of his fall, Richard improvises a public de-coronation, solemnly divesting himself of his royal regalia.

> Now, marke me how I will undoe my selfe.
> I give this heavie Weight from off my Head,
> And this unwieldie Scepter from my Hand,
> The pride of Kingly sway from out my Heart,
> With mine owne Teares I wash away my Balme,
> With mine owne Hands I give away my Crowne, ...
> All Pompe and Majestie I doe forsweare. (13.4.1.2025-29, 2033)

Richard's improvisation briefly wins him control of the stage and frustrates the scenario devised by his enemies. It is performed in that space created by the displacement of a usurpation. His displaced status accords him the peculiar freedom together with the peculiar weight of this terrible, unbearable performance. His auto-divestiture might be said to dramatize the limits of ceremonial power, the breakdown of the continuity which a coronation is supposed to ensure.

Richard's antagonist, Bolingbroke, is trapped by the realist heresy, by the disjunctive assumption that a coronation in itself has no force and no meaning. It will require many years and insurrections before he acquires a kind of weary wisdom and recognizes the partial power of a symbol. In the closing hours of his life, he will be shocked to discover his son, so to speak, trying the symbol on. Henry IV, broken by his underestimation of ritual continuities, pays for his mistake with a reign overshadowed by civic turbulence and inner guilt. The last king of the series, Henry V, lies awake on the eve of Agincourt soliloquizing on the burden of the royal role heavy with confining formality and symbolism.

> And what have Kings, that Privates have not too,
> Save Ceremonie, save generall Ceremonie?
> And what art thou, thou Idoll Ceremonie?
> What kind of God art thou?
> What are thy Rents? what are thy Commings in?
> O Ceremonie, shew me but thy worth. (17.4.1.2016-19)

Where is the profit of all that ritual paraphernalia, now perceived as totally void of meaning and depleted of magical efficacy? One might single out that question as the dominant problem of the tetralogy. Henry V will never recover the reverence for the performed signifier felt by his grandfather, John of Gaunt. Perhaps the real tragic protagonist of the history plays is the dim, noble, mutable presence of the ceremonial society.

Something of the same drama tinges Cervantes's *Don Quixote*, which reminds us that the ludic in literature can overlap on occasion with something very close to the tragic. The scene near the beginning of the novel which describes the hero's supposed investiture into the order of chivalry is a classic travesty of ceremonial faith. Don Quixote has stopped at a seedy provincial inn in the belief that it is a castle; he has greeted two prostitutes as great ladies and requested the innkeeper-castellan to dub him a knight after the requisite nocturnal vigil by his armour. He has placed his makeshift accoutrements by the innyard well and has dealt brutally with two mule drivers who approached it to water their drove. When this occurs, the nervous innkeeper decides to proceed immediately with the investiture and his improvisation does not lack resourcefulness.

> Advertido y medroso desto el castellano, trujo luego un libro donde asentaba la paja y cebada que daba a los harrieros, y con un cabo de vela que la traía un muchacho, y con las dos ya dichas doncellas, se vino adonde don Quijote estaba, al cual mandó hincar de rodillas; y, leyendo en su manual — como que decía alguna devota oración —, en mitad de la leyenda alzó la mano y diole

sobre el cuello un buen golpe, y tras él, con su mesma espada, un gentil espaldarazo, siempre murmurando entre dientes, como que rezaba. Hecho esto, mandó a una de aquellas damas que le ciñese la espada, la cual lo hizo con mucha desenvoltura y discreción, porque no fue menester poco para no reventar de risa a cada punto de las ceremonias; pero las proezas que ya habían visto del novel caballero les tenía la risa a raya. Al ceñirle la espada dijo la buena señora: — Dios haga a vuestra merced muy venturoso caballero y le dé ventura en lides. (*Don Quijote* 95-96)

The parodic implications of a scene such as this extend beyond the "madness" of its central figure and beyond the anachronism of a single rite. One might well make out in this scene an anticipation of the death of ceremonial symbolism. Yet the force of the scene and of the entire novel lies in the simultaneous recognition of a deep human need for this symbolism. For Cervantes's pitiless honesty shows the appeal of this chivalric ceremonial and the delight of its creative make-believe even as he shows the absurdity and the danger of its perpetuation. The prostitutes who serve as damsels are a little frightened but they are also vastly amused, as countless other characters throughout the novel will be amused when they participate in the charade. By the end, Don Quixote is destroyed because all the others can play with his fiction only if he regards it seriously as a myth. By displacing as far as possible the form of investiture, however mangled, from its traditional context, Cervantes isolates and ridicules the potential equivocation of any ceremony. We are led first to see the absurdity of the serious investiture, then almost as soon, the delight of its imitation. Only slowly do we realize that this travesty has been a trap. The novel first brings us to expect the facile demystification of a Boccaccio story, a reduction of a mystery to brutal "realism" and transparence. But in fact, that process in *Don Quixote* is attended by a process of remystification. The new emergent mystery, however, is secularized, anti-institutional, and tragic; it centres on the compulsive human need for myths which will always prove vulnerable. The creative improvisation of the innkeeper, the prostitutes, and all the other subsequent characters who *play along* is ambiguous because it depends on a faith which is not playful and which exacts a progressively high price, in the end the price of life itself.

In the scene at the inn, Don Quixote wants the privilege of access to a social institution and mode of life represented as outmoded. Not all rites of passage were or are similarly outmoded. But perhaps one has the right to interpret Cervantes's irony as extending beyond the institution of chivalry, as extending even to the dream that a physical gesture, a stroke on the shoulder, could yield true access to a moral condition. The novel reveals itself as a tragedy of failed magic.

But I would prefer not to close on this note of failure, since the kind of literary play I have been tracing seems to me essentially fertile. The ceremonies improvised by Renaissance artists may have been precariously grounded, but they constitute a resourceful response to the semiotic crisis of their era. Most of these writers, unlike Shakespeare as history-writer and unlike Cervantes, hold out a hope that the rigid repetitions of the past can flow into future inventive adaptations. One passage which leads us to be hopeful about that flow occurs at the close of Book I of Spenser's *Fairie Queene*, when, after the dragon is disposed of, the residents of the besieged city emerge to thank their saviours. Una is honoured by a row of comely virgins dancing toward her and playing timbrels as they dance. When they reach her, Spenser writes:

> Then on her head they set a girland greene,
> And crowned her twixt ernest and twixt game;
> Who in her selfe-resemblance well beseene,
> Did seeme such, as she was, a goodly maiden Queene. (I.12.8)

In the last phrase, Spenser is glancing both at the royal sovereign of England and at the May Queen of folk festivity. But this particular coronation, extending a right of entry, lies somewhere in the middle, "twixt ernest and twixt game," open to a nourishing past but appropriating it for new contexts. This space where the ludic meets the formal productively belongs to a lost semiotics, still saturated with formal performed signs but no longer, at all levels, presenting them as determinant.

The miniature history traced in this essay would need, of course, more quotations, more precise local analysis, more qualifications, and counter-examples, before it could aspire to something like historical exemplarity. One purpose of the essay, in fact, is to dramatize the effective absence of a missing sub-discipline which the humanities grievously need — namely, historical semiotics. We possess many sketchy contributions like the foregoing paper which this future sub-discipline might incorporate, but to my knowledge we have no organized effort, no single scholarly journal, no academic program, which might focus the cross-disciplinary collaboration that is required. I have tried to suggest here a few of the consequences stemming from one tortuous, infinitely complex *mise-en-question* which a future team of scholars would have to explore. But the spasmodic waning of one immemorial practice of signification had, of course, further immeasurable consequences, and these in turn produced others. If literature remains a disorderly but autonomous system, and I believe that it does, future scholarship will nonetheless compel us increasingly to think of representation as a meta-system, and we will never exhaust either the problems or the enlightenment that development will introduce into our reflection upon the past.

STEVEN RENDALL

Reading in the French Renaissance: Textual Communities, Boredom, Privacy

Recent research on the history and "ethnography" of reading has questioned the contrast often drawn between literate and oral cultures, stressing the extent to which modern Euro-American conceptions of reading as a silent, private activity are bound to specific historical conditions.[1] In particular, there is much evidence to suggest that in medieval Europe reading was *normally* a public activity, performed out loud for the benefit of listeners. On this view, Augustine's surprise at Anselm's silent reading[2] should be understood as reflecting less his astonishment at the ability to read without voicing the words than his puzzlement as to why Anselm should have chosen to read in this way rather than in the usual one.

This point is connected with another of direct relevance to my topic in this essay: in several European languages, the verb for "reading" includes within its semantic field the notions of telling, recounting, and advising or counselling. German philologists have long maintained that Middle High German "lesen" usually means "to read aloud" and sometimes "to narrate, recount, tell" (Green 84, 316 ff.). Nicholas Howe has pointed out that Anglo-Saxon *raedan* shares with Gothic *garedan*, Old High German *ratan*, Old Saxon *radan*, Old Norse *rada*, and Old Frisian *rêda* the meanings of "to give advice or counsel" (61). Howe further notes that the Modern English verb "read" has moved away from these senses to "occupy the semantic category that in Gothic is divided between the two verbs **raedan* and *lisan*, and in Modern German between *raten* and *lesen*" (62). That is, it has gravitated toward the sense of the Latin *legere*, from which the verbs for reading in the Romance languages are derived (Italian *leggere*, French *lire*, Spanish *leer*, etc.). But if we recall that in the Middle Ages these Romance verbs were usually still construed as referring to a public oral performance (a sense preserved in Modern English *lecture*: cf. Howe, 65ff.), we can see that their meaning was less distant from that of their Germanic counterparts than it might at first appear to be.

35

Brian Stock's concept of "textual communities" composed of "a text, and interpreter, and a public" (*Listening* 37) offers a useful way of understanding the context implied by medieval Europeans' use of words for reading. In this context, Stock notes, "the text did not have to be written; oral record, memory, and reperformance sufficed" (cf. Green 316 ff). For Stock, such reading was connected with the public's adherence to certain beliefs, knowledge, and goals; this adherence was both assumed and produced by the reading performance. This helps us see more clearly how reading was connected with giving advice and counsel: the audience understood what was read by reference to commonly held ethical and prudential principles.

We might reasonably expect to find residues of these medieval practices of reading in the Renaissance, as well as significant departures from them in the direction of modern practices. In this paper I shall approach this question by examining Renaissance representations of scenes of storytelling and their reception by audiences. The considerations set forth above seem to me to justify this rather oblique approach: reading in the Renaissance was still often conceived as an oral performance of a text and as complemented and completed by the audience's reception.

Now it happens that at the dawn of the Renaissance in France, Marguerite de Navarre's *Heptaméron* dramatizes not only the activity of storytelling and the setting in which it takes place, but also the "reading" or reception of the stories told, as the characters listen to and comment upon them. Moreover, there are grounds for seeing storytelling itself in the *Heptaméron* as the oral performance of a text. In the prologue, the narrator explains that the storytellers agreed to recount only "true" stories (explicitly contrasting this with the practice of the storytellers in Boccaccio's *Decameron*), that is, stories they have either witnessed themselves "or heard from somebody worthy of belief" (10). The vast majority of the tales fall into the latter category. Thus, even if the storytellers are not offering a rendition of a traditional tale (as in fact many of them are), they may be repeating something they have heard from another source. In either case, they are producing readings — that is, (re)performances of a text in the sense defined by Stock.

I shall take the *Heptaméron* as my starting point, and I do so for an additional reason. As we shall see, the connection between reading/storytelling and idleness or boredom is explicitly thematized in this text, and this connection seems to me related to the later conceptions of reading *literature* as a leisure activity pursued alone, silently, in the privacy of one's own home — and often, in the bedroom.

In the prologue to the *Heptaméron*, the frame narrator explains that her storytellers are all noble ladies and gentlemen who have travelled to a spa in Southern France for their health. On their way back to Paris and the Court, they are caught in a violent storm that washes out a bridge, and are forced to wait in a nearby monastery until they can resume their journey. One of their number proposes that they tell stories while they wait, and so every day they assemble under some spreading trees by the riverside and tell the stories the frame narrator later repeats. This kind of scenario is, of course, familiar to every reader of Chaucer or Boccaccio, and much of what I am about to say about Marguerite's construction of the setting and purposes of storytelling would be equally applicable to the *Canterbury Tales* and the *Decameron*. In all three works, characters tell stories to *pass the time*. But the *Heptaméron* lays particular stress on the *hygienic* function of telling and listening to stories, and its connection with idleness and boredom.

As Marguerite's travellers contemplate the prospect of remaining idle for ten or twelve days while the bridge is rebuilt, they begin to suffer from boredom (ennui). One of the travellers, Parlamente, "who was never idle or melancholic," says that they need a pastime (passetemps) to alleviate the boredom (ennui) they will have to bear, "for if we don't have some pleasant and virtuous occupation, we are in danger of falling ill" (de Navarre, *L'Heptaméron* 7).[3] Still worse, the young widow Longarine adds, they will become morose (fascheuse), "which is an incurable illness" (7). Thus, whereas in the *Decameron* the bubonic plague rages outside, in the *Heptaméron* the plague of melancholy threatens from within; it is endemic in the characters themselves, and can be kept at bay only through some kind of occupation or "business." For, as Robert Burton put it in his *Anatomy of Melancholy* some sixty years later, "the mind can never rest, but still meditates on one thing or other; except it be occupied about some honest business, of [its] own accord it rusheth into melancholy" (*Anatomy of Melancholy* 1932, 1: 242).

As Burton also notes,

> idleness is an appendix to nobility; they count it a disgrace to work, and spend all their days in sports, recreations, and pastimes, and will therefore take no pains, be of no vocation; they feed liberally, fare well, want exercise, action, employment ... and company to their desires, and thence their bodies become full of gross humours, wind, crudities, their minds disquieted, dull, heavy, etc. care, jealousy, fear of some diseases, sullen fits, weeping fits, seize too familiarly on them. (1: 244)

The idleness faced by Marguerite's nobles is, however, of a more radical sort, and hence more perilous; for they are stranded without even their customary "sports, recreations, and pastimes." Moreover, unlike Burton, they regard the court as a busy place — so busy, Parlamente says, that a project of producing a French version of Boccaccio's *Decameron*, conceived by the crown princess and "madame Marguerite," had to be abandoned because of the "grandz affaires" following the peace signed with England in 1546, the birth of a son to the crown princess, "and several other matters worthy of the court's attention" (9). It was partly in order to repair the deleterious effects on their health occasioned by such frenetic activity that these courtiers went to "recreate" at the spas near Pau; but now they have fallen into the other extreme, and are confronted by a dangerous lack of occupation.

Parlamente's husband, Hircan, first proposes that they pass their time in dalliance, but she replies that they should leave aside "the pastimes that only two can participate in, and discuss one in which everyone can take part" (9), such as telling each other stories. And so in the *Heptaméron* it is idleness that gives rise to storytelling, as it does also in the *Decameron*. It may be worth noting in this connection that Burton mentions among the remedies for melancholy the reading of "merry tales ... such as the old woman told of Psyche in Apuleius, Boccace novels, and the rest, which some delight to hear, some to tell, all are well pleased with" (2: 81).

One might at first think this in conflict with the German critic Walter Benjamin's account, set forth in his well-known essay "The Storyteller," which argues that the roots of storytelling are in the workplace, among cobblers at their lasts and peasants shelling peas. For Benjamin, however, this is so because such work is routine and boring, and thus produces the special kind of relaxation and receptivity most conducive to listening to stories. The listener's ability to integrate the story into his own experience, Benjamin says in a passage that recalls the medieval practices of reading considered at the beginning of our discussion,[4]

> requires a state of relaxation which is becoming rarer and rarer. If sleep is the apogee of physical relaxation, boredom is the apogee of mental relaxation. Boredom is the dream bird that hatches the egg of experience. A rustling in the leaves drives him away. His nesting places — the activities that are intimately associated with boredom — are already extinct in the cities and are declining in the country as well. With this the gift for listening is lost and the community of listeners disappears. (91)

In the Renaissance, the "community of listeners" had not yet disappeared from the workshops and cottages. For instance, as Natalie Zemon Davis has noted, the institution of the *veillée* was alive and well in sixteenth-century France. This was

> an evening gathering within the village community held especially during the winter months from All Saints' Day to Ash Wednesday. Here tools were mended by candlelight, thread was spun, the unmarried flirted, and some man or woman told stories.... Then, if one of the men were literate and owned books, he might read aloud. (Davis, *Society and Culture* 201)

The advent of the printed book greatly increased the likelihood that the *veillée* would include reading aloud, often from a translation of Aesop's fables, from the *Calendrier des bergers*, or even the *Roman de la rose*; and as early as the 1530s, the vernacular Bible began to be read in such gatherings (Davis 202). We should observe here that telling stories and reading aloud from books took place in the same context, and that no sharp distinction was drawn between these two activities.

Such communities of listeners are clearly related to Stock's "textual communities," though we should remember that the latter concept includes both a context of belief and the listener's response to reading. As Elizabeth Long recently has written, "Reading in groups not only offers occasions for explicitly collective textual interpretation, but encourages new forms of association, and nurtures new ideas that are developed in conversation with other people as well as with the books" (194). This is, of course, precisely analogous to the situation described in the *Heptaméron*, where each tale is subjected to extensive discussion and debate by the group of storytellers. Moreover, in the *Heptaméron*, discussion and debate often make the story a pretext for developing new perspectives on the issues it raises and for arriving at consensus or, alternatively, at a clearer understanding of differences of opinion.[5] Finally, it seems reasonable to suppose that Marguerite's "textual community" of storytellers and listeners served as a model for the relation between the *Heptaméron* itself and its readers, whether the latter read the text silently and alone or aloud and in a group.

The *Heptaméron* thus suggests that in the Renaissance, such textual communities continued to exist among the upper classes as well as among the common people. Even in the seventeenth century, writers could still expect their works to be read in public gatherings, and to be rewarded by the attention of those who listened to them, even if the works were very long. For example, Honoré D'Urfé's pastoral novel, *L'Astrée*, first published in 1607, was a great success for its time, despite its immense length (it ran to more than five thousand pages in the 1635 edition), and was read aloud in early seventeenth-century aristocratic salons, where devotees would show up garbed as their favourite characters, complete with shepherd's crooks and victual pouches. Of course, at such sessions D'Urfé's novel was not read *in toto*, and that raises other questions about Renaissance reading practices which I have touched on elsewhere (see Rendall in the list of works cited). But the fact remains that in such cases reading was still a public performance that responded to the aristocrats' need to find a way of filling, or killing, time.

The pastoral setting of D'Urfé's novel makes clear the implications of the pilgrimage in the *Canterbury Tales*, the retreat to a country villa in the *Decameron*, and the isolated monastery in the *Heptaméron*: the move from city and court to country allows a temporary suspension of normal "business" (cf. Barber, ch. 1) and creates the leisure in which stories may be told and listened to. *Negotium* temporarily gives way to *otium*; storytelling takes place in an *interlude* separating two moments of "business." Moreover, the setting of storytelling in the *Heptaméron* has many of the characteristics of the pastoral oasis or *locus amoenus*: trees, shade from the midday sun, soft green grass, running water. And so *L'Astrée* can be seen as belonging to the same tradition, particularly since its characters also tell stories to each other.

The length and number of the stories told by the characters in *L'Astrée* are one reason it takes d'Urfé five thousand pages to narrate events that occur over a period of only about four months. The amazingly slow pace of the main narrative has led most modern readers to find *L'Astrée* impossibly boring, and to marvel at the fact that early seventeenth-century readers did not. This is one way to measure the distance separating modern culture, based since the eighteenth century on the conviction that time is money and must not be wasted, from an earlier culture concerned not so much with saving time as with spending it. Burton's repeated strictures on aristocratic idleness presage a view that became much more dominant later on; the gentry "are all for pastimes," he writes, "'tis all their study; all their invention tends to this alone, to drive away time, as if they were born some of them to no other ends" (2: 70). But even in so aristocratic a fiction as *L'Astrée*, there are signs of a certain apprehension that storytelling, rather than charming away its audience's boredom, might actually produce it.[6]

For example, telling her story to another character, Astrea says, "There is no point, good Diana, in telling you everything we said, for that would take too long, and you might find it tiresome" (Bk. IV). Asked to tell the story of his relations with his beloved, Corilas says: "I am afraid you will find it tedious to listen to the petty details of our village life" (Bk. V). And when Sylvia urges

Celadon to tell her the story of Celion and Belinda, he says it is so long she may find it boring, but she replies: "On the contrary, we could find no better way to spend our time while Galatea is reading the letters she has just received" (Bk. X). In every case the tale gets told, and at length, so that the chief effect of these protests is to highlight the audience's *desire* for narrative, which must overcome the storyteller's reticence.

The note sounded occasionally in D'Urfé is loud and clear in Boileau, whom I take here as a representative of seventeenth-century neo-classicism. The figure haunting his *L'Art poétique* (published in 1674) is that of the bored reader or listener. A writer who fails to vary his style will "put us to sleep," he tells us, and "few people read such authors, born to bore us to tears," whereas a writer who succeeds in this regard will find his book "surrounded by buyers" (IV). Similarly, if you write a play that does not touch the audience's feelings, "Your cold arguments will only make lukewarm a spectator already too lazy to applaud much, and who, rightly worn out by your rhetoric's vain efforts, falls asleep or criticizes you" (III). "A fool at least makes us laugh, and can cheer us up," Boileau opines, "but a cold writer can do nothing but bore us" (IV). This may be sound advice, but my point here is that when Boileau imagines failure, he sees it in the form of a bored reader or listener, and this is the scarecrow he uses to warn prospective writers that they had better take his advice.

These issues simply don't arise in the *Heptaméron*, and they are no more than adumbrated in *L'Astrée*, where no one ever seems to be bored by listening to stories, no matter how long and involved they are. Now, of course, I don't want to argue that stories never bored people in the Renaissance, or that in the seventeenth century writers and readers universally adopted a bourgeois attitude toward time and abandoned an aristocratic one. The evidence I've presented here is far too slim to establish such a sweeping and overly simple conclusion. It might reasonably be objected that Marguerite was unlikely to represent her stories as boring their listeners, and that from her example one can conclude little on that account. Nevertheless, I think the texts I have examined illustrate a certain shift in the relation between boredom and reading or listening to stories — whether or not one sees this as a process of historical development — that can help us better define practices of reading in the Renaissance. Let me now try to characterize this shift as I see it.

First of all, in the *Heptaméron*, as in the *Canterbury Tales* and the *Decameron*, and still in *L'Astrée*, boredom is produced by life, not by literature. It is a potentiality endemic in the human psyche and thrives on idleness, whether this is a function of the artisan's or peasant's routine work or of aristocratic leisure. It constitutes a threat to the individual's mental and physical health, and literature is seen as a remedy, not a cause. Boileau's *Art poétique*, on the other hand, stresses instead the ways in which literature can cause boredom, and the writer's need to retain his audience's attention and keep it from falling asleep. Second, in the *Heptaméron* and *L'Astrée*, the role of memory is much closer to that described by Benjamin. For Benjamin, boredom allows the storyteller's listeners to forget themselves and lend the tale their full attention, and this in turn promotes the audience's integration of the tale into its common memory and experience. In other words, memory is a collective, social phenomenon that absorbs and is at the same time augmented by the story. In the *Art poétique*, on the other hand, Boileau writes that a play must "constantly arouse us with surprising strokes; let the dramatist hurry in his verses from one marvel to another; and let everything he says be easy to remember, and leave in us a long memory of his work" (III). The implication is that the audience's indolence (the spectator, we know, is "already too lazy to applaud much") is not the writer's ally but his foe. The audience does not eagerly await his words, but virtually challenges him to interest it and to imprint his work upon its memory.

Finally, we might recall Parlamente's distinction, in the prologue to the *Heptaméron*, between pastimes in which only two can participate and those in which any number can take part. By the first category, Parlamente refers to sexual intercourse (she assumes, perhaps wrongly, that her husband is not suggesting an orgy), but we might now be inclined to see it as including *reading*, insofar as the latter is conceived on the model of a private communication between the author and an individual reader. As I have suggested, this conception of reading was less common in the Renaissance than it is today (I have suggested elsewhere that in France it arises in the late seventeenth century; see "Fontenelle and his Public"). It is striking in this regard that even when Boileau is talking about a theater audience, he still fixes his gaze on the individual spectator nodding off in his seat, rather than on the collective response.[7] This may be taken to reflect a more general cultural shift that focuses increasing attention on the individual and on private life.

We thus return to the point raised at the outset, concerning the modern understanding of reading as an essentially private, solitary, and silent activity. In a stimulating article entitled "Textual Interpretation as Collective Action," Elizabeth Long maintains that the image of the solitary reader has prevented us from acknowledging the continuing importance of reading as a group activity. As she points out, this image "suppresses recognition of the infrastructure of literacy and the social or institutional determinants of what's available to read, what is 'worth reading,' and how to read it" (193). Examining graphic representations of reading, she observes that these take two distinct, gender-coded forms. The first of these depicts the solitary male scholar in his study, meditating on "serious" texts (theological, scientific, historical, etc.). The second, which begins with late medieval representations of the Virgin or Mary Magdalen reading, develops in the seventeenth century into a conventional image of the solitary female reader, often in her boudoir, reading novels, poems, or letters — that is, the sort of text we have called, since the eighteenth century, "literature." This latter "scene of reading" is firmly anchored in the private home, and even in the most private part of the home (the boudoir was the closest an eighteenth-century woman came to having "a room of her own"), and thus it tends to isolate reading from political activity or any other form of practical engagement with the world.[8]

This may help us grasp the significance of Marguerite de Navarre's representation of the "textual community" gathered in a field adjoining a monastery.[9] The stories are told out of doors, in a public (even if isolated) setting, and they are collectively interpreted by the listeners (each of whom, we should remember, tells stories in his or her turn) in relation to important moral, prudential, social, and political issues. That is, they are interpreted as offering "counsel" that is not bound to any particular individual but forms part of a common lore. Moreover, in no case are the stories interpreted primarily in order to determine the teller's *individual* meaning; while the listeners often discern an "agenda" in the storyteller's choice of a tale or comments on it, they are chiefly concerned to articulate their reactions to the tale as such, as a public document for discussion. The authority of the text does not preclude debate and further development; indeed, it calls for it. The "receptiveness" boredom creates in these listeners or readers is thus not a form of passivity, but rather an active desire for wisdom that can be incorporated into their collective experience and memory — and for the social intercourse through which this incorporation takes place.

Should we then conclude that Renaissance reading was a paradise where idleness and boredom gave rise to productive social interaction and collective wisdom, and which was lost some time in the seventeenth century? To do so would be to engage in a delusion paralleling the one that posits a golden age of orality corrupted by literacy, which James Clifford has called "ethnographic pastoral" (118; qtd. in Howe 74). Long's argument suggests that a more promising approach would be to assume that the model of reading implicit in the *Heptaméron* and other Renaissance texts continues to be relevant to understanding reading practices, although in our cultural discourse on reading it has been largely suppressed by the image of the solitary reader.

LISA NEAL

Reading *Ultima Verba*: Commemoration and Friendship in Montaigne's Writing

Nam verae voces tum demum pectore ab imo
Ejiciuntur, et eripitur persona, manet res. (Lucretius)

I. THE DEATH SCENE AND ITS "LANGUAGE"

Studies treating the theme of death in the *Essais* are numerous and varied in tone and perspective.[1] Some critics have likened the work to a tomb for Montaigne's friend Etienne de la Boétie, while others have characterized it as the author's way of leaving to posterity his own last testament. Over the past several decades, many scholars have also used Montaigne's frequent pronouncements on death to debate whether or not the *Essais* are evolutionary in nature.[2] No one, however, has examined Montaigne's attitude towards death in relation to the tradition of *ultima verba* in early modern Europe. In this essay, I will examine Montaigne's presentation and explanation of the last words of others and the privileged status he accords them; he seems to perceive them as transparent and transmissible, provided that they are recorded by the dying person's friend. This privileging, however limited the context, implies a view of language that seems incompatible with Montaigne's frequently expressed opinion that words are equivocal, ambiguous, and ever open to multiple interpretations.

The *Essais* are riven by the conflict between these views of language which in turn give rise to two distinct paradigms of reading: on the one hand, if words are semiotically unstable, then their meaning must depend on their reception, on the person hearing, reading, or quoting them.[3] According to this view, every reader transforms the meaning of each utterance: "Ce n'est non plus selon Plato que selon moy" (Montaigne, *Oeuvres complètes* 1: 26, 150).[4] Terence Cave labels such a model of reading "generative," locates it in the later sixteenth century, and suggests that the *Essais* are its epitome insofar as they "invit[e] the reader to constitute himself as a subject through the act of reading" ("Mimesis of Reading" 159). But if, on the contrary, language reflects the author's essence

45

and individuality — if discourse is the mirror of the soul, *oratio speculum animi* — then the author's meaning will be impervious to change as the text passes from one generation of readers to the next. In keeping with this view, Gérard Defaux argues that Renaissance writers like Montaigne do in fact believe that writing makes the author present in the text: "Il suffit de savoir lire: toujours l'oeuvre célèbre l'ouvrier" (214).

Resolving the conflict between these two views of language (and between the corresponding groups of scholars) is not my goal here. I wish to suggest that Montaigne's preoccupation with, and his pronouncements about, last words reveal a desire that written language be unequivocal, stable and, above all, transmissible to others through reading. I will focus on the figure of the friend who, in his role as a witness to the death scene, is, I believe, the model for a reader Montaigne would consider ideal, though rare: a reader who completely understands the author's words, who feels the author's presence in them and is able to convey that presence to others in a commemorative text.

If language can ever be the "mirror of the soul," in other words, convey meaning reliably, we might expect it to be at death. In both the Classical and Christian traditions, writers tend to assume that words spoken at death can be counted on to represent the truth about the person who utters them. Last words thus enjoy a special status which continues even today when we attribute special significance to death-bed confessions. When Socrates remarks at the beginning of the Phaedo that a philosopher should be willing to die because his death will be the affirmation of the principles by which he has lived, death is to be understood as a standard by which posterity should judge a person; in other words, death is a point before which nothing definitive can be determined about a life. The association of the *hora mortis* with judgment is exploited in fifteenth and sixteenth century treatises on the art of dying, *ars moriendi*, in which allegorical images of angels and devils vie for the soul of the individual lying in bed surrounded by family members, peers, priests, and even pets.[5] Death is here depicted as a struggle between the forces of good and evil with the victor being the moral force best corresponding to the true nature of the life in question. In early modern Europe, death is viewed as the point at which the character of an individual is revealed to God, but as in the classical tradition, this revelation is also made to other humans, including the immediate audience in the bed chamber as well as future readers of the treatises. Throughout history, the death scene has a decidedly exemplary function; it is traditionally represented as a single moment revealing the moral quality of all the moments preceding it, rather like a condensed biography. Indeed, in the numerous biographies Humanists published during the Renaissance, a special category was often accorded to details of the individual's death scene. Erasmus, for instance, ends each of the groups in his *Apopthegmes* with the person's eulogy, or with memorable things he had said about death. Montaigne was an avid reader of such biographies and, by his own admission, paid particular attention to the accounts of death contained in them:

> Et n'est rien dequoy je m'informe si volontiers, que la mort des hommes: quelle parole, quel visage, quelle contenance ils y ont eu; ny endroit des histoires que je remarque si attantifvement.... Il y paroist à la farcissure de mes exemples; et que j'y a en particuliere affection cette matiere [la mort des hommes]. Si j'estoy faiseur de livres, je feroy un registre communté des morts diverses. (1: 20, 88)[6]

What is crucial for our understanding of Montaigne's attitude toward last words is that in the Western tradition the *hora mortis* is considered an instance, and perhaps the only one in life, when words are spoken that can be counted on to represent reliably the speaker's innermost character. In an essay, the title of which comes from Ovid, "Qu'il ne faut juger de nostre heur, qu'après la mort," Montaigne compiles a number of *sententiae antiquae* to convey the traditional notion that the death moment provides an index of character: "C'est le maistre jour. C'est le jour juge de tous les autres: c'est le jour, dict un ancien, qui doit juger de toutes mes années passées" (1: 19, 78-79). Lucretius, cited in the epigraph to this paper, puts it succinctly: "At last true words surge up from deep within our heart. The mask falls away and reality is left" (1: 19, 78). Montaigne repeats this notion in his own words and goes on to emphasize the extent to which the words uttered at death are of a different nature from those used in everyday speech:

> En tout le reste il y peut avoir du masque: ou ces beaux discours de la Philosophie ne sont en nous que par contenance.... Mais à ce dernier rolle de la mort et de nous, il n'y a plus que faindre, il faut parler François, il faut montrer ce qu'il y a de bon et de net dans le fond du pot. (1: 19, 78)

In this passage, Montaigne presents last words as *true*, as nondissimulating, unequivocal signs of the character of the deceased: "Au jugement de la vie d'autruy, je regarde tousjours comment s'en est porté le bout; et des principaux estudes de la mienne, c'est qu'il se porte bien" (1: 19, 79). This attitude is, as we mentioned, fundamentally different from his frequent descriptions of the word as detached from the thing, as standing for many things, just as one example can illustrate many, often incompatible, general laws. Statements that illustrate these points abound in the *Essais*. Among the most frequently cited by scholars: "Le nom c'est une voix qui remerque et signifie la chose; le nom, ce n'est pas une partie de la chose ny de la substance, c'est une piece estrangere joicte à la chose, et hors d'elle" (1: 16, 601); "Quelque diversité d'herbes qu'il y ait, tout s'enveloppe sous le nom de salad" (1: 46, 265); "Par divers moyens on arrive a pareille fin" (1: 1, 12).[7]

II. FRIENDSHIP AND COMMEMORATION

What is it about the words uttered at death that leads Montaigne to invest them with a privileged significance that he does not accord even the Bible, whose language, he claims, is subject to myriad interpretations because of the variety of its readers? ("En la parole la plus nette, pure et parfaicte qui puisse estre, combien de fauceté et de mensonge a l'on fait naistre?"; 2: 12, 569). The answer lies, I believe, in the relationship between the speaker of last words and his witnesses. In a number of the death scenes Montaigne describes in the *Essais* — for instance, those of Socrates, Seneca, Eudamidas, and Epicurus — the presence of *friends* appears to be of paramount importance. Montaigne implies that, for the deceased's reputation to be preserved and prolonged, his friends must transmit the details of his death scene to the public. It seems that only a friend can be relied upon to represent and interpret accurately the words and behaviour of the dying; the friend is thus the essential intermediary between a dying speaker and the public. If one accepts the premise that the authorial presence of the deceased can be conveyed in a commemorative text about him written by his friends, then one might also believe that future readers of this text might be able to recover this presence.

Montaigne is not the first to make the claim that friends are endowed with a special ability to portray, and in so doing convey to others, the essence of their deceased friends. Commemoration and friendship are associated in a long tradition; Cicero, for example, writes that a deceased man is not truly dead if he has friends to commemorate him: "[friends] though dead, are yet alive; though absent, are at hand; so great is the esteem on the part of their friends ... [which makes] the death of the departed seem fortunate and the life of the survivors worthy of praise" (23). Making the absent present is the project of representation, the very project of which Montaigne is at times so wary; believing that the presence of an individual can be posthumously transmitted in words requires a belief in the reliability of linguistic representation. Cicero's statement reveals his own belief that language can act as a vehicle to convey the character of the deceased, at least when the words come from friends. Leon Battista Alberti, the Renaissance painter and theorist, follows Cicero in emphasizing the importance of friends as transmitters of the presence of the deceased, although for him the medium of transmission is visual. In fact, Alberti draws a parallel between the portrait itself and the friend, since both "represent the dead to the living many centuries later, so [the dead] are recognized by spectators with pleasure and deep admiration for the artist" (*On Painting* 63-64).

This tradition associating friendship with commemoration is grounded in a dual hope. First, it is hoped the commemorative work can act as a kind of death portrait that realizes the Humanist ideal of *oratio speculum animi*. As Alberti says, the friend's account of the deceased must "resemble" the deceased so that he is "recognized with pleasure." Now, resemblance and recognition (from *similare*, to imitate; and from *recognoscere*, to know again) would seem to require that readers or spectators have prior knowledge of the person being commemorated, and indeed, Montaigne implies on more than one occasion that he intends his own book to be read by his family and friends after his death, in other words by people who can recognize the author in the book. In "Au Lecteur" he writes,

> Je l'ay voué [ce livre de bonne foy] à la commodité particuliere de mes parens et amis: à ce que m'ayant perdu (ce qu'ils ont à faire bien tost) ils y puissent retrouver aucuns traits de mes conditions et humeurs, et que par ce moyen ils nourrissent plus entiere et plus vifve la connoissance qu'ils ont eu de moy.

In essence, he suggests that for his book to be meaningful to readers as a self-portrait, they must have known him in life.

But this does not appear to be the case concerning commemorative accounts done by others, at least to judge by Montaigne's references to the death scenes of Socrates and Seneca. Socrates' friends must have created an account of his death which resembled, or was consistent with, the quality of the man's life, for how else would Montaigne and his fellow sixteenth century readers know that Socrates' "teneur de vie incorruptible et [sa] saincte image de l'humaine forme" was not "corrupted" by "ornemens [du] parler" (3: 12, 1031)? Seneca's friends also can be acknowledged as the transmitters of an account which confirmed the virtue he displayed throughout his life. Montaigne goes into some detail describing Seneca's death scene in which the philosopher qualifies his friends as "sinceres et veritables," saying:

> Je vous laisse au moins ce que j'ay de plus beau, à scavoir l'image de mes meurs et de ma vie, laquelle je vous prie conserver en vostre memoire ... et que l'eure estoit venue où il avoit à montrer, non plus par discours et par disputes, mais par effect, le fruit qu'il avoit tiré de ses estudes, et que sans

doubte il embrassoit la mort, non seulement sans douleur, mais avecques allegresse. (2: 35, 726)

In the cases of Socrates and Seneca, the accounts Montaigne has read of their *hora mortis* seem to confirm the image Montaigne has of these men, though the account of Seneca's last words, which Montaigne calls "très-excellans" did not survive to the sixteenth century (a loss that Montaigne calls "facheuse"). It thus seems possible to judge the quality of a person's death scene — and by extension his life — without reading the very account written by the friend-witness; it suffices to read another account, provided it was inspired by a first-hand testimony made by the deceased's friends. This implies a broader meaning of the term *resemblance* used in reference to commemorative accounts, a meaning expressed in a letter by Petrarch, for example, in which he speaks of resemblance or likeness as being a kind of *aria* (Gombrich 8). It is this *aria*, then, that is portrayed by true friends, and which can henceforth be copied and perceived by others.

A second hope for the commemorative work is also expressed in the above passage concerning Seneca: that the quality of the death scene will ensure the perpetuation of the deceased's good reputation. Montaigne seems to value a good reputation as a kind of life-after-death — "J'estime toutefois que ce soit une grande consolation à la foiblesse & brieveté de ceste vie, de croire qu'elle se puisse fermir & allonger par la reputation & la renommee" (1361) — and, in a letter written to Henri de Mesmes seven years after the death of La Boétie, he acknowledges his responsibility to preserve the reputation of his late friend:

> Ayant aymé plus que toute autre chose feu M. de la Boétie ... je penserois lourdement faillir à mon devoir, si à mon escient je laissois esvanouir & perdre un si riche nom que le sien, & une memoire si digne de recommandation, & si je ne m'essayois par ces parties la, de le resusciter & remettre en vie. (1362)

Again, the power of a commemorative account to convey a person's presence and moral qualities — in short, his *aria* — to future generations of readers depends on a certain transparency of language that only the friend can ensure. As is often pointed out, the loss of la Boétie left Montaigne bereft of a future commemorator to convey his image to others. "Il n'y a personne à qui je vousisse pleinement compromettre de ma peinture: luy seul jouyssait de ma vraye image et l'emporta. C'est pourquoy je me deschiffre moy-mesme, si curieusement" (961, n.3).[8] As scholars frequently suggest, La Boétie's death may be the catalyst for Montaigne's entire writing project. In short, he had no friend to commemorate him.

In contending that his relationship with La Boétie existed from the moment of their meeting and that it was marked from this moment by perfect understanding — "[une] intelligence, si promptement parvenue à la perfection" — Montaigne repeats the commonplace that perfect friendship is characterized by immediate familiarity and a sense of completeness.[9] The two men, writes Montaigne, were "well-acquainted" at their first meeting: "à nostre premiere rencontre ... nous nous trouvasmes si prins, si cognus, si obligez entre nous, que rien dès lors ne nous fut si proche que l'un à l'autre" (1: 28, 187). Ullrich Langer has expressed the sense of the completeness of friendship thus:

> The development of friendship is the unfolding of what is already there, a sort of repeated showing of its completedness: just as the similarity of the friends ties them to each other, so does temporal development fail to introduce anything different, for each successive event is a confirmation, a demonstration of what has been perfected. (29-30)

Consequently, friends do not need to rely on reasoning and empirical evidence in order to know each other perfectly; they *always* have completely understood and known one another. A person knows what his friend would do in a given situation without having observed him in an identical or similar situation. In this vein, Montaigne writes in "De l'Amitié": "Il n'est pas en la puissance de tous les discours du monde de me desloger de la certitude que j'ay des intentions et jugemens du mien [mon ami]. Aucune de ses actions ne me sçauroit estre presentée, quelque visage qu'elle eut, que je n'en trouvasse incontinent le ressort" (1: 28, 188). The import of this for the reception of last words by a friend is that, if the friendship is true and perfect, a person's last words can serve only to confirm the image his friend has always had of him.

As we recall, Montaigne refers to his own role with respect to his departed friend: "de le resusciter & remettre en vie" (1362). In order to do this, the true friend must be able to grasp the overall configuration of the other; this other is thus never reduced to an example of a universal or to an essence but instead retains his wholeness and individuality. Indeed, Montaigne does not judge La Boétie on the basis of any one of his attributes, actions, or statements; he professes to know instinctively what his friend's words or actions mean.

In keeping with the goal of conveying the absolute singularity of the deceased, the friend may edit or correct the dying man's words (which may not, in fact, be *his last*). Ironically then, a friend may be considered "faithful" and "true" not because he reports *verbatim* what the dying man utters, but because, by virtue of his complete familiarity and fusion with the deceased, he is able to create an account of his *hora mortis* which conveys an overall image of what that man was in life. The edited or corrected image of the deceased friend is intended neither to convey the details of one particular action nor an idealized view of the person, but rather the sum of all his many characteristics. The notion that a global impression of an individual is different from the impressions one can derive from observing particular instances of this person's behaviour is expressed in Renaissance writings on portraiture. Petrarch, in the letter mentioned above, claims that the *aria* of a person is decidedly not the imitation of the exact traits of the individual at any given moment of his existence.[10]

If we draw a parallel between the commemorating friend and a reader, we would have to say at this point that, in acting as editor of the dying man's words, the friend "reads into" them (or adds to them) what he believes should be expressed. Now this may seem antithetical to the tradition of *ultima verba* inasmuch as these words are thought to be true in and of themselves and impervious to myriad interpretations by different readers. One can, however, reconcile the incompatibility by understanding that the friend who recounts the last words is not motivated by any desire outside the friendship; he desires only to convey the plenitude, the sense of identity or *aria*, of the speaker. This a-teleological nature of perfect friendships has been recently compared by Ullrich Langer to a kind of reading that Montaigne seems to promote, a reading that has no goal outside itself. "Reading is not directed towards an end outside itself, it is precisely not 'desire' of something else" (168). Langer furthermore points to the importance of friendship as a model for Montaigne's whole writing project: "When Montaigne attempts to define the 'sentiment' which indicated a perfect friendship, in a sense much of the project underlying the *Essais* is involved in that definition" (169).

The ways in which Montaigne describes the union of true friends — "Cette parfaicte amitié, dequoy je parle, est indivisible" (1: 28, 190) — recalls the way classical rhetoricians use metaphors of fusion and consubstantiality to explain a model of reading in which the meaning of a text is ideally transmitted to a reader without losing the plenitude of the author. Erasmus refers to a certain kind of language as being able to penetrate the minds of listeners and, by extension, readers. Although he does not refer to ultima verba specifically as being endowed with this special power, he does use the term pectus, the breast or heart, in a sense similar to that expressed by Lucretius when, in his description of *ultima verba*, he writes: "At last true words surge up from deep within our heart / The mask falls away and reality is left." Terence Cave elaborates on the connection Erasmus draws between reading and the notion of pectus which he describes as

the focus of the self which is presumed to guarantee profound understanding....
The text is made consubstantial with the reader and is then re-uttered in a

speech-act grounded in the living presence of the speaker, a process which achieves its end in that vivid penetration of the listener's mind which is in itself a mark of authenticity. (*Cornucopian Text* 85-86)

The reception of last words by friends would appear to provide a perfect test case for the notion of *pectus* and the kind of reading it makes possible. In other words, if ever there should be immediate, intuitive understanding and transparent communication between two individuals, it is at a death scene witnessed by a friend who is able to listen to the *ultima verba* with his heart and, through the heart, understand them.

III. PROBLEMS IN READING *ULTIMA VERBA*: PECTUS OR PERFORMANCE

In 1563, Montaigne wrote a letter to his father in which he describes La Boétie's last days and words and his own role as friend and witness. We could not ask for a more appropriate example of *ultima verba*.

In the letter, the frequency of the metaphor of the *heart* is striking. The *heart* is contrasted to the *mouth* in a way that emphasizes the commonplaces of friendship we have enumerated: the depth and completeness of perfect understanding, the fusion of the friends, and the lack of self-interest within the friendship union. A schematic enumeration of the instances of the term *cueur* demonstrates the extent to which it is over-determined: From his friend, Montaigne inherits a book collection which "part de bon cueur" and which Montaigne receives, "le cueur serré." During his dying moments, La Boétie admits that the words that the two men have shared in their short friendship are carried not only in the mouth, "mais engravez bien avant au cueur." This reinforces the classical notion of the heart as the source of a true language and also as the repository where memories of friends are stored. By claiming, "Il y a fort long temps que j'y estois preparé, & que je sçavais ma leçon par cueur," La Boétie claims to have followed the Socratic imperative to study dying and death in preparation for one's own demise. Near the end of the letter, La Boétie tries to tell his wife a story, but "le cueur luy failloit," and he has no more words for her. It is rather Montaigne who is destined to receive La Boétie's most significant, ultimate, words. Analyzed on this level, the letter appears to reinforce certain Classical notions of friendship as well as the tradition of death-bed scenes: it combines a Stoic emphasis on the courage of the dying man with details — "tout horreur et tout effroy" — reminiscent of the Christian *ars moriendi*.

At the beginning of the letter Montaigne assures his reader (his father, Pierre Eyquem) that he is qualified to recount La Boétie's last words: "Quant à ses dernieres paroles, sans doubte si homme en doit rendre bon conte, c'est moy" (1347). He is qualified first because he witnessed the death scene and heard La Boétie's words; secondly, and more importantly, because of the great friendship the two enjoyed — "pour la singuliere & fraternelle amitié que nous nous estions entreportez" — which enables him to fully understand his friend and guarantee the great moral integrity he displayed throughout his life. "J'avois trescertaine cognoissance des intentions, jugements & volontez qu'il avoit eu durant sa vie, autant sans doute qu'homme peut avoir d'un autre ... je les sçavois estre hautes, vertueuses, pleines de trescertaine resolution, & quand tout est dit, admirables." Montaigne ends this lengthy sentence by acknowledging that, from the onset of his friend's last illness, he expected that his *ultima verba* would reflect his high character: "je prevoyois bien que si la maladie luy laissoit le moyen de se pouvoir exprimer, qu'il ne luy eschapperoit rien en une telle necessité qui ne fust grand, & plein de bon exemple: ainsi je m'en prenois le plus garde que je pouvois."

In the first paragraph of the letter, Montaigne leaves the reader in suspense as to the actual quality of La Boétie's *ultima verba*. What seems clear, on the other hand, is that this account of a death scene fulfils one traditional requirement; it is recounted by a true friend who can attest to the moral quality of the dying person's life. Given the importance that Montaigne himself places on the "dernieres paroles" of his friend, I quote the final passage of the letter in entirety.

Lors entre autres choses il se print à me prier & reprier avecques une extreme affection, de luy donner une place: de sorte que j'eus peur que son jugement fust esbranlé. Mesmes que luy ayant bien doucement remonstré, qu'il se laissoit emporter au mal, & que ces mots n'estoient pas d'homme bien rassis, il ne se rendit point au premier coup, & redoubla encores plus fort: "Mon frere, mon frere, me refusez-vous doncques une place?" Jusques à ce qu'il me contraignit de le convaincre par raison, & de luy dire, que puis qu'il respiroit & parloit, & qu'il avoit corps, il avoit par consequent son *lieu*. "Voire, voire, me respondit-il lors, j'en ay, mais ce n'est pas celuy qu'il me faut: & puis quand tout est dit, je n'ay plus d'estre.---Dieu vous en donnera un meilleur bien tost, luy fis-je.---Y fusse-je desja, mon frere, me respondit-il, il y a trois jours que j'ahanne pour partir." Estant sur ces destresses il m'appella souvent pour s'informer seulement si j'estois pres de luy. En fin il se mist un peu à reposer, qui nous confirma encores plus en nostre bonne esperance. De manière que sortant de sa chambre, je m'en resjouïs avecques Madamoiselle de la Boëtie. Mais une heure après ou environ, me nommant une fois ou deux, & puuis tirant à soy un grand soupir il rendit l'ame, sur les trois heures du

Mercredy matin dishuitiesme d'Aoust, l'an mil cinq cens soixante trois, apres avoir vescu 32 ans, 9 mois, et 17 jours.... (1359-60; my emphasis)

The passage begins with La Boétie imploring Montaigne to give him a "place." Faced with this request, Montaigne worries that his friend is losing his powers of reason — "j'eus peur que son jugement fust esbranlé" — a concern he then voices to his friend, telling him that "ces mots n'estoient pas d'homme bien rassis." This puts in question the status of these last words as *verae voces*, since their truth value would seem to depend on the lucidity of the speaker. Secondly, it casts this final interchange in the form of a dialectical *agon*. Thus Montaigne notes that La Boétie "ne se rendit point au premier coup," and that he even counterattacks, "redoubla encores plus fort." Montaigne finds himself forced to resort to argument: "il me contraignit de le convaincre par raison." All this seems wholly incompatible with the complete understanding characteristic of perfect friendship, which, as we have seen, is supposed to be dependent on neither interpretation nor argument. Thirdly, Montaigne's doubts about his friend's mental state introduce a further element that has little place in traditional death scenes: the friend's possible misunderstanding of the dying man's words. Indeed, all three factors seem antithetical both to the tradition of the death scene as well as to the kind of understanding from the *heart* that is supposed to characterize interactions between friends. As Richard Regosin notes in another context, "A fundamental characteristic of the perfect union of friendship is that it is most profoundly a prelinguistic or extralinguistic phenomenon" (1977, 28).

And yet much of this final interchange turns on the meaning of words, in particular the word "place." Why, in his response, does Montaigne transform the word "place" (that La Boétie repeats) into "lieu"? This enigmatic shift has not, to my knowledge, ever been investigated in the critical literature on this text. The meaning of "place," in the two instances where it appears in the text, cannot be precisely determined,[11] whereas Montaigne himself defines the meaning of "lieu" as a physical location and, adopting a somewhat argumentative style, he tries to convince his friend — "par raison" — that he does indeed occupy a "lieu" by virtue of his body's spatial extension: "puis qu'il respiroit & parloit, & qu'il avoit corps, il avoit par consequent son *lieu*." Faced with this translation, and perhaps deformation, of his words, the dying man announces that he has indeed a "lieu," but that is not the one he needs. He then says that he no longer has any "being" ("estre"), a statement which may be interpreted on either an ontological or social level (in other words, either as a comment on his lack of existence or rather his lack of a place in the world). To this Montaigne responds that God will soon grant him a better one ("Dieu vous en donnera un meilleur bien tost"). It is not absolutely clear if the masculine direct object pronoun "un" is meant to refer to "estre" or "lieu," though the pronoun in the following sentence — "Y fusse-je desja" — indicates that La Boétie understands the antecedent as "lieu." For all the unresolved questions about this exchange, it is at least evident that La Boétie is not delirious, since his responses are all logically linked to his interlocutor's statements.

What is striking in this exchange is that, quite simply, the dying man's words are not clear to Montaigne, who records the lack of understanding with no comment. Furthermore, his apparent misreading of La Boétie is not limited to a verbal level, but extends to his behaviour as well. When La Boétie, no doubt exhausted, becomes silent, Montaigne interprets the behaviour as a positive sign: "qui nous confirma encores plus en nostre bonne esperance." What Montaigne understands as a sign of improved health — his silence — announces on the contrary his imminent demise. La Boétie dies about an hour afterward ("une heure après ou environ"), pronouncing Montaigne's name "une fois ou deux."[12]

Does this letter satisfy the dual objective of accounts of death scenes and portraits — that they should convey the integrity of the deceased by resembling the image of what he was in life, and communicate this image to posterity? Compared to most of the death scenes recounted in the *Essais* as well as to those in well-known classical accounts, for example Plato's *Phaedo,* to which this letter has been compared,[13] La Boétie's death scene presents an image of the deceased that is not — dare we say — as definitive? Questions are likely to arise in the reader's mind as to the precise meaning of his last words.

Montaigne's apparent inability to understand his dying friend's words points to the kind of duplicity of meaning that the notion of *pectus* and the ideal of friendship are supposed to counter. Montaigne's account of La Boétie's death may well testify to the writer's hope that last words constitute a special or transparent language that can ultimately be interpreted with perfect clarity by a friend-witness; it nonetheless points to the instability of all language — even the ostensibly privileged language of death — and to the impossibility of remaining impervious to the vagaries and varieties of readers' interpretations. This is the most obvious and significant consequence of Montaigne's misreading of La Boétie's *ultima verba.*

A second consequence concerns the nature of what La Boétie might have been trying to convey with the word "place": a last wish. Earlier in the letter, Montaigne notes that La Boétie had asked him to remember him to his acquaintances: "[les] gens de bien qui m'ont aymé et estimé pendant ma vie. Je vous prie ... de leur rendre tesmoignage de la bonne volonté que je leur ay portee jusques à ce dernier terme de ma vie" (1350). The final plea for a "place" might be understood in light of this more fully articulated request. There is a long tradition of death-bed requests, the most well-known example being Socrates's request that Crito offer a cock to Asclepius,[14] and such requests constitute a part of the conventional role to be fulfilled by the dying person. One notable example appears in "de l'Amitié" in the story of Eudamidas's last wish that his friends take care of his mother and daughter. Montaigne lauds Eudamidas for having requested a favour of his friends: "Il laisse [ses amis] heritiers de cette sienne liberalité, qui consiste à leur mettre en main les moyens de luy bien-faire. Et, sans doubte, la force de l'amitié se montre bien plus richement en son fait qu'en celuy d'Aretheus" (190-91). The point here is that, by failing to understand La Boétie, Montaigne effectively prevents him from performing this aspect of the dying man's role — a last request — for which Eudamidas and others through history have been praised.

Despite the fact that La Boétie may be deprived of one role traditionally accorded to the dying, Montaigne claims that his friend is his example in death: "Cela me serviroit d'exemple, pour jouer ce mesme rolle à mon tour" (1353).[15] The mention of *roles* in death scenes points to an incompatibility, if not a flagrant contradiction, inherent in the tradition of last words. On one hand, they are perceived as a spontaneous and true expression of the inner self, the *pectus*. On the other hand, *ultima verba* are referred to as a learned and rehearsed performance, a kind of script memorized as part of an established role. Speaking of what should be taught to a young pupil, Montaigne advises: "il me semble que les premiers discours dequoy on luy doit abreuver l'entendement, ce doivent estre ceux qui ... luy apprendront à se connoistre, et à sçavoir bien mourir et bien vivre"(1: 26, 158). Montaigne draws the title for his essay, "Que philosopher c'est apprendre à mourir," from the famous maxim attributed to Socrates,[16] the same person he lauds for *not* having learned by heart the last oration he delivered to the men who were about to condemn him, "Et sa riche et puissante nature eust elle commis à l'art sa defense, et en son plus haut essay renoncé à la verité et naïveté ... pour se parer du fard des figures et feintes d'une oraison apprinse?" (3: 12, 1031).

The imperative to accept last words as an unequivocal, unfeigned, and spontaneous sign of the deceased's character thus stands in contrast to the imperative to *learn* them, to regard them as exemplary texts to be read and studied in preparation for one's own death. The two imperatives are perhaps not mutually exclusive, but, as we see in Montaigne's writing, they do belong to two distinct semantic fields: as *verae voces*, they are described in terms of truth, nature, purity, sincerity, and incorruptibility; as objects of study, they are associated with practice and preparation, and, in a more negative vein, with figures and fictions.

Pectus or performance, spontaneous or orchestrated? The tradition of last words incorporates both aspects, as does Montaigne's text. A decade after quoting La Boétie saying "Il y a fort longtemps que ... je sçavais ma leçon par cueur," Montaigne repeats the allusion to "coeur," saying "Je remets à la mort l'essay du fruict de mes estudes. Nous verrons là si mes discours me partent de la bouche, ou du coeur" (1: 19, 79). Part of this statement suggests that *ultima verba* may not naturally and inevitably emanate at the moment of death; that they must be learned ("le fruict de mes estudes") while the very next sentence implies that the words spoken at death can never be definitively prepared — "nous verrons là" — only at death will we see, or hear, what happens.

IV. MONTAIGNE'S REFUSAL TO PLAY HIS ROLE

Montaigne's own death is, perhaps not surprisingly, a subject of contemplation and discussion in the *Essais*. What is a surprise, however, given the stress he places on last words and the presence of a friend-witness at the bed-side, is that he eschews such a scene for himself.

> Si toutes-fois j'avois à choisir, ce seroit, ce croy-je, plustost à cheval que dans un lict, hors de ma maison et esloigné des miens. Il y a plus de crevecoeur que de consolation à prendre congé de ses amis. J'oublie volontiers à dire ce grand et eternel adieu. S'il se tire quelque commodité de cette assistance, il s'en tire cent incommoditez.... Il n'y a donc pas beaucoup de mal de mourir loing et à part. (3: 9, 956, 959)

Jules Brody has pointed out the extent to which Montaigne's attitude toward death scenes differs from that of his contemporaries; he argues that Montaigne's rejection of the ceremonial or performative aspect of the death-bed spectacle would have been perceived by sixteenth century readers as "une formelle mise en cause, sinon un rejet catégorique, de l'efficacité ... d'une 'vulgate de la mort' qui s'élaborait depuis plus de cent ans au sein de la culture catholique européenne" (102).[17] The question remains: *why* would Montaigne wish to abandon what had been for centuries a social norm and a literary convention — the death witnessed and recorded by a friend?

In response to this enigma, one could simply argue that Montaigne's concern about language — the relativity of meaning given the variety of readers' interpretations — leads him to fear that his own last words might not be read by posterity in the spirit they were delivered and with the meaning he intended. He may well boast that at death, "cessera tout le droict et interest que j'ay à la reputation" (3: 9, 956), he nonetheless promises to return from the grave if his posthumous reputation does not correspond to him, if his death-portrait, as it were, does not resemble him: "Je ne veux pas après tout, comme je vois souvent agiter la memoire des trespassez, qu'on aille debatant: 'Il jugeoit, il vivoit ainsi; il vouloit cecy; s'il eust parlé sur sa fin, il eust dict, il eust donné; je le connoissois mieux que tout autre.... Je reviendrois volontiers de l'autre monde pour démentir celuy qui me formeroit autre que je n'estois, fut-ce pour m'honorer" (2: 12, 569). This fear can be related, of course, to Montaigne's repeated claim that since La Boétie's death, he has no friend who could be relied upon to fully understand his final words and then convey them, and with them his presence, his *aria*. Montaigne appears to hold onto the hope of finding a friend before he dies; that friend will be a reader of his book. "Outre ce profit que je tire d'escrire de moy, j'en espere cet autre que, s'il advient que mes humeurs plaisent et accordent à quelque honneste homme avant que je meure, il recherchera de nous joindre" (3: 9, 959). According to this argument, the truth of *ultima verba* would not be in question, but the possibility of their being reliably transmitted to those who survive him would be.

However, the *Essais* also suggest another reason why Montaigne might wish to die "loing et à part." Simply put, the moment of death may *not* be more important, or more revealing of character, than any other moment in life. Montaigne says as much: "[La mort] est bien le bout, non pourtant le but de la vie; c'est sa fin, son extremité, non pourtant son object" (1: 12, 1028). Now such a statement does seem to put in question the tradition by which the *hora mortis* is considered to be both a means by which to judge the quality of the life and also an appropriate object of life-long study. Should we see death as life's goal, "le but" or rather as nothing more than the end of life, "le bout"? The apparent incompatibility of these stances has led a generation of scholars to try to prove that Montaigne's thought on this question "evolved" from one to the other. Pierre Villey, a major proponent of this argument in the early years of this century, wrote that Montaigne's attitude toward death "se transformera complètement. En 1588, [elle] est exactement contraire à ce qu'[elle] était en 1572" (Villey 390). A problem arises with the evolutionists' argument, however, when one discovers that Montaigne endorsed both views throughout his two decade writing career.[18]

The debate nonetheless reveals the complexity of Montaigne's relationship to the tradition of the *hora mortis* and *ultima verba*. As Villey himself notes, "[Montaigne] se plaira à recueillir des exemples de morts qui ont contredit le reste de la vie" (Villey 81). Now there are several ways to understand Montaigne's attraction to death scenes which seem inconsistent with the lives in question. Villey presents this as proof that the death moment becomes less privileged in Montaigne's thought, but it could simply be a further case of

Montaigne's nominalism (the lack of link between particulars and universals) which marks his writing from the outset.[19] Another way to understand the examples of "inconsistent deaths" in the *Essais*, and by extension to shed light on the enigma of Montaigne's wish to die alone, would be to return to the traditional assumption that last words are "true."

If last words are true, in the sense that they do not lie, then there exists the possibility that his last words might give the lie to his life; they could run counter to the image he has of his own life, the image for which he would wish to be remembered. And if people believe that last words do not lie, then the presence of well-meaning friends might do nothing to alter an interpretation of *ultima verba* which would be unflattering to the dying individual. This is precisely what happened in the case of Epicurus, at least as the story is recounted in "de la Gloire." "Voyons les dernieres paroles d'Epicurus, et qu'il dict en mourant: elles sont grandes et dignes d'un tel philosophe, mais si ont elles quelque marque de la recommandation de son nom, et de cette humeur qu'il avoit décriée par ses preceptes" (2: 16, 603). It seems that after spending his life expressing contempt for posthumous glory, Epicurus's last words and requests of his friends show him to be subject to the vanity he had so decried; he admits taking pleasure in the remembrance of his discoveries and teachings, and he requests that his friends and disciples celebrate his birthday and regularly meet in honour of his memory (and that of Metrodorus). Montaigne comments: "Ce qui me faict interpreter que ce plaisir qu'il dit sentir en son ame, de ses inventions, regarde aucunement la reputation qu'il en esperoit acquerir après sa mort, c'est l'ordonnance de son testament." Now, Montaigne also expresses concern for his posthumous reputation, but that is not the point, since he did not spend his life creating an image of himself as a person disdainful of glory as he maintains Epicurus did. Montaigne observes that the last words are inconsistent with Epicurus's life; it is as if the words rewrote his life-story because, according to the tradition of *ultima verba*, a person's life must be evaluated by its consistency with his death. As Montaigne puts it in "De la Cruauté": "Toute mort doit estre de mesmes sa vie. Nous ne devenons pas autres pour mourir" (2: 11, 404). And yet, immediately following this statement which expresses a traditional view of the *hora mortis* (that a person's life should be judged in terms of his demeanor and words at death), Montaigne turns tradition upside down: "*J'interprete tousjours la mort par la vie.*"

Perhaps the only safe way for Montaigne to make his exit is "quietement et sourdement" (1: 19, 79), unwitnessed both because he has not a friend but also because he does not want his death to be seen as "le maistre jour ... le jour juge de tous les autres." Montaigne thus leaves us, not an account of his last words, but rather an account of his life and thoughts so that we may judge him on that basis. Lacking a friend, he must rely on future readers to interpret this account. Will these readers receive Montaigne's writing in the spirit of the tradition of *ultima verba*, of unequivocal words that express the essence of their author? Only if these readers assume the traditional role of friends, a role Montaigne was unable to fulfil "à la lettre."

EPILOGUE

Montaigne did not die alone on horseback, as he had wished, but in bed (September 13, 1592). There is no eyewitness account, but Montaigne is said to have uttered the name of his friend, Pierre de Brach, in his last words. Upon learning this, Brach wrote to Justus Lipsius saying:

> Il m'a faict cet honneur d'avoir faict mention de moy jusques à ses dernieres parolles, ce qui me donne plus de regret de n'y avoir esté, comme il disoit avoir regret de n'avoir personne pres de luy à qui il peut desploier les dernières conceptions de son ame.[20]

But, friend or no friend, Montaigne would not have been able to articulate his last thoughts because, according to Etienne Pasquier, he was stricken with aphasia during his last days.

Gender and Genre

CARLA FRECCERO

Gender Ideologies, Women Writers, and the Problem of Patronage in Early Modern Italy and France: Issues and Frameworks

To enter history, one must have access to discourse, whether that access takes the form of being written about or of writing. One's "name" or one's writing must also be preserved, protected, and published. In early modern times, this was usually accomplished through the institutions of patronage and canonization. The "pater" in patronage suggests to us all, in this time of intense speculation about gender difference, that the relation between women and this act or condition of fathering was and is problematic. Women could themselves be patrons, and thus "fathers" to writers and artists. They could also be muses, inspirational amorous figures of absent presence who engendered poetic creation in men, paternal beings — phallocratic women — who enabled a "feminized" male poet to appropriate the creative labour of birth.[1] Finally, and relatedly, women's names could be preserved for the annals of history as the object of a male poet's love. Here, too, the woman was a figure; her name, extracted from the patrilineal designator that would locate her in history, acted as a sign of the poet's own fame and artistic mastery.[2] Thus, while it seems evident in early modern Europe that certain women could indeed be "fathers" to writers, it is not so clear that women could be "fathered" in their turn, except perhaps as silent and obedient daughters. As Linda Nochlin bluntly put it, "Why have there been no great women artists?" (145-78).[3]

I would like to speculate about some of the problems of patronage for women authors in a context determined by incipient nationalism and capitalism, interstructured with existing economic, political, and social systems distinctly and definitively marked by patriarchy.[4] I will explore some of the necessary frameworks within which to think about the question of women and patronage, and how the ideological encoding of cultural practices informs observable social relations.

Recent studies of gender in the early modern period have been able to delineate some parameters of the category woman focusing, in particular, on the

65

relation between "woman" and speech or writing. By surveying the ideologies governing this relation, it is possible to understand what it might have meant to be a woman writer in early modern Europe, both for the woman herself and for the society as a whole. Such an understanding may, in turn, shed light on the peculiar "absence" to which Nochlin refers, and on the problematic relation between women authors and male patrons.

Jacques Lacan, in a stunning analogy between personal and historical absence, suggests the path of investigation that has been taken up by new historicist studies of gender:

> The unconscious is that chapter of my history that is marked by a blank or occupied by a falsehood: it is the censored chapter. But the truth can be rediscovered; usually it has already been written down elsewhere. Namely:
> — in monuments: this is my body. That is to say, the hysterical nucleus of the neurosis in which the hysterical symptom reveals the structure of a language, and is deciphered like an inscription.... (50)

Lacan's literary formulation points to the domain of symptomatic representation as a field where the question of a historical absence may be raised and read, not simply or only by looking for "actual" women in history, but by examining the traces, inscriptions, and symptoms of that absence "elsewhere." What is yielded in this fashion is a form of ideology not always readily accessible in pronouncements of the official culture, since those pronouncements often conceal or elide the degree to which they govern a highly conflicted site of struggle. Indeed, recent studies in the history of women, gender, and sexuality, focus importantly on the body as one such site.[5]

As Mikhail Bakhtin has shown, relations in the body politic are mapped out onto actual bodies in discourse. He distinguishes between the classical (closed and ordered) body as the language of the ruling class that privileges the head as the seat of reason, and the grotesque or open body of the language of carnival and the people, privileging the lower bodily strata and the body's orifices (see *Rabelais and His World*, especially chapters five and six). Thus the body becomes a site of struggles for power. Bodily metaphors can then be read as ideologically symptomatic, just as ideologies can be mapped onto the body. Peter Stallybrass, in an important corrective to Bakhtin, examines how gender is inscribed in the oppositions between these bodies as well (123-42; see also Stallybrass and White).[6] The ways in which gender functions in the conflict between "classical" and "grotesque" bodies in discourse points to symbolic (and symptomatic) uses of the category woman, as well as to the ways in which women were affected by the inscription of ideology onto the body.

Thomas Laqueur and Stephen Greenblatt have argued against an overly totalizing view of ideologies of gender in early modern Europe, charting rather the heterogeneous and dynamic discourses of sexual difference in theological, philosophical, and anatomical texts (Greenblatt, *Shakespearean Negotiations* 66-93; Laqueur, "Orgasm" 1-41; see also Laqueur, *Making Sex*).[7] Thus, they fruitfully engage in a polemic against the view of dominant ideology as all-determining, a position which feminists have also adopted in order to focus their attention, not only on the forms of male domination of women in history, but also on the (historical and individual) agency of women in their struggle and negotiations with structures that seek to contain them. Furthermore, the adoption of a Foucauldian model of power as a productive force works against both static notions of domination and suppression, and the idea that either pole, as such, is "simply" visible and operative; rather, disciplinary regimes and those governed by them could be seen to be mutually constitutive and diffuse (cf. Foucault, *The History of Sexuality*). Nevertheless, in the case of European early modernity, particularly in France, but perhaps elsewhere as well, I think it is possible to invoke the Gramscian notion of hegemonic ideology — a concept that importantly "restores" the place of agency in charting the workings of domination — to describe patriarchy, a ruling practice, philosophy, world-view — in short, an ideology — whose contradictions become more or less apparent at different points in time and whose articulation and enforcement depends also upon class interests.[8]

Early modern Italy and France inherit medical, philosophical, and theological discourses defining "woman." Alberti, Castiglione, Rabelais, and the participants in the *querelle des femmes* conduct encyclopaedic surveys of these sources: the Aristotelian view of woman as partial man, the Pythagorean monad/dyad opposition that constructs woman as other to man's same, Galen's view of the wandering womb and uncontrollable female desire, Genesis' conception of woman as the helpmeet of man, and finally St. Paul, the scripture perhaps most frequently cited as precedent for the political suppression of women.[9]

Discourses about "woman," such as those found parodically represented in Rabelais's third book, represent her as a necessarily but also sinfully insatiable creature. Stallybrass notes that, "woman's body, unlike the prince's, is naturally 'grotesque'. It must be subjected to constant surveillance precisely because, as Bakhtin says of the grotesque body, it is 'unfinished, outgrows itself, transgresses its own limits'" (126). He also points out that "the connection between speaking and wantonness was common to legal discourse and conduct books" (126). Thus, also there is a kind of displacement upward, whereby the open mouth signals the dangerous openness of the woman's body: "Silence, the closed mouth, is made a sign of chastity" (127). Francesco Barbaro's humanist treatise *De re uxoria* (*Concerning Wifely Matters*) makes this connection: "It is proper that the speech of women never be made public; for the speech of a noblewoman can be no less dangerous than the nakedness of her limbs" (Kohl *et al.* 205).[10] Thus the "open," public, speaking woman was represented as a threat.

Christian doctrine also promoted a view of woman as sinful seductress, the daughter of Eve. St. Paul, in I Corinthians 14, adds silence to the injunctions against women: "Let your women keep silence in the churches: for it is not permitted upon them to speak; but they are commanded to be under obedience..." (34).

Ruth Kelso and Joan Kelly, groundbreakers for the study of women in early modern Europe, have indicated the ways in which changes in economic and political conditions in the fifteenth and sixteenth centuries widened gaps between the "public" and the "private" spheres. Kelly explains, in response to the question, "Did women have a Renaissance?":

> The state, early capitalism, and the social relations formed by them impinged on the lives of Renaissance women in different ways according to their different positions in society. But the startling fact is that women as a group ... experienced a contraction of social and personal options that men of their classes either did not ... or did not experience as markedly.... (19-20)[11]

Whether or not women were more restricted in the fifteenth and sixteenth centuries, it does seem that early mercantile capitalism in Italy, combined with prevailing notions about "woman," made possible a detailed articulation of woman as property within the private domain of a man's household. Leon Battista Alberti's fifteenth-century treatise *Della Famiglia* (*On the Family*) obsessively articulates the connections between private property, goods, children, and wives. In the following passage, he aggressively promotes a strategy of containment for the merchant-class wife:

> Women, on the other hand, are almost universally timid by nature, soft, and slow, and are more useful, therefore, for staying at home to care for our possessions, as if Nature had thus provided for our existence, decreeing that man should bring things home and the woman care for them. Let women defend their possessions and themselves, entrenched in the home with leisure, diffidence, and anxiety. (*Albertis of Florence* 215-26)[12]

This early text of economic management expresses considerable anxiety with regard to wifely cooperation in the protection of class interests. There are numerous passages that deal with the importance of secrecy for control or possession of wealth and goods, where women are cited as the potential gap or opening through which loss can occur. Women must be enlisted to protect and conserve; their capacity to circulate (wealth, goods, information) poses a threat. Once again, the focus is the mouth:

> No matter how trifling a secret I had, I never shared it with my wife or with any other woman. I disapprove of those husbands who consult their wives and do not know how to keep any secret to themselves. They are mad to seek good advice and wisdom in women, even more so if they think a wife can guard a secret with greater jealousy and silence than her husband. O foolish husbands, is there ever a time when you chat with a woman without being reminded that women can do anything but keep silent? (218)

Alberti's treatise, through contradictions in the discourse on woman (she is by nature "timid" and yet she cannot keep silent) and anxious arguments for her control, suggests that woman's place was at issue in this period and that there was indeed resistance to that place. This was in part a function of class anxiety, a counteraristocratic move to promote bourgeois industriousness over leisurely self-indulgence. Ann Jones notes that "Certain women of the high nobility recognized that the wives of princes played highly visible and articulate roles" ("Surprising Fame" 75). Citing examples from a sixteenth-century treatise written for the daughter of a Genoese shipping magnate, she argues:

> Writers aiming advice at fathers and husbands in lower ranks limited women's exposure to language and learning even further. They opposed the frivolous and potentially dangerous pleasures of poetry and philosophy to the sober, useful work assigned to the daughters and wives of the petty gentry and urban merchant class.... [Giovanni Bruto] opposes domestic virtue to public ambition; he links literary fame to lascivious self-indulgence. (76)

As Natalie Zemon Davis so aptly notes, "In the little world of the family, with its conspicuous tension between intimacy and power, the larger matters of political and social order could find ready symbolization" (*Society and Culture* 127).

Class conflict and political instability often converge during this period in the discourse on woman. Thus, in Castiglione's *Courtier*, the court lady becomes the subject of Book III, which is framed by the question of the courtier's social and political role in relation to his prince.[13] Machiavelli, in the *Discourses*, entitles a chapter: "How States are Ruined on Account of Women" (Book 3, ch. 26), which recounts a situation of class conflict leading to governmental demise.

He concludes: "women have been the cause of great dissensions and much ruin to states, and have caused great damage to those who govern them" (489). Davis describes how, in France, family patriarchy extends itself as a metaphor for other political hierarchies:

> Jean Calvin, himself a collapser of ecclesiastical hierarchies, saw the subjection of the wife to the husband as a guarantee of the subjection of both of them to the authority of the Lord. Kings and political theorists saw the increasing legal subjection of wives to their husbands ... as a guarantee of the obedience of both men and women to the slowly centralizing state.... (*Society and Culture* 128)

The subordinated woman, chaste and silent, figures the "classical body" of the well-ordered state with its stable hierarchies, while the promiscuous, outspoken or "unruly" woman (as Davis calls her) figures the "grotesque body" of the people and the threat of revolution.[14]

This ideological map of woman in early modern Italian and French discourses charts the territory through which women writers negotiated their "unruly" desires. For, as Mary Wiesner points out, "While male writers, officials, theologians, workers, and professionals were attempting to limit women's activities to the private realm, women consistently defended their public role" (1). Davis suggests, for example, that some aristocratic women realized the economic and political importance of their bodies in contracting alliances and consolidating state power, and exploited that importance by "giving themselves away" ("Boundaries" 62), thus reappropriating notions of the body as property. She makes the point that "if women can think of giving themselves away, then they can also begin to think of having stronger ownership rights in their bodies" (62).

In exploring the relation between patron and writer in early modern France, I focus on those women writers who were best known, who were "canonized" that is, even before the current interest in women's writing made profitable the search for discredited or previously unknown works by women. While historical bias may account for the proportionately lower numbers of early modern women writers within even the privileged, educated classes, nevertheless there are women who occupy chapters in the official, patriarchal literary history of the period. By examining the conditions of their entry into public spheres and the mobilization of prevailing gender ideologies around them, it is possible to understand why the dominant models of economic support and promotion for male writers were rendered problematic for women. It is also possible to see what historical instabilities during this period produced such a proliferation of proscriptions against the "unruly" woman and created gaps in which a significant number of women's voices could be heard.

Women writers of the noble classes in early modern Europe could confine themselves to religious topics and thus acquire the ecclesiastical protection of one powerful institution of support (or censure) through "canonization" (the word originally meant official sanction by the Church). Christine de Pisan (late fourteenth, early fifteenth century) and Marguerite de Navarre (sixteenth century) both entered publication in this manner.

But what about secular writings and the secular institution of patronage? If, as I mentioned, there was a belief that "women's speech opened them to irresistible sexual temptation; that articulateness led to promiscuity" (Jones "Surprising Fame" 78), then the fact that a woman wrote could call into question her honour. Furthermore, the explicit economic link between artist and patron whereby the artist's production is exchanged for economic support made a woman whose patron was male vulnerable to accusations of prostitution. Christine de Pisan, one of France's earliest professional writers, constantly complains of having to defend herself against such accusations.

Indeed, in sixteenth-century Italy and apart from female rulers and queens, those women whose patrons most successfully provided them with fame, publishing their reputations, were courtesans, and their patrons were multiple as well as male.[15] Jones, whose studies of Veronica Franco and Tullia d'Aragona have focused on the ways in which they negotiated their precarious literary fame, writes of the courtesan:

> Her reputation, on which she based the high fees that distinguished the courtesan from the common prostitute, depended on a male clientele, the Venetian and Florentine literati and courtiers with whom she traded sexual favors in return for literary recognition. ("Surprising Fame" 87)[16]

The independence of the Venetian Republic may be adduced as explanation here for the relative freedom from ecclesiastical censure these women enjoyed. Political and economic conditions may have functioned contradictorily in creating the class of courtesan writers and the space in public discourse for their work to circulate. On the one hand Italy, unlike France, was not undergoing monarchical centralization; there was no "ideological state apparatus," as Althusser calls it, that reinforced family patriarchy by analogy with the state (127-86). Urban patriotic identification was possible and served class interests in the competition for cultural status. Courtesans were also a tourist attraction. Merchant capitalism and the money economy worked against static family arrangements in some cases (witness the anxiety of Alberti's treatise regarding the integrity of proximate family business relations), while at the same time producing more rigid distinctions between public and private; Venetian sumptuary laws severely restricted wives in public circulation and display. Courtesans, as one tourist noted, could be enlisted in the service of domestic control. The English traveller Thomas Coryat assessed the situation thus: "they do grant large dispensation and indulgence unto them.... For they thinke that the chastity of their wives would be the sooner assaulted, and so consequently they should be capricornified (which of all the indignities in the world the Venetian cannot patiently endure) were it not for these places of evacuation" (Jones, "City Women" 303). Furthermore, courtesans and their children were a source of inexpensive labour in the city. Thus, changing economic, political, and social relations may have simultaneously further restricted women while opening up spaces for their participation in aspects of the cultural economy.

Conditions in sixteenth-century France produced a different set of writer/patron relations. In this century of monarchic consolidation, the analogous relations between king/subject and husband/wife produced a different cluster of meanings around the figure of the unruly woman. Within the aristocracy, relations between men and women were matters of state; Marguerite de Navarre, writing in the mid-sixteenth century, often figures the struggle between women's self-determination and their inscription within a political system in her collection of novellas, *The Heptameron* (see Freccero, "Marguerite de Navarre"). At the end of one such story, a male interlocutor remarks: "in order to maintain peace in the state, consideration is given only to the rank of families, the seniority of individuals and the provisions of the law, and not to men's love and virtue, in order that the monarchy should not be undermined" (Margarite de Navarre, *The Heptameron* 374). Marguerite's life, like that of many queens, was centrally bound up with state politics, much of it indirect and "unofficial," except in the kingdoms, such as Navarre, which were at the time still independent domains of rule within the territory now known as France.[17] The gradual merging of these states into the nation state over the course of the sixteenth century lends credence to Kelly's sense of a waning political autonomy for female rulers in the Renaissance; it also may have made possible Marguerite's literary production with the sanction of her brother, Francis I, king of France. The woman's exclusion from active participation in matters of state left her free, in a sense, to participate in literary production without as great a risk of censure, although Marguerite's poem, "Miroir de l'âme pécheresse" (1531), was condemned by the Sorbonne. Her brother's intervention — his protection and patronage, in other words — saved her from the fate of other heretical writers. Indeed, it is in the sixteenth century that the king's "privilege" (*le privilège du roi*) begins to replace individual patronage as the most effective means of copyright protection and protection from censure, though not necessarily financial support.[18] In Marguerite's case, however, the injunction against secular prose fiction held; her collection of short stories was not published in her lifetime, and it was her daughter, Jeanne, a protestant political leader and mother of King Henry IV of France, who commissioned the first "authorized" edition of *The Heptameron*.[19]

As in Italy, the canonized women poets in the secular tradition came from an urban, commercial centre, Lyon. Pernette du Guillet, writing in the 1540s, did not seek patronage: her husband published her poems in 1545, after her death. Jones recounts how "her printer claimed to make [her poems] public only at the insistence of her mourning husband, and he hedged them around with epigraphs commemorating her life-long chastity" ("City Women" 301). The fiction of address that may have preserved her fame for anthologies of French literature was her stance of modest discipleship towards Maurice Scève. Scève thus became a "poetic" patron whose renown conferred praise and provided protection for Pernette's claim to fame (Jones, "Surprising Fame" 81).

Louise Labé's situation was more ambiguous, in part because she played a more boldly public role in her work. Unlike her Italian counterparts, she was not a courtesan; a bourgeoise, married to a rope-maker, she published her writing herself, eventually obtaining the royal *imprimatur* that replaced ecclesiastical canonization in the growing secular state. Her patrons were the noblemen, scholars, poets, and publishers of the city of Lyon. Again, the more fluid economic, social, and political relations of an urban centre permitted her to capitalize on class pride and civic patriotism for social and professional advancement. Yet a myth of sexual profligacy grew up around her as well. Jones recounts how "she was violently criticized during a trial in Geneva at which her cousin accused her of leading her into lechery and finally to the murder of her husband," and that there were rumours that "she granted her favors to all the well-born men who frequented her house; she disguised herself in men's clothes, and provided her own and other women's sexual services to the local clergy" ("City Women" 302). Literary historians continue to debate the myth, while granting her nevertheless a place among France's prominent poets. Antoine du Verdier, writing in 1585, says, "It is not for having been a courtesan that I grant her a place in this library, but only for having written" (Guillot 117; translation is mine).

Louise Labé herself writes a preface to her work appealing to a rich landowner's daughter, Clémence de Bourges, for patronage, asking her to be a chaperone because, she writes, "women do not willingly show themselves alone in public."[20] Unlike the Venetian courtesans, Louise Labé and her promoters work to dissociate the poet from prostitution. It may be that such a class of women would have had too destabilizing an effect in a nation subject to the already destabilizing forces of the Lutheran and Calvinist Reform movements, where public discourse, like the municipal brothels, was carefully monitored by the state. Kelly and Davis (1975) note how laws were passed in sixteenth-century France restricting women from participation in commercial activities as well. While the civic autonomy of Lyons may have provided the material preconditions for a woman writer's success, it could do so only if the woman remained outside of economic and political circulation.[21]

In sketching the framework for a study of the relation between women writers and the system of patronage in early modern Italy and France, I have confined my remarks to the relations between male patrons and female writers. Noblewomen in early modern Europe also acted as patrons, but this phenomenon does not present a challenge to prevailing gender ideologies, as women's exclusion from public economic and political spheres has often given them the role of supporters and promoters of culture, particularly in the arts and letters. It is through these roles, in fact, that women have often contributed to shifts in ideology that have made possible both their greater participation in public spheres and the closing of the gap between public and private.[22] The situation of women writers, however, should indicate the necessity of constructing new frameworks within which to examine patronage and canonization: the economic, political, and social systems of promoting cultural artefacts; and of understanding that these systems themselves constitute obstacles to the historical investigation of women's production in early modern Europe.

Transitional periods in economic, political, and social relations will often make gender visible; indeed we have seen how the "unruly" woman's presence in public discourse often functions as a sign of such transitions. It is for women, however, to measure the gains and the costs of our entry into discourse through the patriarchal promotion systems we inherit. It is not possible to look back and measure a progressive enfranchisement; the current promotion of women's writing and writing about women in the U.S. publishing industry is occurring simultaneously with the feminization of poverty and the increasing racial and political oppression of women of colour. The challenge for those of us who are so privileged would be to break down those systems of support which are also systems of exclusion, to refigure the tropes of paternal/filial succession and to question propertarian claims upon bodies and writing.

KATY EMCK

Female Transvestism
and Male Self-Fashioning in
As You Like It and *La vida es sueño*

In Neil Jordan's film *The Crying Game* (1992), a lonely transvestite male comes to stand in for the straight hero's own lack of identity; his lack of stable social allegiances and of a role that fits his nature. The transvestite is at the centre of this strangely contentless film where people are invariably the opposites of what they first appear to be. Transvestism, as a signifier of shifting identity and reference, of deceptiveness and inauthenticity as opposed to unity and self-coherence, is both a peculiarly postmodern motif and a quintessentially Renaissance trope. In it, the performative aspect of identity is accentuated. While the representation of female transvestism in the Renaissance is usually understood as concerning anxieties about female transgression *per se*, I wish to look at it as profoundly allied to male identity, to show how this motif of female insurgency, power and deceptiveness becomes resonant of male social identities under construction.

In particular, in the two plays I wish to discuss, *La vida es sueño* and *As You Like It*, the transvestism of the heroines Rosaura and Rosalind is basic to the development of central and autonomous male subjects, Segismundo and Orlando, respectively. I will argue that the female transvestite functions in *As You Like It* and *La vida es sueño* as a trace of and a form of anxiety about "self-fashioned" male identity.[1] In *As You Like It* and *La vida es sueño*, Rosalind and Rosaura, who take their fates into their own hands by adopting the signifiers of male identity, reflect the needs of their marginalised male counterparts. Segismundo and Orlando eventually attain to pre-eminent positions in their courts, that is, to vested patriarchal authority, via a theatrical sleight of hand that is in some senses enabled and presupposed by the heroines' agency. Moreover, the narrative of the active and mobile cross-dressed heroine whose agency in some crucial respect outstrips that of her male counterpart occurs in a number of other important Renaissance texts.[2] However, it does not occur with the same fullness of expression. In *La vida es sueño* and *As You Like It*, female transvestism echoes

75

the heroes' own self-transgressing ambition, their problematic relation to patriarchal authority, and a more generalised social mobility and sense of transition which threatens to overwhelm categories of identity even as it transforms them into new configurations of stability.

While the extent and true nature of female cross-dressing in early modern Europe is hard to determine, recent scholarship has suggested that there was no shortage of instances (see Dekker and van de Pol; Howard 418-21). What seems even more relevant in this context is the degree to which the *idea* of female cross-dressing and the mobility it allowed becomes an anxious refrain in moralistic and, in particular, anti-theatrical tracts of the time. Where the English theatre included boy actors dressed as women dressed as men, it was *de rigueur* in almost any Spanish comedy to include a female actress who played a cross-dressing woman. For moralists, female cross-dressing becomes a potent symbol of a social and moral disorder frequently associated with a public theatre which, in England and Spain, cut across class boundaries and allowed its audiences to imagine themselves in different roles and stations of life and, in theory at least, to actually try them out. Father Juan Ferrer in 1613 describes the pernicious influence of cross-dressed women in the comedies thus:

> Otro dano es tambien el atravimiento y desverguenza que en nuestro tiempos se ha visto en muchas, y es andar algunas mujeres representar en habito de hombres por las calles e por las casas, con tanto dano de sus almas y de las ajenas. (Romera-Navarro 281)

The disquieting female mobility and self-disguising roleplay which he evokes is, in Phillip Stubbes' *Anatomie of Abuses*, associated directly with a more broadly-based transgression of sumptuary laws in Elizabethan England.[3] For Stubbes, human pride is at the root of this problem. Pride, and clothing that is self-aggrandising beyond the social rank of the wearer, are both associated with a mobile, metamorphic quality which disorders social relations and goes against the edicts of God and nature.[4] Uniformity and conformity in clothing are praised and associated with a divine order, while variety, difference, and change are the devil's work. Self-artificing and self-transformation are at issue here, and while the arena in which they are played out is merely that of fashion, the pride of place which Stubbes gives fashion in his anatomy of abuses, and his bellicose denunciations of it as a contravening of God and nature, convey the extent to which sumptuary issues in the Renaissance were moral and social issues in the largest possible sense. The "rise of the individual" in the Renaissance at a quite profound level comprises a disobeying of the sumptuary laws which inculcated the order of degree.[5] For Stubbes, self-artificing involves self-dissimulation. Not only women, but men, are no longer what they seem, and the early modern sense of the possibility of "self-betterment" is cast as an invidious social imposture. Transgression of class role is associated with female insurgency. Women's perceived rejection of their subordinate status in Renaissance Europe and, specifically, their emulation of male clothing fashions, at times comes to stand in for a host of anxieties about the new social mobility and instability and, in particular, about the perceived sumptuary excesses of male social aspirants.[6] Women seem to be taking on the badges of masculine office and men descending into increasing effeminacy. The humanistic spirit of self-sovereignty and its concomitant impulse to question authority is frequently projected onto women, both in its optimistic form and its anxious understanding of the social disruption implied by individualism. Lisa Jardine, in noting that French treatises defending women "make [a] correspondence between the merits and abilities of the female sex, and acceptance of the right of all men to rise through wealth and ability" (164), indicates the link in early modern thinking between female and male self-fashioning.

The structure of both plays is similar, with the heroes rebelling against oppressive patriarchal authorities and subsequently rising to eminence. However, their rebellions and their eventual achievements of self-determinability are amplified by the roles of Rosaura and Rosalind. Female rebellion here embodies the desire for expanded self-sovereignty in a world where the power of domestic patriarchs and of monarchs was being absolutised.[7] Patriarchal subordination was a condition of young men's as well as women's lives, and this is thematized in the oppressions of Segismundo and Orlando as well as those of Rosaura and Rosalind. Constance Jordan makes the point that for Renaissance feminists and humanists, women's subordination to "fallible yet absolute governor[s]," their husbands (and, one might add, fathers), made of them "quintessential political subject[s]" (308). In certain instances, then, women can embody *men's* humanistic claims of individual merit against subjection to vested authority. Yet it is important to recognise that in *As You Like It* and *La vida es sueño*, it is the more disruptive implications of this problematic which are projected and displaced onto the heroines.

In both plays the heroes progress from rudeness and marginality to title and wealth. The movement is legitimated and naturalised by plots of patrimonial dispossession and injustice.[8] Segismundo, the rightful prince of Poland, has been bestialised by a life in prison because his father, King Basilio, has feared his son's future rebellion against himself. Orlando is disbarred from education and a place in society by his elder brother, kept in a state of rusticity "that differs not from the stalling of an ox" (I.i.10).[9] Being without state or status but desiring self-determinability, these young men are from that class of adolescents commonly perceived as insurgent in the early modern period; as a threat to civil order (see Fletcher and Stevenson 33).

Rosaura and Rosalind test out the waters of rebellion in ways that echo and at times exceed the male protagonists. They substitute for and deflect some of the burden of that disorder, with their male disguises mirroring the rise in status and the access to self-determinability which the male protagonists desire. It is Rosaura who opens *La vida es sueño*, dressed as a man and crossing the border from Muscovy into Poland in order to force her seducer, Astolfo, to marry her and redeem her honour. Like Segismundo, Rosaura has had her patrimony concealed from her by her father and is symbolically dehumanised and stripped of a socially legitimate identity. In *As You Like It*, Rosalind and Orlando are associated within strikingly similar terms of reference. She is a victim of patriarchal tyranny — banished from the court of her usurping uncle, Duke Frederick, she too is dispossessed of patrimony and is delivered into the double marginality of male disguise and exile from court. Her liberating flight from the court precedes Orlando's and the condition of self-exile betokened by her transvestism mirrors his own exile from legitimate identity.

Both Orlando and Segismundo are liminal figures. This is echoed by the female subjects, whose transvestism echoes their borderline gender status, as does the heroes' and the heroines' mutual positioning on the border between Arden and the court of Duke Frederick, Poland and Muscovy. In particular, Segismundo's passive role at the whim of his autocratic father and king is literalized by his imprisonment, and contrasts fully with Rosaura's active transgression and her geographical mobility. As a man, Rosaura can play out the active and socially transgressive desire of the hero.

Rosalind's and Rosaura's movement "beyond the pale" is involved with erotic desire. Rosalind's exodus into Arden, "to liberty and not to banishment," (III.iii.138) follows hard on the heels of her falling in love with Orlando. Rosaura's famous entry on a horse she cannot control, which opens the play, is an allegorical figure of uncontained sexual passion; her affair with Astolfo. While, within the terms of early modern codes of femininity, Rosalind's and Rosaura's independence presupposes their (suggested and stated, respectively) lack of chastity,[10] the paralleling of their experience with that of the male subjects, not to mention their sartorial masculinization, may suggest that at another level they are functioning as projections of the male protagonists' dilemmas and desires. The representation of both heroines as desiring and adventurous subjects masculinizes them, and their desirableness in the eyes of the male heroes suggests a narcissistic identification. Indeed, the larger phenomenon of Renaissance viragophilia could also be put down to a narcissistic identification on the part of men. To be called a *mujer varonil* in Renaissance Spain is a term of praise, and the adjective itself points to the reason for male approbation of such a transgressive figure; her independence and her will to rise above her subordination reflect the ideals of Renaissance men and manhood. Thus, Segismundo and Orlando's falling in love with these dynamic heroines propels them into self-achievement, so that desire here functions as a displacement of social self-elevation onto amorous identification with adventurous, transgressive women. The representation of Rosalind and Rosaura suggests a contradictory overlapping of cultural codes. Although the unruly, because independent, woman threatens male sovereignty, that sovereignty is also the law of the father which oppresses the hero, and the independent woman is allied with the hero in his struggle to overcome patriarchal and political tyranny.

Yet where she attempts self-determination via the playing of a role, his transcendence of oppression appears spontaneous. Similarly, his rise in status is the just manifestation of his noble rank. Thus the lurking structure of rebellion and transgression of degree, the sense of social instability, is ultimately obscured by recourse to an apparently more stable set of social meanings. Moreover, the hero's alienation from the court, his rustification, suggests that his virtue is not an achieved or learnt but a natural quality. This constitutes a reversion to an older and hence more authentic-seeming notion of self as "kind" rather than action (the emergent early modern notion) (see Whigham 186), and it colludes with the Castiglionian art of *sprezzatura*, which is, in Frank Whigham's words, "designed to imply the natural or given status of one's social identity" (33), and to deny that any labour, effort, or self-interest has been put into it. In "...the fashion of these times, / Where none will sweat but for promotion" (*AYL* II.iii. 59-60), Orlando's and Segismundo's distance from the court is justified by the corruption of the court, and suggests their redemptive innocence even as their "rudeness" must be adapted to the court, which is the predetermined point at which they finally arrive, as if by magic.

In Puttenham's *Arte of English Poesie*, that handbook of rhetoric and courtly self-fashioning, a gender-based slippage of meaning similar to that in *As You Like It* and *La vida es sueño* occurs. Here, rhetorical and courtly self-attainment tends to be understood as deceptiveness rather than as the spontaneous attainment of natural birthright. Art slips into artifice. Where this association comes to the surface in Puttenham's text, it is coded as feminine and is strongly associated with self-disguising surfaces, in particular, sartorial adornment. Thus, poetic ornament is like female dress and the colours of rhetoric are associated with ladies' make-up (149), while the art of poetry is in turn like that of the "very courtier, which is in plain terms, cunningly to be able to dissemble" — and the courtier, of course, dissembles his true identity and motives through the effeminizing splendour of his "new fashioned garments" (305). In the Spanish and English plays, this aspect of the hero's identity is displaced onto the heroines, the doubleness of whose transvestism embodies a rise in social agency through artful counterfeit.

The heroine's androgyny can be seen as a figure of unconscious male anxieties and desires. Francette Pacteau shows how androgyny is simultaneously a fantasy of autonomy and a motif of castration. At the unconscious level of primary processes, the androgyne constitutes an absorbing of the identity of the other, a self-completion which alleviates the anxiety of castration. Thus, early modern and, particularly, humanist, desires for autonomy frequently make use of Plato's myth of the primordially complete hermaphrodite, as well as of the positive alchemical and mystical understanding of the hermaphrodite (see Wind *Pagan Mysteries* 1958, 212).[11] However, androgyny is also a defence mechanism that has its own incoherence built into it. Within the inevitability of secondary processes, of language and social meanings, it is always a split figure, oscillating uncertainly between the terms of male and female (Pacteau 70-71). The putative fusion of these terms is unrepresentable in language and inconceivable within a social reality which depends on gender differentiation as its foremost binary opposition, and unrepresentable in a historical period when gender roles are being strenuously polarised and naturalised, both in polemical tracts and within the terms of a naturalistic aesthetic system.[12] Moreover, in a society in which the female body denotes castration, the real gender of the female transvestite suggests an underlying powerlessness; the inauthenticity and, indeed, the deceptiveness of the power which the male disguise is meant to project. Rosaura and Rosalind, as the alter-egos of Segismundo and Orlando, embody both the male arriviste's castration and a fantasy of autonomy that is unattainable within the social.

In the early modern period, youth was perceived as a time of sexual ambiguity, or even femininity. Thus, English boys at the age of seven would graduate from girls' clothing to breeches. Both Stephen Greenblatt and Stephen Orgel write about the state of childhood in the Renaissance as being symbolically feminine. Yet Greenblatt also claims that identity in this period was conceived of as "teleologically male," implying that maleness is achieved upon the ground of a feminine origin. Indeed, he draws on the currency of Galenic medicine in this period, with its assumptions that the female sex organs were an inversion of the male sex organs, and extrapolates from this that the line between the genders was "alarmingly blurred" ("Fiction and Friction" 75). His argument that there was only one gender, the male one, in Renaissance thought, deconstructs itself at the points I've alluded to — the femininity of the male child and the permeability of the boundary between the genders. According to Galenic biological theory, sex is perilously reversible. Jean Howard provides the best gloss on Greenblatt's argument:

> The interesting possibility raised by Greenblatt's work is that in the Renaissance gender differences may not always or necessarily have been built upon a self-evident notion of biological difference as was to be true in the nineteenth century. This simply means that gender had to be produced or secured — through ideological interpellation when possible, through force when necessary — on other grounds. If women were not invariably depicted as anatomically different from men in an essential way, they could still be seen as different merely by virtue of their lack of masculine perfection (softer, weaker, less hot), and their subordination could be justified on those grounds. (423)

These grounds are more slippery than those of biological essence. A man can be soft and weak, both morally and physically, but he cannot have a vagina. The grounds of gender difference in the Renaissance are more mutable. Thus, where a polemicist like Philip Stubbes relies on notions of divinely-sanctioned, natural sexual difference (the absolutist equivalent of nineteenth-century biological theory), he displays an odd belief that metamorphosis might be engendered by a change of clothing — "Our apparell was given us as a signe distinctive to discern betwixt sex and sex, and therefore one to wear the apparel of another sex, is to participate with the same, and to adulterate the veritie of his owne kinde" (38). Natural — essential — difference, which should by definition be immutable and self-evident, is not merely glossed over but *adulterated* (which implies a chemical or physical change) via a simple and, to all intents and purposes, merely *superficial* change of clothing. Where divinely sanctioned difference is adulterable, and there is no essential biological difference, sexual difference comes to be much more strongly grounded in social signs. Hence the preoccupation with clothing.

The identification with women that is latent in early modern thought is both exemplified in and displaced onto the cross-dressed heroines of *La vida es sueño* and *As You Like It*. Masculinity becomes something socially attained rather than inherently given. For young men, marriage was particularly key to the attainment of the symbolic and real sovereignty, the economic self-determinability, which was increasingly understood as the masculine ideal. In the early modern period, it was commonly understood that all those who lived within a household but were not the head of it — wives, servants, grown-up offspring — were in the role of children to the *pater familias* (see Schochet, "Patriarchalism" 415-16). Where the gender binary in the Renaissance is, more than anything, defined hierarchically (with women being by definition subordinate), a man in a subordinate or childlike position is, logically, feminised. Becoming the head of a household released young men from the sexual indeterminacy, the femininity, of the child. Marriage and sovereignty, both at a state and a domestic level, are the markers of Orlando's and Segismundo's eventual success. However, their *passage* from the effeminized condition of subordination and powerlessness into masculine authority is embodied in the heroines' own ambivalent identities and mediated by their agency. Indeed, it is because the anxiety of castration and the compensatory desire for the self-completeness of the androgyne are displaced onto female figures that the heroes can develop in a continuous and teleological fashion towards identities that are non-contradictory and powerful.

The heroes emerge into masculine authority through the maturing and civilising processes which the heroines enable in them. Rosaura, when she stumbles across Segismundo in prison in the opening scene, awakens him to a quest for self-mastery that is also her own. The metaphors of birth which surround him here indicate that the play is tracing the course of his maturation into full humanity. It is his three encounters with Rosaura, in her various guises, male and female, which precipitate the significant steps in his progress from bestiality to humanity.

Equally, Segismundo's frequently alluded-to monstrousness is matched by her own, as a cross-dressed woman. Significant in the light of this relationship is the fact that monstrosity and bestialization are connected to fashion, hermaphrodism, and theatricality in Renaissance moral thought. Thus, Phillip Stubbes declares that "newe-fangled fashions" "deform" and "disguise" people, making them into "savage beastes" and "stearn monsters" (7) and that women who wear men's clothes are "monsters of both kindes, half women, half men" (38). In 1589 in his "Tratado de la Tribulacion," Father Pedro de Rivadeneyra declares that theatre is bestialising, and barely conceals his fears that it can engender an actual metamorphosis in the audience. These sentiments are also visible in English anti-theatricalists such as Stephen Gosson and Anthony Munday (see Levine 123). Fashion (in this case the bewildering variety of clothing and hence, gendered identities which Rosaura sports), hermaphrodism and theatricality signify the deviation from a norm which is conceived of as natural and God-ordained. They also testify to the tenuousness of that norm. Both *La vida es sueño* and *As You Like It* play on what Stephen Orgel has defined as the early modern sense of "the fragility, the radical instability of our essence ...

and the metamorphic quality of our sinful nature" (16). This "metamorphic quality," which is monstrous because it appears to threaten the social order,[13] is both embodied in the theatricality of the cross-dressed heroines in *La vida es sueño* and *As You Like It*, and harnessed, through them, to bring about the heroes' eventual success. It is that Protean will to self-creation of which Pico's *Oration on the Dignity of Man* is the most famous example. It is also that aberrant lack of essence which Stubbes' treatise on fashion castigates and which is exemplified in the figure of the cross-dressed woman.

As with Segismundo, Rosaura's monstrousness is coeval with her lack of a properly socialised identity; of an identity which conforms to a social hierarchy where women do not bear arms and travel alone, and where sons do not rebel against their fathers. Yet, as Segismundo progresses towards humanness and identity during the course of the play and is no longer referred to as a monster, Rosaura comes to take over this function. In their final encounter, where she appears dressed as a woman but bearing arms and claiming the power of a man, she is twice referred to as a monster. In this meeting on the battlefield of Segismundo's Oedipal revolution against Basilio, her long, personal confession unmasks the historicity, process, and contingency of the reality which his father has hidden from him by incarcerating him and making him believe that his experiences in the real world were only dreams. Rosaura's simultaneous masculinity and femininity, embodying both agency and subjection, literalizes the division of the self within history which has been Segismundo's primary, but until now opaque and unexplained, experience.

Yet, significantly, Segismundo disavows the heterogeneous nature of Rosaura's discourse; even though it is this discourse that enables his transformation. The feared but productive confusion of male and female identities which she has embodied and their relationship has manifested is short-circuited and a hierarchical boundary between identities is drawn. Thus, he curtails speech with Rosaura in order to repress his unruly desire for her. This enables him to have the moral grace to hand her back to Astolfo, in turn forgiving his father and imprisoning as a traitor the soldier who freed him from the tower. This signals the return to an autocratic order and, from an intense concentration on Rosaura, focalised through Segismundo, the drama turns all the characters' eyes on Segismundo and orchestrates their voices in choral admiration of him, thereby underlining his newfound unity and completeness and ratifying his monarchial singularity. He becomes a transcendent subject, his own author. Segismundo's transcendence supersedes Rosaura's enabling immanence and his connection to division, marginality, the strife of political process and the underlying conflicts of self-fashioning is elided. Yet it is precisely these realities — embodied in and understood through Rosaura — which have formed the ground of his successful achievement of princeliness.

In *As You Like It*, Rosalind, dressed as the boy Ganymede, coaches Orlando into maturity and self-consolidation, at which point the play returns to an emphasis on the male subject, deprivileging femininity. Whereas Rosaura educates Segismundo in metaphysics, teaching him the nature of freedom as moral choice and action, Rosalind educates Orlando in reality. In her guise as Ganymede she mocks his bad Petrarchan poetry and conventional romantic idealisations of "Rosalind," debunking his self-aestheticization and the vaunted spirituality of his love. Like Segismundo's self-sacrifice in restoring Rosaura to Astolfo, Orlando's self-sacrificing battle with a lion in Act V is the definitive moment of his self-transcendence and maturation. This transcendence ushers in the heroine's return to femininity: she faints when she hears of the fight. The uncertainty of his identity as a man, which makes room for Rosalind's commanding androgyny, is resolved. As in *La vida es sueño*, there is no longer a need for a cross-dressed heroine to mediate the hero's identity, his passage from marginality to social importance through the fantasy-structure of androgyny.

The resolution of male identity necessitates the suppression of a parity between the male and female protagonists which threatens the supremacy and autonomy of the male subject. Rank and patriarchal authority are reasserted in a number of ways. Duke Senior, Rosalind's dispossessed father, dominates the final moments of the last scene and provides it with its closing words. The announcement of the restoration of his Dukedom means that Orlando, by marrying Rosalind, should succeed to the title. There is a clear continuity between Duke Senior's refound authority and Orlando's future pre-eminence. The Duke enunciates a kindly paternalism that will restore the fit between well-being and rank. All shall

> ... share the good of our returned fortune,
> *According to the Measure of their States*. (V.iv.174-75; my italics)

And at the end of the scene, male ascendancy and class hierarchy is once again ratified when Jacques leaves the wedding celebrations and addresses his goodbyes to the male partners in each of the four couples in order of social importance, ignoring the women entirely. Thus, there is a powerful movement of ideological, as well as formal, closure in *As You Like It*. The final emphasis on a pre-eminent male voice mirrors the denouement of *La vida es sueño*. Here Basilio simultaneously orchestrates several marriages, resolving contradictions in a final and transcendent unity, an authority that appears unassailable.[14]

Yet the traces of the fashioning of patriarchal sovereign subjects are everywhere apparent in *La vida es sueño* and *As You Like It*. They are not only embodied in the figure of the self-fashioning transvestite heroine, but displayed in the "world[s] turned upside down" with which she is primarily associated. This phrase is taken from Natalie Zemon Davis' seminal essay on the literary and social function of the image of the unruly woman in early modern Europe (Davis, "Women on Top"). Her references to the use of female dress to legitimate male rebellions in early modern Europe is extremely suggestive of the ways in which femininity could come to stand in for a specifically male sense of oppression in the Renaissance. Lope da Vega's *Fuenteovejuna*, where a peasant uprising against brutal masters is spearheaded by the village women, is a case in point. And the specific association of the cross-dressed woman with struggle against social injustice and subordination is exemplified in Moll Frith, the heroine of Dekker's and Middleton's *The Roaring Girl*, who cries, "I am too headstrong to obey" (II.ii.39). Moll is linked with righteous rebellion by virtue of her own actions as well as by her association with other early modern women who represented "protest against social injustice" (see Howard 437-38). Natalie Davis suggests that the figure of the unruly woman is symptomatic of the "struggle over change" in early modern Europe and asks rhetorically, "can the unruly woman have been so much an issue when sovereignty was less at stake?" ("Women on Top" 183). Certainly, the issue of sovereignty, which traverses images of role reversal, pervades the two plays. For the transvestism of the heroine, which symbolically constitutes a third possibility,[15] a possibility of meaning which exceeds the complementarity of binary gender divisions and, concomitantly, of binary high/low class divisions, amplifies the "democratic" urgings of the dramas; elements within them which challenge authority and suggest the blurring or transgression of social limits.

This both derives from the "category confusion" (the phrase is Marjorie Garber's) suggested in transvestism, and from the ambiguous status of femininity itself within the class and political systems of early modern Europe. Walter Cohen has suggested that in Renaissance Spain and England, noblewomen could symbolise the mediation of class difference, articulating a movement between the elite to which they belonged socially and the non-elite to which they (usually) belonged educationally and politically (112). Thus, where Rosalind travels with a court fool whose links to the lower classes are made manifest in his marriage to the goatherd Audrey, Rosaura travels with the clown, Clarion. And it is significant that Rosaura's most complete embodiment of the hermaphrodite, in the scene where she proclaims herself as the impossible third term, both man and woman, is a scene of revolution initiated by subordinates. Segismundo has been freed from his prison by soldiers in order to lead them in battle against the king. Rosaura, charging onto the scene of battle on her horse, is construed as an elemental force, of "confusion" and "chaos" (III.ix), her turbulence and sexual ambiguity symbolising the political processes of reversal that are at work, including Segismundo's own transgressive arrogation of power.

Class reversal is reflected in a lighter vein in *As You Like It*, where rigid separations between court and country, peasant and aristocrat, break down and a shepherd is a match in argument for a court fool, and classically-named yokels mirror and outdo the Petrarchan ecstasies of gentle Orlando. In his *Anatomie of Abuses*, Philip Stubbes, attacking social climbers in Elizabethan England, not only links social mobility with a Rosalindesque violation of rules of apparel, but suggests the linguistic, as well as social tenor, of Shakespearean comedy in his disapproving epithet for contemporary transgressions as "a confuse mingle-mangle of preposterous excesse." Like Rosalind's verbal jugglings, as well as her disguise, and like *La vida es sueño*'s semiological chiaroscuro which is both introduced by and epitomised in Rosaura, this describes a disruption of the way signs — who possesses them and what they refer to — secure the "natural" stability of social difference. As Patricia Parker has shown, the mobility of the sign in the Renaissance is directly associated with an (alarming) mobility of the social order, and this mobility is frequently conceived as feminine (see *Literary Fat Ladies*).

"Reality," like the gender of the heroines, becomes a play of ornamental transferences, of linguistic and literal masks which slip between levels. Time and again, signs demonstrate their excess over the "natural" hierarchies, the class and gender-based realities, which the plays attempt to contain in formalistic endings that purport to secure the sovereignty of the hero. If all reality is illusion and all worldly power transitory in *La vida es sueño*, and if the whole of *As You Like It* hangs on Touchstone's "If" (V.iv.103) and the "truth" of "feigning," then the certified social selves of Orlando and Segismundo are fragile indeed.

But the lack of a fixed self is also pleasurable, a kind of tourism of possible roles, and the theatricality of transvestism signals a release from oppressive, conventional, and socially-determined identities. In Francette Pacteau's words, it "belongs to the realm of primary processes: psychic energy happily shifting from one representation to the other" (63). Thus, Rosaura and Rosalind each preside over worlds of linguistic play, position-shifting, and slippage; the fluidity of the Lacanian Imaginary, which can disrupt the Symbolic order, the domain of the law. The fictional worlds of *As You Like It* and *La vida es sueño*, worlds of playful pastoral rejuvenation and life as a dream, respectively, suggest a realm of fantasy on the border between the unconscious and social forms. The plays mobilise potentially disruptive unconscious desires and pleasures in order to reinvest the Law with "truth." Thus, at the level of the unconscious to which the fantasied components of play and dreaming appeal, the plurality of the androgyne can operate, not as mere contradiction and loss of self, as it does in the reality of the Symbolic order, but as a mythical completeness capable of effectuating magical transformations and solutions within the Symbolic. Rosaura's activation of Segismundo's moment of grace at the end of *La vida es sueño*, and Rosalind's "magician uncle" and mobilisation of Hymen at the end of *As You Like It*, are both magical solutions intrinsic to the power of their ambiguous identities. Yet, as Phyllis Rackin points out, an "idealised image of the androgyne" (29) cannot be maintained within the conventions of realism, where s/he becomes grotesque, an aberration of nature. And a Lacanian understanding of reality as the symbolic order underlines the fact that the "nature" mimetic conventions represent is indissolubly allied with the legality of social existence, existence in and as language. Rosalind and Rosaura's relinquishing of their disguises signals the return to a "true" femininity that in turn represents a return to society's "natural" state. They are both reintegrated into society via marriage and their supremacy is suppressed in favour of male voices, as the reality principle demands. The cross-dressed heroine finally seems to secure the patriarchal subject in a pre-eminent position, transforming from a projection of his desire for autonomy into an object of exchange in the patriarchal economy which depends on her legal and symbolic exclusion.

Yet the fundamental provisionality of a Renaissance symbolic order that strenuously improvises patriarchs and princes as unassailable sovereign subjects returns as unsuccessfully repressed material even within the plays' forms of closure and containment. There are suggestions of throwaway parody. When, as his final order-restoring act, Segismundo arrests the soldier who rebelled on his behalf, the effusions of Basilio, Astolfo, and Rosaura inflate his newfound "wisdom" to such a degree that they become ironic —

Basilio.	Tuo ingenio a todos admira.
Astolfo.	Que condicion tan mudada!
Rosaura	Que discreto y que prudente! (III.xiv)

His response to their flattery measures the self-defensiveness and provisionality of his newfound authority.

Que os admira? que os espanta,
Si fue mi maestro un sueno,
Y estoy temiendo en mis ansias

Que he de dispertar y hallarme
Otra vez en mi cerrada
Prision? Y cuando non sea,
El sonarlo solo basta;
Pues asi llegue a saber
Que toda la dicha humana
En fin pasa como un sueno... (III.xiv)

Restored honour all around, a double marriage and the rigorous expunging of seditious members of the lower classes, all of which suggest an achievement of order, are here measured as fragile formalisms imposed on flux.

Significantly, *As You Like It* ends with a similar sense of gratuitously-imposed order. The symmetry of the fourfold marriage effectuated by Rosalind and Hymen is so encompassing as to seem arbitrary, and suggests a reduction of individuality. Finally, Rosalind's playful epilogue, with a naturalness significantly missing from the formal ending, reminds the audience of the continued reality of the multiple "Rosalind," who was to all intents and purposes killed off when she came out in a dress once more. Reopening the theme of gender-role transgression, she makes it clear that, as a woman, she should not really be delivering the epilogue and then seamlessly becomes the boy actor she "really" is again. In saying, "if I were a woman I would kiss as many of you as had beards that pleased me, complexions that liked me, and breaths that I defied not" (V.iv.18-20), Rosalind, who is now admitting her masculinity, is still undermining it by keeping alive the possibility that she "is" a woman. She is also allowing audience members, male and female, to be titillated by the idea that a thoroughly sexually ambiguous boy actor "would" kiss them. She can be all things to all people. The theme of mere, fleshly desire, which has been sublimated in favour of transcendence and closure, is here reasserted, while overt interaction with the audience engages the excess of social process and exchange over aesthetic forms. "Rosalind's" erotic play on her identity with the audience suggests the pleasurable incommensurability of selves that always exceed their formal and ideological determination. The "third term," as an incommensurable reality which cannot be contained in gender binarisms or class binarisms of low to high, or controlled by figures of the sovereign masculine subject, here parades its disturbing, and intensely pleasurable, irrepressibility.

Continuities and Discontinuities

JONATHAN HART

The Ends of Renaissance Comedy

Nothing human is alien to me. (Terence)

Tragedy has as its argument history, and comedy fiction....
Equivoke and the uncertainty arising from ambiguity have always
held a large place among the crowd, for it thinks that it alone
understands what the other one is saying. (Lope de Vega, *Arte nuevo
de hacer comedias en este tiempo* [1609] sects 10, 24)

Qui sent, pleurt; qui pense, rit. (French proverb)

There is no denying the order brought to bear at the end of most Renaissance
comedies. Criticism has often emphasized the happy ending of comedy and the
movement from order through disorder to order (see Frye, "Argument";
Jagendorf). This assumption is sound, but it needs qualification. One of the
recent qualifications has been, in the English-speaking world at least, to see the
ends of comedy, both the endings and the purpose of the plays, as a kind of
ideological containment. While these arguments, which find their inspiration in
Derrida's breaking down of binary opposites and in Foucault's analysis of power,
are suggestive and have provided new perspectives with which to view literary
texts in general, and Renaissance comedy in particular, the interests of my essay
lie elsewhere (see Belsey). I would like to argue that in Italian, Spanish, English,
and French comedies of the early modern period, the very structure of the plays,
the way they end, involves disjunction, stress, and rupture. The ends of comedy
represent a return to order, but a restoration with loose ends. They are often
asymmetrical and leave doubt in and with the audience. Here the exception,
while not proving the rule, complicates it, and the comedies are not simply
apologies for utopian hope or the existing social and political order. What I am
proposing — to see the tragic in the comic, disorder in order, as an unsettling of
the end of comedy — is not novel. The difference is one of emphasis, serving
as a reminder that the complex ways of representing and seeing the endings of

comedy from sixteenth-century Italy to seventeenth-century France can be forgotten in a fascination with order and pattern.[1]

The pleasure principle of comedy may predominate in the happy marriage that ends New Comedy and becomes popular in the romantic comedy of Shakespeare and his contemporaries, but, the agonistic principle, to use Harry Levin's phrase, pushes the ends of comedy towards Freud's reality principle (*Playboys and Killjoys* 131). The stresses, ruptures, and the mixing of generic imperatives occur in many Renaissance comedies, including the ones most discussed here. Rather than discuss the whole range of comedy, I shall concentrate primarily on two kinds or aspects, first the "romantic pastoral" — Guarini's *Il Pastor Fido* (1590), Shakespeare's *As You Like It* (1599) and *Twelfth Night* (ca. 1600-01), particularly Calderon's *No hay burlas con el amor* (ca. 1634-35) — second, and more briefly, "satirical comedy" — Ben Jonson's *Volpone* (1607) and Molière's *Tartuffe* (1664).[2] These comedies represent the poles of romantic comedy and romance (tragicomedy) and that of satire. Even in the most romantic of these comedies there is an admission of agon and reality.

I

Pastoral and romantic comedy involve compensation and escape from the tensions of the world. The idyll of the pastoral contains implicit and explicit reference to its opposite. This absent other might be a social order that needs renewal, a household in which the senex blocks the romantic yearnings of the young, or a world that has fallen from some kind of golden age or Eden. The tragic stress or potential chaos often occurs when the city or court threatens to impinge on the pasture or forest, what Northrop Frye has called the "green world." Sheer confusion can seem, to the characters at least, a threat to their happiness. But even at the end, after the comic recognition has resolved the near catastrophe, there are loose ends and suggestions that the dark and tragic side of life is still there and can reassert itself at any time. This tragic potential is only suggested and in varying degrees, sometimes to the point of being in a very minor key.

Romantic comedy or what I have also called "romantic pastoral" represents the tragic or disorder on a sliding scale. These darker elements coexist with the more dominant celebratory aspects. If one accepts the origins of Greek comedy that critics like Francis Cornford set out, then the romantic element of comedy can be related to the Greek religious rites that probably involved ceremonies of sexual initiation for the young, whose *komoidia* or revel songs developed into Greek comedy (see Cruickshank and Page xiv). Although I am concentrating on the period of romantic comedy from about 1590 to 1635, *Gl'Ingannati* (1537) contains many of the elements of plot that Shakespeare later uses in *Twelfth Night*, a comedy from the turn of the seventeenth century. Before Shakespeare's play, *Gl'Ingannati* represents a brother and sister parted by accident and ultimately reunited, a heroine who disguises herself as a boy and has to court a woman for the master she herself loves. The ending, however, lacks a comic scapegoat, like Malvolio, swearing revenge. Comedies share conventions but also distinguish themselves.

In *Il Pastor Fido*, Baptista Guarini represents characters who are blind and chase illusions in their pastoral Arcadia and whose recognition brings about a peripeteia. Guarini doubles the action. At first, Silvio alone seeks Amarillo's love, but then Mirtillo is also in love with her. By a peripeteia, Mirtillo's fortunes are reversed and, through faithfulness, he wins Amarillo's hand. Dorinda loves Silvio without much hope, but through a perepeteia, she finds that he loves her. Silvio, blind in love and in the hunt, has wounded the disguised Dorinda with his arrow and wounds himself when he sees what he has done, a more concrete version of Romeo's poisoning of himself after he sees the sleeping Juliet and thinks her dead. When Dorinda asks Linco, an old servant of Montano, Silvio's father, not to carry her home disguised in the clothes she is wearing, Silvio says:

> Tu dunque in altro albergo,
> Dorinda, poserai che'n quel di Silvio?
> Certo ne le mie case,
> o viva o morta, oggli sarai mia sposa;
> e teco sarà Silvio, o viva o morto. (IV.ix; 318)

Here is a moment of love in life or death, tragedy in comedy and comedy in tragedy, a kind of transcendence of love Shakespeare's Romeo and Cleopatra espouse in their respective plays. The marriage of spirits is part of Guarini's tragicomedy. Linco reinforces this Neo-Platonic element and also emphasizes the reversal and the doubling of the plot ("E come a tempo" IV.ix; pp. 318-21). As Amarilli is lost to marriage, life, and virtue, Dorinda can become Silvio's wife. Linco prays to the gods for a cure for them both. They are wounded in a pastoral paradise in a kind of oxymoronic love where pain and pleasure, life and death are joined.

Corisca, a nymph who is in love with Mirtillo, is willing to sacrifice Amarilli. Guarini has her repent, and she is left by herself, so that there are not three couples paired, leading to a culmination at the end with the pairing of Mirtillo and Amarilli. To Mirtillo, Corisca says: "Assai lieta son io/ del perdon recevuto e del cor sano" (V.x; 408). Despite the asymmetrical ending, which J. H. Whitfield has observed, love triumphs (23). Guarini separates the pairing of Silvio and Dorinda from that of Mirtillo and Amarilli by an act. Despite this double climax, which is reflective and splintering, the playwright is still proud of what he conceives to be an observance of Aristotle's unities in the play. In *Compendio della poesia tragicomica* (1601), Guarini asserts: "a me pare che'l Pastorfido n'habbia gran parte, essendosi in lui, con tanta esquisitezza osservato il precetto dell'unità, che c'insegna il grande Aristotile" (qtd. in Whitfield 40).

The end of *Il Pastor Fido* represents the shepherds twice calling on Hymen to bless the marriage before and after Mirtillo's speaking of the joy and anguish he has experienced at once and his wondering, before Amarilli, whether he is in a state of sweet wakefulness rather than in a dream of bliss. At the very end, the Chorus also emphasizes the pairing of pain and pleasure in Guarini's tragicomedy ("Oh fortunata coppia" v.x; 410). Here the Chorus moralizes about what a foil the couple's fears play to their joys, the blindness of mortals in love and life, true joy born from virtue after suffering. In this pastoral romantic comedy, which Guarini calls a tragicomedy, the tragic elements express themselves thematically and structurally, for instance, in the words of the Chorus and in the double mirror of the two couples, where likeness and difference appear.

Shakespeare also writes a romantic and pastoral comedy about faith in love: *As You Like It* (1599). Here disguise involves less talk of pain than in *Il Pastor Fido*, but both plays rely on Hymen's blessing, in the shepherd's choric prayer in Guarini's play and in person in a masque in Shakespeare's. The recognition scene in *As You Like It* involves Rosalind's disguise as Ganymede in which she promises to bring Rosalind forth and then appears, with Hymen and Celia, as "herself" (V.iv). The dramatic irony underscores the audience's knowledge and the exploration of identity in this comedy:

> Duke Senior. I do remember in this shepherd boy
> Some lively touches of my daughter's favor.
> Orlando. My lord, the first time that I ever saw him
> Methought he was a brother to your daughter. (V.iv.26-29)

Jaques' satirical presence and humour qualify the romance and give the comedy another dimension. He is wry about the movement towards the multiple pairings of lovers: "There is sure another flood toward, and these couples are coming to the ark" (V.iv.35-36). He calls Touchstone and Aubrey "very strange beasts," that is, fools. Touchstone displays the wit of a fool on the topics of women, marriage, and court before Jaques and Duke Senior, but must leave off when the god of marriage, Hymen, enters. Touchstone has used "If" thematically and rhetorically to hold together his tale of the courtier and has spoken about "If" as a peacemaker full of virtue, and now Shakespeare pins his recognition scene on the anaphoric "Ifs" of Duke Senior, Orlando, and Phebe as they discover Rosalind's identity. The playwright uses these serial "Ifs" to lead from the climax of the Duke's recognition of his daughter and Orlando's of his love to the anticlimax of Phebe's cognitio that Rosalind cannot be hers because Ganymede is a woman: "If sight and shape be true,/ Why then my love adieu!" (V.iv.120-21). As Ganymede, Rosalind exacted a "compact" from everyone before she left to change her costume, so that on refusal of Ganymede/Rosalind, she must marry the shepherd Silvius (V.iv.5-34). Hymen bars the confusion of identity that Rosalind's triple "if ... not," in regard to father, husband, and woman, questions. Even Hymen, as he blesses the four couples with marriage and fertility, cannot resist a joke about the match between Audrey and Touchstone: do we know which is winter and which is foul weather (V.iv.135-36)? Duke Senior welcomes Celia and Rosalind while Phebe greets Silvius.

The next movement in the ending occurs with the entrance of Orlando's brother Jaques de Boys. He announces that Duke Frederick marshalled a great power to take the forest and to put his brother, Duke Senior, to the sword; but, after meeting a religious man, "was converted/ Both from his enterprise and from the world" (V.iv.161-62). This report — which allows narrative to soften the romance nature of the conversion, the ultimate in reversals — includes the information that Duke Frederick has given back the crown and lands to his banished brother. This is a sequel to Oliver's conversion, so that this Jaques, and not the satirical one, is just in time, as Duke Senior tells him, for his two brothers' weddings. Duke Senior's proclamation applies as much to romantic comedy in general as to *As You Like It* in particular: "First, in this forest let us do those ends/ That here were well begun and well begot" (V.iv.170-71). They return to order, love, and good fortune. After Duke Senior asks the couples to dance, melancholy Jaques says he wants to join Duke Frederick in his religious life away from court for the sake of what is "to be heard and learn'd" (V.iv.185). In a role that would usually fall to Duke Senior, Jaques gives his blessing to the restored Duke and to the other males in the pairs of lovers. He cannot resist a parting shot in his interrupted badinage with Touchstone:

> And you to wrangling, for thy loving voyage
> Is but for two months victuall'd. So to your pleasures,
> I am for other than for dancing measures. (V.iv.193)

But the Duke's response, "Stay, Jaques, stay," (V.iv.194) meets with Jaques' ambivalent response and not outright rejection. Jaques will not stay to see this dancing pastime, but he will stay to hear out the Duke at his cave: "What you would have I'll stay to know at your abandon'd cave" (V.iv.195-96). By pronouncing the shortness of Touchstone's proposed marriage and by not remaining for the marriage dance, Jaques does provide a satirical qualification to the comic order. The comic dance, as Anne Barton reminds us and as this essay argues, cannot contain all elements of human experience; but whether Jaques goes off to search with Duke Frederick is much more ambiguous than most critics, like Barton, assume (368). In his discussion with the other Jaques, Jaques has stated his intention of joining Duke Frederick, but in his reply to Duke Senior shows that he respects this brother's authority. Jaques will attend him in the Duke's cave to know his wishes, which may be for Jaques to stay. If Jaques may be moving beyond the world of comedy, he is still perched on its outskirts. He may go and he may leave, but that, like the marriage itself, is left for the future in allusion. "Proceed, proceed. We'll begin these rites,/ As we do trust they'll end, in true delights" (V.iv.197-98).

Like other begging choruses in Shakespeare's oeuvre, the Epilogue to *As You Like It* plays games with the audience (see Hart, *Theater and World* 151). Just as Jaques qualified but respected the authority of Duke Senior at the end of the play, here Rosalind says that "It is not the fashion to see the lady as the epilogue" (1-2); but in challenging the convention, she softens the challenge through normative analogies, the lord as prologue, and the bush as the vintner's sign. Although a good play does not need an epilogue, Rosalind says, it can benefit from its supplement. Rosalind's wit shows that she begs as she denies it and implies that the audience knows what she is doing and enjoys it. She asks the men and women to let the play please as they love each other. But then the boy actor playing Rosalind is given the opportunity to make part of the delight of the play a playing with the gender boundaries of the comedy, which has relied on the dance of heterosexual marriage at the end to achieve order:

> If I were a woman I would kiss as many of you as had beards that
> pleas'd me, complexions that lik'd me, and breaths that I defied not;
> and I am sure, as many as have good beards, or good faces, or
> sweet breaths, will for my kind offer, when I make curtsy, bid
> me farewell. (18-23)

Here is the "If" that ends as conditionally as the "If" that begins Shakespeare's *Twelfth Night*. The boy actor is dressed as a woman and is thus in Shakespeare's fiction (when not dressed as the boy Ganymede), but in the after-shadows of the Epilogue, the character must also give way to the boy actor who lives in the world. The boy actor is, nevertheless, still in role because he will curtsy if they applaud Rosalind for her offer. The offer is fictional, an appeal to the desire of the men in the audience. They do not expect an actual parade of kisses. The last ambiguity is that this offer to the men (though women also have good faces and sweet breaths) ends the play, as if the applause is for the offer of kissing and not the pleasure of the play. But it also has to be an appeal to the women in the audience, as the appeal for applause and approval is also to them. It is hardly likely that Shakespeare expects only the men in the audience to applaud. In this play with gender boundaries, the playwright elides the difference between the offer of kissing and the play itself as well as the differences between men and women on stage and in the audience. The end of the body of this comedy and the Epilogue allow for wit and satire, the dance and the critic, conventional marriage and other desires.

The fifth and final act of *Twelfth Night* has more tragic force than the end of *As You Like It* and pushes harder towards catastrophe before the comic anagnorisis resolves the confusion over identity through the double image of Sebastian and Viola, which leads to the pairings of Sebastian and Olivia, Viola and Orsino. Feste clowns with the Duke just as Touchstone has with Jaques, playing on grammar and logic, in this case for gold, as Orsino waits for Olivia. After Feste and Fabian exit, Cesario/Viola recognizes Antonio as the man who rescued him (her, though she is still in disguise as Cesario, Orsino's servant). Unfortunately, for Antonio, the first officer identifies him as Orsino's enemy who, among other things, "did the *Tiger* board, / When your young nephew Titus lost his leg" (V.i.62-63). When Viola says that he did her kindness but then "put strange speech upon me" (67), the audience knows that Antonio mistook her for her brother Sebastian. Orsino calls Antonio "Notable pirate, thou salt-water thief!" (69), an appellation Antonio denies. His tale begins to reverse the catastrophe in which he finds himself, by the very information Antonio provides, rescuing "That most ingrateful boy there by your side" and about giving him his purse and later being refused it back (77). The audience knows what has happened, but this begins Viola's amazement. Olivia and her attendants interrupt Orsino's declaration of the impossibility that Viola (Cesario) had spent three months at Antonio's side, when the youth had tended the Duke for that same period. Olivia is still spurning Orsino and eyeing Cesario (Viola). Orsino would make a sacrifice of Cesario because Olivia loves him and not the Duke. There is, of course, another comic misunderstanding because Olivia has already mistaken Sebastian for Cesario and the brother has not spurned her as his disguised sister has. When Cesario rebuffs Olivia here and wants to follow his true love, Orsino, Olivia heightens the drama when she calls him, reminds him with "husband." This name stuns Orsino and puts the ever-denying Cesario on the defensive. To heighten the dramatic irony even more, Shakespeare has the Priest enter. He responds to Olivia's appeal by declaring that she was betrothed to Cesario less than two hours ago.

Shakespeare extends the dramatic irony as far as he can take it in order to get the most play from this comic stress. Orsino tells Cesario to go with Olivia but not to cross his path. Cesario protests because he is Viola, who is in love with the Duke. Olivia still thinks that Cesario protests out of fear of his master because of his social superiority. But Shakespeare interrupts this strand to bring in Sir Andrew Aguecheek with another story. Narrative plays a key role in this ending. Andrew accuses Cesario of hurting Sir Toby and him. Cesario also denies this accusation, but has to face Toby and Feste. Toby's accusations — "H'as hurt me, and there's th'end on't" (V.i.196-97) — are loud and he is led, on Olivia's order, to be tended for his injury. Just when Shakespeare could play on the dramatic irony even more by stringing out the accusations of Andrew and Toby, he has them leave the stage with Feste and Fabian, and brings about the moment of ultimate confusion that leads to recognition: Sebastian comes on stage. Here is the central moment in the comedy:

> Sebastian. I am sorry, madam, I have hurt your kinsman,
> But had it been the brother of my blood,
> I must have done no less with wit and safety.
> You throw a strange regard upon me, and by that
> I do perceive it hath offended you.
> Pardon me, sweet one, even for the vows
> We made each other but so late ago.
>
> Duke. One face, one voice, one habit, and two persons,
> A natural perspective, that is and is not! (V.i.209-17)

Sebastian gives the answer that Cesario is expected to give. With his words Sebastian satisfies Olivia but baffles Orsino. There are two such men in the Duke's view, as nature has produced an optical doubling that is and is not an illusion. Sebastian's warmth towards Antonio also corroborates Antonio's earlier self-defence before Orsino. Antonio pursues Orsino's puzzlement: "How have you made division of yourself? / An apple, cleft in two, is not more twin / Than these two creatures. Which is Sebastian?" (V.i.222-24). In love with one Sebastian, Olivia finds the existence of two "Most wonderful!" (225). Sebastian himself is baffled —"Do I stand there?" (226) — and it is now for Sebastian and Cesario to give the last clues to the characters and end the dramatic irony. They match backgrounds and lament the loss of each other without knowing it.

Shakespeare does string out this recognition to give the audience pleasure over the characters' discovery, especially that of brother and sister. In typical fashion, Shakespeare contrasts the joy the audience experiences in dramatic irony with the sadness the characters feel at a sense of loss. They have lost each other and remember the loss of their father without embracing each other as who they are. The audience already feels the recognition while "Cesario" and Sebastian are still in the tale of catastrophe. Sebastian's lines illustrate this contrast: "Were you a woman, as the rest goes even, / I should my tears let fall upon your cheek, / And say, 'Thrice welcome, drowned Viola!'" (239-41). Cesario/Viola recognizes her brother and eight lines later begins to reveal her feminine identity as Viola. She has an "If" of her own as she replies to Sebastian:

> If nothing lets to make us happy both
> But this my masculine usurp'd attire,
> Do not embrace me till each circumstance
> Of place, time, fortune, do cohere and jump
> That I am Viola. (V.i.249-53)

She continues that she will confirm this claim with the evidence of the captain who saved her and who has her "maiden's weeds" (255).

Sebastian seeks to interpret this moment of recognition for Olivia as this revelation of identity affects her even more than Orsino since she has married Sebastian thinking him Cesario. So Sebastian reminds Olivia that she has been mistaken but that Nature allowed her to fall in love with someone with the likeness of Sebastian. In fact, she has married Sebastian because he looks like Cesario. But Sebastian will not be deterred in his mediation: "You would have been contracted to a maid, / Nor are you therein, by life, deceiv'd, / You are both betroth'd both to a maid and a man" (261-63). The sexual ambiguity that As You Like It flirts with in the body of the play and the Epilogue becomes explicit in the climax of Twelfth Night. But before Olivia can respond, Orsino responds as, in his interpretation, Olivia stands amazed. The Duke calls upon another romance element, "this most happy wrack" (266), which will benefit him. The ambiguity is like that in Rosalind's Epilogue: "Boy, thou hast said to me a thousand times / Thou never shouldst love woman like to me" (267-68). Orsino cannot help but yoke boy and woman in the same sentence. Still Olivia does not speak. Instead, Rosalind swears once more her love for the Duke, who wants to see her woman's clothes — just in case. Viola says that the Captain who has them in prison is under the order of Malvolio, a member of Olivia's household.

And so the theme of Malvolio, who had suffered a plot against him as he dreamed of Olivia's love, re-emerges. Rather than respond to Sebastian and the revelation of Viola's identity, Olivia remembers Malvolio and asks that he be brought to her so that he can release the Captain, who has Viola's feminine clothes. Olivia admits that in her frenzy she forgot Malvolio. Feste discusses Malvolio's "madness" and would read Malvolio's mad letter as if he were mad. Fabian, another of Olivia's servants, reads the missive, which begins — "By the Lord, madam, you wrong me, and the world shall know it" — and which is signed — "The madly-used Malvolio" (V.i.301-02, 311). Olivia does not see much madness in Malvolio's reply and when she finally replies to the revelations that Sebastian and Viola have uncovered, she asks the Duke "To think me as well a sister as a wife" (317), and offers to pay for both weddings at her house. The Duke offers Viola his hand, so she can now be "Your master's mistress" and, to Viola, "A sister! you are she" (326).

But here a stress arises in the celebration that grows out of the characters' perception of the identities of Sebastian and Viola. Malvolio enters with Fabian and makes his famous accusation against Olivia, which echoes his letter, that she has done him "wrong, / Notorious wrong" (328-29). He wants to know why she has abused him by encouraging him with a letter and then imprisoning him "in a dark house" (342). Olivia, who says it is Maria's hand and judges even-handedly, tells Malvolio:

> Prithee be content.
> This practice hath most shrewdly pass'd upon thee;
> But when we know the grounds and authors of it,
> Thou shalt be both the plaintiff and the judge
> Of thy own cause. (V.i.351-55)

Fabian confesses that Toby and he devised the plot against Malvolio, with Maria's aid, but did it for laughter rather than revenge, thereby letting the other characters know what the audience already knows. Fabian asks that the injuries on both sides be weighed. After Olivia says to Malvolio, "Alas, poor fool, how have they baffled thee!" (369), Feste quotes some of the foolish lines that Malvolio has spoken in the play, and now the other characters recognize them for what they are because they understand the context of the trick or plot. The Fool, who says he played Sir Topas, finishes his satire on revenge, by turning Malvolio's accusations against him: "And thus the whirligig of time brings in his revenges" (376-77). To which Malvolio answers: "I'll be reveng'd on the whole pack of you" (378), and exits.

Whether that whole pack includes Olivia herself, or only the tricksters, is not entirely clear. Olivia still takes Malvolio's side, echoing Malvolio's own words to Feste at IV.ii.87-88 — "Fool, there was never man so notoriously abus'd" —when she says: "He hath been most notoriously abus'd" (379). This echo juxtaposes the plot with the exposure of the abuse. But it is not Olivia who decides what must be done, although it seems that Fabian's and Feste's pleadings have not had any demonstrable effect on her. Instead, it is Orsino who is more concerned with the evidence of the Captain, whom Malvolio imprisoned (something too often forgotten in the commentary), the evidence of the forged letter, and the wrong done against Malvolio. He does not seem concerned about the Captain, except that he can present the evidence of Viola's clothes. The Duke is speaking with the major voice of comedy when he asks (it is not clear whom) to pursue Malvolio "and entreat him to a peace" (380), so that the wronged steward's acrimony and pledge of retaliation will not usurp the music and marriage that define the order at the ends of comedy but will be played in a minor key. Knowledge of the captain will, the Duke says, allow a marriage at a suitable time, which, he assures Olivia, they will attend.

Thus the marriage is delayed as the comic scapegoat has escaped with the last clue. Malvolio's angry flight also suspends the question of gender. The cognitio or comic recognition of Cesario's female identity is deferred, so that, cross-dressed, the woman under the man's clothes must wait to become Viola and Orsino's wife.[3] He addresses her as a man impatient for his return to womanhood:

> Cesario, come —
> For so you shall be while you are a man;
> But when in other habits you are seen,
> Orsino's mistress, and his fancy's queen. (V.i.385-88)

The boy actor remains in the role, so there is another layer in the garment of desire.

After these lines, the characters leave the stage, except for Feste, who sings a song. This song follows Malvolio's swearing of revenge and the damage control Olivia and the Duke may perform as members of the ruling class. As critics have long noted, this is a political scene as well because Malvolio dresses like a Puritan and may be said to represent those who dissented within and without Elizabeth's Church of England. This is another irruption or stress, a political rebellion (although Malvolio would have been very happy to marry Olivia), that has resonances for later audiences that Shakespeare did not live to see. But this darkness is combined with foolishness. The Clown ends the play. Shakespeare used a similar refrain in the song that ends this comedy to one in the very middle of *King Lear*, where Kent and the Fool take the king into a cave out of the storm. In that play the Fool calls the king grace and himself a codpiece, "a wise man and a fool" (III.ii.40-41). The wind and rain in the tragedy are the chaos at the centre of the play. Unlike Feste, Lear's fool also alludes to sexual transgression and disorder.

Why Shakespeare chooses to end *Twelfth Night* with Feste, the Clown who brought back revenge and threw it in Malvolio's face until he fled, is not clear. Shakespeare's clowns are prone to satire and their wit can unmask and can show a wistful bent whether the context they find themselves in is happy or terrible. Feste sings a song about rain. His representation of the changes in life is a difference version in the genre of Jaques' speech on the seven ages of man.[4] Feste's rendition follows the progress of the song's protagonist from when he was a tiny boy and his foolishness was taken as a toy, to "man's estate" when men shut their gate against knives and thieves (perhaps even fools), to marriage where he learned that he could never thrive by bullying, to old age when drunkards were still drunk (perhaps like Toby and Aguecheek). But no specific allegory is attached to the song, and it is built on tautology: rain usually rains and drunkards are usually drunk. This is one kind of wit Shakespearean fools use. It is a kind of beautiful nonsense, apparently pregnant with meaning and rich in its simplicity. The song ends with a stanza that moves from the beginning of the world to pleasing the theatre audience:

> A great while ago the world begun,
> [With] hey ho, etc. [the wind and the rain,]
> But that's all one, our play is done,
> And we'll strive to please you every day. (V.i.405-08)

Like Rosalind's epilogue, Feste's song asks for applause, but *Twelfth Night* ends with Malvolio's sworn revenge, attempts to contain it and to bring about order in gender roles and with marriage, and a sweet and sad song about rain, spoken by the actor who is and is not in character as the Clown who tricked Malvolio and mocked him into his exit. Shakespeare thereby balances Feste's claims and Malvolio's, although Feste gets the last word. The celebratory nature of the comedy cannot escape the accusations and the shadow of the comic scapegoat even in his very absence. The mixed nature of this comedy is a productive problem, like the problematic at the end of *Henry V*, so that to use the term "problem comedy" or "problem play" to describe it, would be positive and not some deficiency that hangs on a theatrically achieved ending by a baffled playwright (see Hart, *Theater and World*, esp. ch. 4).

The cross-dressing and sexual ambiguity in *As You Like It* and *Twelfth Night* is part of a representation of these elements on the Renaissance stage throughout Europe.[5] Calderón's *La vida es sueño* (ca. 1635) deserves more attention in this regard. It is reminiscent of *As You Like It*, perhaps by coincidence. As in the relation between Rosalind and Orlando, that between Segismundo and Rosaura involves a mixing of gender boundaries through disguise, and the recognition of the heroine's identity, now as a woman and without boyish disguise, brings about the harmonious marriage that graces so many comic endings. But the breaking down of gender boundaries qualifies the rules of that conventional marriage. Even though it seems that order and convention have triumphed, can the audience forget the world of cross-dressing and the joy and laughter it produced (see Emck; Davis, "Women on Top")? The representation of a return to the "normal" cannot entirely suppress female transgression. The rupture of carnival leaves an opening for the forbidden and the celebration of inversion. When in *A Midsummer Night's Dream* (1595) Theseus proclaims, "The lunatic, the lover, and the poet / Are of imagination all compact" (V.i.7-8) before the play of the rude mechanicals, he is calling attention to whether the dream in and of the *Dream* is a fiction. The audience considers whether the comic dance of pre-marriage is a dream both while it is going on and as they make their way out of the theatre. Puck's epilogue completes the stylized and literal comedy of Pyramus and Thisbe at Theseus' bidding. Puck speaks of actors as shadows and asks for applause from the audience, which he hopes will be less critical than the young lovers are of the production by the rude mechanicals. The very coexistence of criticism with pre-nuptial celebration of the marriage dance after the events of the midsummer dream produces an order of a different kind from a straight marriage dance. Shakespeare has Prospero observe at the end of the wedding mask: "We are such stuff / As dreams are made on; and our little life / Is rounded with a sleep" (*Tempest* IV.i.156-57). Even in romance, the characters call attention to the globe dissolving and not leaving a rack behind. Calderón also observes the metaphysics of dream: the moment of recognition is that life is a dream (see Cope). This metaphor hardly possesses the solidity of comic order. But can the dream of the class and gender inversion of pastoral comedy, the land of desire, be so easily forgotten even if a rack of it, and anything else, will not be left behind? How much does the Lord of Misrule and gender transgression represent catharsis for a day or a kind of shadow structure that is often there at the end of comedy? To see the unseen is the paradox of recognition.

Before looking at satirical comedy, the essay will examine a comedy devoted to laughter and manners and with only hints of darkness and tragedy, although it has its fair share of satire and parody — Calderón's *No hay burlas con el amor* (1635). This comedy of intrigue and situation culminates with an ending that borders on farce. It represents themes of treachery and deceit with a lightness that Malvolio's presence does not allow in *Twelfth Night*. *No hay burlas con el amor* is a comedy that almost overthrows the argument of this essay as it tries to evoke laughter in the representation of all things, from Leonor's tricking of her older sister, Beatriz, to Don Alonso's wound from a street-fight arising from jealousy growing out of a misunderstanding of a love situation. By laughing at events that would be serious in life, even though their exaggeration heightens the dramatic irony, farce edges towards absurdity. The farce and the debate over the role of women in love and society in *No hay burlas con el amor* belong to a kind similar to Shakespeare's *The Taming of the Shrew* (1590-94), which itself draws on George Gasgoigne's *Supposes* (1566), an adaptation of Ariosto's comedy, *I Suppositi* (1609). Calderón, however, does not make much of the battles of the wills between Don Alonso and Beatriz and emphasizes their love at first sight, and he does not develop the same motifs from Roman New Comedy that Ariosto, Gasgoigne, and Shakespeare do. Nonetheless, these Renaissance comedies rely on false suppositions about characters and the situations in which they find themselves. There is, however light and pleasant we find farce, something disturbing, at least to modern audiences and perhaps to those during the Renaissance, between the machinery of laughter, slapstick jokes, and situations, and the less comic content, such as cruelty and deceit. Even if the transformations of the characters — in *No hay burlas con el amor* of Beatriz from a beautiful woman conceited with her command of language and knowledge to a woman in love, and of Don Alonso from a womanizing noble cynical about women and love to a man in love — are not explored in depth, their presence in the comedies implies that they could be and that they help constitute a shadow structure. Some of the laughter, as in the more farcical examples of English Restoration comedy, is uneasy. For the most part, the audience laughs and makes taboo topics less threatening and apparently more controllable by subjecting them to ridicule.

Comedy can also laugh at its own conventions, which is what Cruickshank and Page suggest occurs in *No hay burlas con el amor*, whose title proclaims that love is no laughing matter (xvi). Comedies of the *siglo d'oro* often share some conventions with Greek comedy. Both involve love among the young that culminates in marriage, a love that is unknown to the older generation or is actively blocked by it. The end includes a marriage that represents the triumph of youth and fertility over the winter of age (xv). Cruickshank and Page point out that at the end of such Spanish comedies, the younger generation overcomes the older generation by joining it, so that the desire to be free finds the need to conform. While these critics think that this paradoxical tension is resolved through laughter, it may be that comic marriages, even in farces and comedies of manners, are an uneasy truce (xiv-xv). In lighter comedy it is probably too solemn to speak about the tragic dimensions of their endings, but it is still possible to see unresolved stresses or potential problems with the new society that the marriage is ushering in.

No hay burlas con el amor inverts class boundaries more than those of gender, but Beatriz has intellectual aspirations that go against conventions for women in the seventeenth century. The inversions of class occur, for instance, when Don Alonso is as cynical about women as a servant usually is (1059-88, 1515-34), while Moscatel, his servant, is in love like a noble and describes his beloved, the servant, Inés, in terms usually reserved for the nobility (697-704, 1094-96). Inés, too, sometimes uses diction more suited to a noblewoman (1251-66). The role reversals, as Cruickshank and Page note, do not turn the classes upside down: having accepted Moscatel's proposal, Inés joins him in conventional stage-servant cynicism when she refers to marriage as one of the worst things (3105-12); moreover, Don Alonzo and Beatriz defy the conventions of their class and gender but seem to end up reconciled to them (xvi-xvii). Typical of the pattern of comedy, the old order moves through disorder to a new order. Sometimes, of course, the new order, except for being one generation later, is not that different from the old order.

As in *Twelfth Night*, in *No hay burlas con el amor* a trick or joke causes suffering for one of the characters, Beatriz. In this instance one women, Leonor, thinks of a way of tricking another, Beatriz. She has the idea of introducing Don Alonso as the pretended lover of Beatriz. With Moscatel, Inés later agrees that this joke was a bad one (1925-26). Afterwards, in an aside, Eleanor recognizes that the joke was a bad idea ("¡Oh, nunca hubiera inventado" 1957-60). But Leonor's first instinct, when Beatriz would not allow her to dissuade her older sister from telling their father, Don Pedro, about Leonor's love for Don Juan, was to defend herself and attribute Don Juan's letter, which the sisters tear in half as the father discovers them, to a fictional lover of Beatriz (907-61). The trick is even more necessary for the plot than the one practised on Malvolio in *Twelfth Night*, as the steward plays the third man — or odd man out — role that Don Luis does in *No hay burlas con el amor*, rather than one of the lovers who participates in marriage at the end. As Leonor's trick unfolds, with Don Juan's help, Don Alonso becomes the invented lover whose feigned love turns to true love when he looks into Beatriz's eyes. The trickster is tricked, and the reversal soon brings in the cognitio. The situation comedy cannot do without the trick as Beatriz needs to be married, so that Don Juan can marry the younger daughter, Leonor.

In romantic comedy a sliding scale exists between disguise and deceit. Rosalind's disguise in *As You Like It* is fairly harmless; the false "disguise" of

Don Alonso as Beatriz's admirer (as devised by Leonor and Don Juan) is a less harmless deceit; the disguise and trick that imprisons Malvolio as a cross-gartered and not star-crossed lover is probably more harmful than it is harmless. With each step, from simple disguise to intrigue, the role of satire, revenge, and cruelty increases. As Beatriz and Malvolio begin as self-righteous prudes, they are ready to be comic gulls, but the more cruel the revenge, the more questionable the comic movement becomes. It is as if the structure of comedy overcomes its comic content. Satire pushes comedy in the direction of tragedy, although in *No hay burlas con el amor* this movement is so incipient that it is only there potentially.

Formally, *No hay burlas con el amor* is effective, as Calderón pushes the comic catastrophe as far as possible before the comic ending. Even though the tone is so light that the audience does not fear a tragic ending, confusion reigns until the last few lines. The technique of this comic structure centres on Leonor's trick in which she reverses Beatriz's accusations against her, thereby impugning the reputation of her elder sister so that their father, Don Pedro, makes a false discovery, beginning with his discovering his daughters tearing a letter and listening to Leonor's lies about Beatriz (897-1022) and ending with him believing Leonor's second denunciation of Beatriz (1419-78, esp. 1413). The final *cognitio* begins when Don Pedro complains about his honour and speaks ambiguous lines that make Beatriz and Leonor fear that he has discovered their loves: "aunque miento en esta parte, / puesto que yo no los traigo: / ellos vienen a buscar me / dentro de mi casa" (2992-95). Moscatel and Inés also contribute to the dramatic irony because in hearing Don Pedro, they, too, think that the daughters have been discovered. It turns out that Don Pedro is angry with Don Luis, who has told him that he must go to the wars rather than marry Beatriz (see 2638-2741). To Beatriz, he says: "pues por ti Don Luis hace / desprecios de ella, y de mí" (3006-07). Just when the sisters discover that their father does not know who their lovers are, Don Juan arrives and complicates the situation by appealing to Don Pedro's honour by asking him to assist him in pursuing three men from his door. Don Juan does so to spare Don Alonso the danger of dropping from the balcony again, but this backfires as Don Alonso fears that these are the men who tried to kill him.

In short, the complication moves towards catastrophe because Don Pedro then discovers Don Alonso and Moscatel. Now Don Pedro says that Don Juan must assist him in a graver matter than the one for which Don Juan had asked his assistance. This is where the danger mixes with slapstick: Don Pedro and Don Alonso fight with Don Juan, not being able to choose between them. This fighting precipitates the arrival of Don Luis and Don Diego. This arrival reminds

Don Pedro that he would like to avenge himself on Don Luis, who says that such a situation was the reason he withdrew his offer of marriage to Beatriz. Don Alonso wants revenge because he now discovers that Don Luis is the man who wounded him. Don Juan then recognizes that Leonor was honourable and his jealousy unfounded. He joins Don Alonso in defending the daughters against their father, who might kill them for his honour. This situation brings about the comic resolution or climax with the recognition of the four lovers ("Don Juan, Don Juan" 3093-3102). Don Pedro refuses to say anything because the two men have promised marriage, something that cannot, in his view, be undone. For Don Luis, it is. The rival says nothing. The daughters have been silent since they each expressed, in a line, their sorrow over the fighting, and they remain speechless. Their father, who does not bless the marriage but is happy for what it does to his honour, does not say any more. The farce ends with the promise of marriage and with brief commentary.

The comments belong first to the two servants, Moscatel and Inés, whose master and mistress are going to be married, and to Alonso himself. The emphasis is on the reversals "de las burlas del amor" as Calderón has the two servants talk about what amounts to the laughing matter, joke, trick, game, or deception of love. Inés and Moscatel return to the role of the wry or cynical stage servants commenting on the folly of aristocratic love. The playwright crafts their lines in a similar fashion, so that Inés's observation of the reversal that brings about the unlikely event of Beatriz's marriage supplements and echoes Moscatel's about Don Alonso's wedding:

Moscatel.	En fin, el hombre más libre,
	de las burlas de amor sale
	herido, cojo y casado,
	que es el mayor de sus males.
Inés.	En fin, la mujer más loca,
	más vana y más arrogante,
	de las burlas del amor,
	contra gusto suyo, sale
	enamorada y casada,
	que es lo peor. (3103-12)

The speeches begin the same way, with "En fin," an "Anyway" that also announces the end of the comedy ("fin"). Moscatel's speech about Don Alonso uses the approximate rhyme of "sale" and "males" as Don Alonso is the most free man who "emerges" from the joke of love injured, lame, and married, the last of which is the greatest of all "wrongs" or "evils." Inés also builds her speech around a similar phrase, echoing the title, and rhymes "del amor" with "lo peor." Her use of "sale" chimes with Moscatel's rhyme. She says of Beatriz that the most mad, vain, and arrogant of women has, from the game or deception of love, emerged in love and married, which is the "worst" thing. The servants represent two reluctant lovers. Although not as witty as Millamant and Mirabel in Congreve's *The Way of the World* (1700), Beatriz and Don Alonso share their initial resistance to marriage, only to find themselves married, even if Beatriz does not have a name that alludes to a thousand lovers and does not insist on a contract that protects her rights as a woman. Despite the cynicism, Moscatel asks for Inés's hand, and adds, if that is the way it has to be, they should not think about it and that the tricks and games of love, which are serious (true), are at an end. Taking Inés's hand may or may not be in marriage, but it is not a repudiation of the attraction that underlies love. Don Alonso addresses the audience directly, asking it not to laugh but to learn a lesson from him: "todos del amor se guarden" (3118). These lines supplement and echo Don Alonso's direct address at the end of Act II to the men in the audience who are in love (2033-38). The last two lines of the play are a condensed version of the poet asking pardon and asking humbly, with some flattery, for the audience's approval. The audience joins the celebration of love after having been warned through satire and ironic comment on love.

Besides the wry satire, especially for modern audiences, the status of women has its stresses in Calderón's comedy. Beatriz is pompous, but she does not deserve to be duped simply because she is a woman who is a prude with intellectual pretensions. The trick against her is a plot device and serves well the symmetrical nature of comic structure. The reversal that the trick ushers in — the accuser, Beatriz, becomes the accused — can be traced in the language: Beatriz says to Leonor: "Eso no, / que tener no puedo yo / hermana libidinosa" (619-20), lines which Leonor later throws back in her face, except Calderón changes "Eso" to "Aqueso" (1414-16). Don Alonso begins by laughing at love and ends by warning against such a course; Moscatel starts by scorning Don Alonso for mocking him for being in love and for deceiving women and finishes by wondering how such a man could wed. But the attitude towards women generally, and Beatriz particularly, in the play is traditional. Don Juan criticizes her for being conceited about her appearance and her cleverness, especially in Latin and the composition of Castilian verse, with an implicit glance at a convoluted style, perhaps worthy of Góngora: "no habla palabra jamás / sin frases y sin rodeos; / tanto, que ninguno puede / entenderla sin comento" (305-08). Moreover, Don Juan's satirical portrait of Beatriz, which follows in contrast a set-piece description of Leonora, lasts about fifty-three lines, and precedes another description of the conflict between the sisters (see 194-392). This three-part description is more than a device to set up the situation or intrigue of the comedy: it is also a means of representing Don Juan's ideal love in contrast with the unfortunate Beatriz, who has the traditional vanity of woman and combines it with that of man. The trouble is that Beatriz and Don Alonso, who hears this long piece, usurp the role of the central lovers, and Don Alonso, himself no champion of new ways for women, does come to love Beatriz. She modifies her speech under the orders of her father and with the help of Inés, her compliant maid, but whether she leaves the old Beatriz behind entirely is debatable.

Just what else is said about women and about Beatriz? It is Don Luis who accepts Beatriz for what she is, yet he loses her, as if the structure of the comedy reinforces the approval of the changes that are imposed on her, first by Leonor's trick and second by her father's orders that arise from believing that ruse's false representation of Beatriz. The reversal in the comedy is problematic from this point of view, even if we admit that Beatriz's vanity about her appearance and her style of speech is excessive. Don Luis asks Don Diego why he should not make arrangements to marry Beatriz, which is, contrary to Don Diego's view, the right thing to do "si en ella veo / virtud, hacienda y nobleza, / gran beldad y gran ingenio?" (462-64). But Don Diego thinks that Beatriz is too clever and he would not like a wife who knew more than he did. This position does not impress Don Luis, who asks when can knowledge be bad? In this debate on the role of women, Don Diego answers that knowledge is bad when it is out of step and explains that women belong to the domestic sphere: "Sepa una mujer hilar, / coser y echar un remiendo, / que no ha menester saber / gramática, ni hacer versos. (471-74). Still, Don Luis will not budge. He thinks that no one should fault an excess in the harmless virtue of knowledge. Don Diego has to shift his ground as he is not winning this debate, so he concentrates on the way Beatriz scorns him, but Don Luis, the thinking man's Romeo, loves her disdain in some kind of unstated convention that she is the unobtainable beloved, perhaps from a sonnet sequence as much as from romance. In defeat, Don Diego utters the plaintive: "Vamos, pues" (486). Don Luis then delivers, in the excessive and idealistic language of lovers (not too different from Orlando's love poetry in *As You Like It*), an ode to the centre of his life ("centro" 486), that is, Beatriz and her house. The style of this brief apostrophe (487-500) is elaborate. Along with Calderón's representation of Beatriz's style, it resembles Shakespeare's use of Lyly's euphuistic and pedantic style in *Love's Labour's Lost*. Don Luis' speech especially plays on the initial and medial repetition of "fuera" or "out of," to stress Don Luis' point that as a lover, being out of Beatriz's centre or house, he is out of his element like the fish, bird, beast, flame, blossom, voice, life, and soul he represents in his extended metaphor. Don Luis uses isocolon and *conduplicatio* in his build up to the climax: his lover is translated to heaven. He is the lover and Beatriz is his heaven. With that ecstasy, he leaves with Don Diego.

Calderón represents Beatriz in all her circumlocutory and periphrastic splendour. There is no denying the satire on such language, even if the playwright did admire an ornate poet like Góngora. Beatriz refuses Leonor's request in outlandish language, but without malapropisms, and Leonor retaliates with her trick. Even Beatriz can accept the conventional view of woman while all but Don Luis (and presumably Don Pedro, until he thinks his daughter's language is connected to her supposed moral turpitude) say that she flouts the natural role of women. She condemns Leonor in unyielding terms ("Deténte; / no te apropincues a mí" 603-16). She speaks of honour as Don Pedro does. Beatriz will tell him of Leonor's breach of honour. Leonor says she has kept her honour.

Even if Calderón is satirizing romantic and courtly love, by allowing Don Luis to lose and Don Alonso to win Beatriz, he keeps Moscatel and Inés in love and the manservant waxing about love throughout, except, at the end, when he joins his own beloved in commenting wryly on the odd couple of Don Alonso and Beatriz. Besides, Don Juan is an idealistic lover of Leonor — his speech is much longer than Don Luis' and as extravagant — and he wins his love (see 192-269). Don Alonso is the playboy of comedy and gives a view of women in keeping with his role: "Verdad es que, en mi concepto, / todas, por qué quererlas, / y todas, por qué dejarlas" (1065-66, see 1059-88; see Levin). Moscatel rightly fears that Don Alonso will pursue Inés, which he does, but she refuses him and teaches her lover a lesson for his false jealousy.

Both Beatriz and Inés resist stereotypes, the lady waiting for marriage and the servant available for sexual dalliance with her superiors. Inés shows herself to be an independent woman ("Dile a tu amo, villano" 1257-66). But Beatriz's independence is under siege when Leonor tricks Don Pedro into believing that her elder sister has soiled his honour with a tryst. The father turns on Beatriz: "biene verse puede, / si a hablar así te acomadas, / que quien no habla como todas, / como todas no procede" (1440-42). Don Pedro will not just judge her by connecting her bad behaviour with her unusual speech, but he forbids study, poetry, and Latin books (1452-55). Calderón creates a comic situation because after all these years, Don Pedro has changed his mind and has decided that to control Beatriz morally, he must do so intellectually. He joins Don Diego's school of thought — women are for the domestic sphere, men for study: "unas *Horas* de romance / le bastan a una mujer. / Bordar, labrar y coser / sepa sólo;

deje al hombre / el estudio" (1456-60). The tone modulates with the sudden reversal. Don Pedro tells Beatriz not to look surprised at his new view and then threatens to kill her if she uses periphrasis, which he must consider to be the heart of her bomphiologia. But Beatriz cannot help herself, despite the patriarchal death sentence, and this drives her father into an exasperated exclamation, interrupted by cacozelia, then followed by another such outcry:

Don Pedro.	¡Perdiendo, Beatriz, el vicio,
	bien enmendada te veo!
Beatriz.	Por tu anticipata ...
Don Pedro.	Creo
	que hoy me has de quitar el juicio. (1474-77)

Beatriz will not obey her father even as she tries to, and Don Pedro is shown to be impotent as his threat is revealed to be a figure of speech, and not an effective one. His authority does not win out. In this passage, Beatriz's Latinate response interrupts her father and then he breaks off her line by rhyming with his previous line. Despite this attempt at order in an ordered poetry — the outer lines include the rhyme of "vicio" and "juicio," her vice will drive him mad because she will not banish it. Calderón gives the father, who is blind to what is going on with his daughters in his house but believes he is right, the rhyme "veo" and "Creo."

Just as Beatriz frustrates her father's authority, so too does Inés rebuff Don Alonso's advances. Being in love with Inés, Moscatel embellishes the words she actually speaks to him, saying that she is too good to be his mistress and not good enough to be his wife, which, as we have seen, is not what she said. Don Alonso's response is both metadramatic and metonymic. He displaces his own sexual desire on to Inés, partly because she is not playing the role of available servant that plays usually represent but, in Moscatel's report especially, she speaks like a defiant countess: "Eso a reyes de comedia / no hay condesa que no diga / de Malfi, Mantua o Milán, / mas no las de Picardía" (1486-89). The pun on "Picardía" plays on "pícaro, pícara" or rogue, which can also include sexual "mischief" (Cruickshank and Page 96). He becomes crude when he says of her: "¡Válgate el diablo, picaña!" (1496). Moscatel, who has listened to such insults, says that like unto like, but Don Alonso can only think of Celia, the last woman he abandoned. Calderón gives the situation a little irony because Don Alonso declares, "Mi firmeza me destruye," which, retrospectively, will be true of his falling for Beatriz (at least from the point of view of a playboy) but in this context he rather roguishly and heartlessly says that he treats women too well when he leaves them (1510). When Don Alonso tells his story about Doña Clara,

Moscatel is not above trading jibes about bartering for women (1536). Don Alonso thinks he will still pursue Inés, even if only to trick or have a joke on her ("burla" is as key to the play and its ending as to its title). But then before he can tell Moscatel what to tell her, Don Juan comes in and speaks of Love, "que, como es niño," smiles today when yesterday he cried (1559). He then tells of Leonor's trick and deception of Don Pedro and announces that Don Alonso must pretend to love Beatriz as part of the ruse. Don Alonso does not want to play that role and he proceeds to satirize lovers: "¡Vive Dios, que antes me deje / morir, que a una mujer siga" (1627-28, see 1595-1642). Don Alonso deprecates Beatriz in ways we have already discussed and takes up the position that Don Diego and Don Pedro have adopted: "que voto a Dios que primero / con diez hombres legos riña / que con una mujer culta" (1651-53). An educated woman is not, at least for now, part of Don Alonso's world, but Calderón is setting up the conversion (reversal) of a great sinner against women to the altar of Love. Don Alonso's use of the word "chistosa" to refer to Beatriz can mean that he thinks that she is pretentiously clever, but it can also mean, as it turns out, that she is witty and fond of joking. Although Beatriz is serious, she does have the last joke on Don Alonso and conceals herself to confront Leonor and him, just as her father had done to Leonor and her.

It is not surprising that in a comedy with a title, *No hay burlas con el amor*, Calderón places a joke at its centre, which has reverberations at the end of the play. The joker is caught in his joke; the trickster is caught in his trick:

Don Juan.	Yo no quiero que tu amor sea, sino que lo finjas, que esto todo ha de ser burla.
Don Alonso.	Mucho el ser fingido obliga, y hacer burla de una loca tan vana y tan presumida...
Moscatel [ap.].	¡Qué presto hizo la razón a la ocasión que le brinda! Tan loco nos venga el año.
Don Alonso.	Cuanto sea engaño y mentira, vaya; mas pensar que tengo de obligarla ni sufrirla, es pensar un imposible.
Don Juan.	Ni nadie a aqueso os obliga. (1665-78)

In an aside, Moscatel hopes that they are not the ones to suffer from this scheme. Just before the love scene, Calderón makes Don Alonso cruel and self-satisfied in his role as trickster and bearer of false love. With alacrity, he suggests that they go at once so he can die laughing at his trick/joke in which her true love responds to his false love. When Moscatel is not sure that this joke will work out happily, Don Alonso berates him for not understanding the joke as revenge for Leonor against Beatriz before he romps with Inés, a statement that keeps up the dramatic tension between Moscatel and Don Alonso in their debate on love with which the comedy begins (1685-96). The playwright plays some more with the different forms of "burla" and "burlar."

Of course, the trick does trap Don Alonso. Whether he is worth trapping or not may be another qualification to the happy ending of the play. How effective his conversion is, seems much more pertinent than Beatriz's change, even though the playwright has both servants comment wryly on the two lovers. Ultimately, even though, as the evidence has been showing, the text sends out intricate signals on the question of love and women, some cultural factors will affect the audience in its view of the ending.

Beatriz's style remains ornate and she continues to use the extended metaphor of the sun, but she thinks she has reformed her speech according to her father's command. Inés, however, finds no improvement (1699-1752). Don Alonso's role as her "galán fingido" begins badly as he says in an aside that he is at a loss to speak his love even if it is false. Nonetheless, he soon regains his composure and speaks to her in a florid style not unlike hers. She calls upon her sun imagery to illustrate the transgression he has committed by being in her boudoir and echoes Góngora in the bargain. Even in his flattery of Beatriz, whom he calls "Peritísima Beatriz" and "dulce enigma," Don Alonso does not think that beauty and knowledge need to dwell in one woman: beauty is enough (1809-15). But in his flattering deception, Don Alonso paraphrases the next two lines of the Góngora ballad, "Cuatro o seis desnudos hombros," to which Beatriz alludes (see Cruickshank and Page 114-17). He is then a sunflower to her sun, bending to bask in her light. Meanwhile, Inés intersperses satirical remarks between his speeches, implying that Don Alonso shows the same excesses of style that Beatriz does and addressing the women in the audience about his deception: "Atención, señoras mías: / entre mentir o querer, / ¿cuál será lo verdadero, / si esto lo fingido es?" (1833-36). Is his love real or false? Who can tell? The irony soon becomes apparent because Don Alonso soon cannot tell himself and is on the verge of falling in love.

Inés and Moscatel play the same role here that they do at the end of the play — they comment on Beatriz and Don Alonso with some scepticism, but here it is in an aside for the benefit of the audience only. Both think Beatriz gullible, but, unlike Inés, Moscatel moves beyond the specific case and generalizes unfavourably about women: "En fin, no hay cosa más fácil / que engañar una mujer" (1873-74). It is possible, although not sure, that this last phrase echoes the familiar expression "engaña a su mujer" or "he's unfaithful to his wife," so that the verb "engañar" carries both the meaning to deceive or trick and to be untaithful to, an ambiguity that would suggest Don Alonso's lack of faith, for which Moscatel has derided him, and his present deceit. Beatriz will not listen to her maid on her high diction, but in the midst of Don Alonso's reference to the planets, the farcical situation complicates itself as Don Juan and Leonor are talking with Don Pedro outside. This news sends Beatriz back into her planetary images and leads Don Alonso to comment wryly that this must be a play by Calderón where a hidden lover or veiled woman must appear. The shock seems to provide an immediate stylistic remedy to Beatriz, who switches, as the situation demands, to brief imperatives, statements, and questions. Don Alonso and Moscatel must hide. Don Alonso locks Don Juan out; Don Alonso takes a moment to kiss Inés; along with Moscatel, he must jump from the balcony to avoid detection. Just before Don Alonso must comply, he warns men about love.

But Beatriz cannot give up her ornate style that easily. At the beginning of Act Three, she catches herself, but then proceeds, and, in an aside, explains her awakening love for Don Alonso (2055-2118). Inés tries to console her with aureate diction: Beatriz wants to tell her of her secret love for Don Alonso, which leads the servant to tell Leonor, "¡Victoria por el amor!" (2165). Even Inés, who plays the independent woman, associates womanhood with love for a man: "en fin, en fin, ha de ser / mujer cualquiera mujer" (2184-85). But the play is not at an end, so that this reversal from no love to love needs complication; Don Juan has heard all and now accuses Leonor of loving someone else (2190-2263, esp. 2226-29). Not to disappoint the audience with asymmetry, Don Alonso explores with his servant his awakening feelings of love, and thus provides a narrative envelope for Don Juan's jealous accusations (2276-2367). Two of the most central lines in the comedy, which point to the reversal, are Don Alonso's "haberme llevado a ser / el burlado yo" (2323-34). The joke is on the joker.

Through the story of the bull, Moscatel points out that Don Juan may have wanted to help Beatriz marry Don Alonso so Leonor was free to marry, rather than enlist Don Alonso's help in avenging Leonor and keeping Don Pedro off the scent of the love between Don Juan and Leonor (2352-57). Inés decides to make Moscatel jealous and teach him a lesson, so she pretends to be receiving Don Alonso's advances (2368f). The game of love is not ready to be resolved yet. But Inés has really come in Beatriz's name, saying so only after Moscatel is gone (2427). Another indication of this reluctant reversal — the false trails are still there, like Inés's flirtation with Don Alonso — is his response to Beatriz's ribbon: "Novedad se me hace extraña" (2449).

The theme of women being deficient keeps recurring. What may propel the comedy for an early seventeenth-century audience may qualify it for a late twentieth-century audience. Inés does not find Beatriz's love as novel as Don Alonso does: "A mí no, porque en sabiendo / que era tu voluntad falsa, / supe que sería dichosa; / que por no acertar en nada, / más con nosotras merece / quien finge, que no quien ama" (2450-55). Here is a woman speaking against women, although the irony may be that Don Alonso is falling for Beatriz and so Inés's observation, even in this specific case, is not entirely accurate. Moscatel returns and misinterprets the exchange between Don Alonso and Inés, so love still remains blind (2455). Inés explains her joke or trick to Moscatel (2475-2513).

Calderón does not want to give up his complications of the movement to a comic ending, which is achieved within a few lines of the very end. Moscatel says he will leave off service in Don Alonso's house because a master in love will neglect his servant, which is a reversal of Don Alonso's threat at the beginning of the comedy to put Moscatel out because a servant in love is not much use to his master (2528-35, see 51-103). The reversal of conventional roles between master and servant is reversed. By his own admission, Don Juan's love for Leonor is finished (2548-50). The reversal is that Don Alonso is now leading Don Juan to Don Pedro's house and not the other way around. Don Alonso even admits that he wants to see Beatriz (2602). The new unexpected matchmaker is Don Alonso. The recognition of his love comes to light. Moscatel is satirical about the obliquity of expression the two nobles use to camouflage their desire to see their beloveds (2616-27). The scene is set for the comic ending, which both the views of women and the use of satire complicate. It is at this point that this essay began its analysis of the end of this comedy. Later, with *Les précieuses ridicules* (1659) Molière would write a satire on the pretensions in speech and style of women, which helped precipitate a controversy over the education of women and their role in the education of a culture (see Cruickshank and Page xix-xxiii). The satirical representation of women in Molière's comedy might, in a minor key, find parallels in *No hay burlas con el amor*.

II

The tricksters of satirical comedy, like Volpone and Tartuffe, practise even greater enormities than Don Alonso does. Satire carries with it a tragic undertow. The Horatian satire of romantic comedy often yields to Juvenalian satire in satiric comedy. The magnitude of sin or treachery or deceit is so great in Volpone,

Mosca, and Tartuffe that they almost become larger than the play. To call a comedy satiric is a matter of emphasis, as we have observed the satiric attributes of comedies that concentrated on pastoral and romantic aspects, the wry observations of Jaques, the trick on Malvolio and his isolation, and Don Alonso's cynical comments on women and the deceit of Beatriz (on satire, see Hart, *Theater and World* 165-69). The satire can contribute to a generic chafing between content and form, reception in the Renaissance and now. The invention of the term "problem play" or "problem comedy" in the last years of the nineteenth century and its currency in the twentieth century shows how a change in audience can demand that Shaw be used to interpret Shakespeare. The satirical aspects of Shakespeare's problem comedies help to make their happy endings more problematic.

This problematic would not have surprised Ben Jonson. In *Timber, or Discoveries* he says: "The parts of comedy are the same with a tragedy, and the end is partly the same. For they both delight and teach.... Nor is the moving of laughter always the end of comedy." (2648-50, 52-53; 589) The end of Jonson's satirical comedy, *Volpone*, is as much about teaching as delight, a movement that involves thought and dramatic irony rather than laughter as a reflex. It is a comedy that spares no targets, male or female, in an attempt to see how blind and greedy human beings can become. *Volpone* is based on variations on a trick that extend throughout the comedy with great intricacy, providing the audience with an ironic view of the dupes, even though, ultimately and beyond the intentions of the playwright, the end of the play might dupe the audience.

The representation of women may also be a problem for a modern audience. Lady Would-be has intellectual pretensions: she is satirized. Celia is a virtuous and obedient wife: for some, she is satirized; for others she is not (III.vii.30-31, V.xii.142-44). At one point, Lady Would-be, a voluble dupe, says to the great eponymous trickster himself: "Here's *Pastor Fido* —" (III.iv.86), and, in aside, Volpone says he will profess silence (see Whitfield 31). She continues to epitomize the world of the court and of romance that the fashion of Guarini's comedy represents:

> All our English writers,
> I mean such as are happy in the Italian,
> Will deign to steal out of this author mainly;
> Almost as much as from Montaignié;
> He has so modern and facile a vein,
> Fitting the time, and catching the court-ear. (III.iv.87-92)

She chatters in a satire with little sympathy for pastoral and romantic notions. Lust, greed, and competition mark Jonson's comedy, so that Lady Would-be's speech highlights the contrast between the opposite poles of comedy — pastoral/romantic and satiric. This passage follows a debate between Lady Would-be and Volpone on the nature of learning and the greatest thing for a woman. For her, the "chiefest ornament" for a woman is music, but for him, the "highest female grace" is silence, as Sophocles writes in *Ajax* (67-81). The satire here, as in *No hay burlas con el amor*, is on a woman who talks a good deal about learning, only to be opposed by men who want them silent or submissive. Learning is not for women in these plays. Volpone would rather sing a beautifully seductive song to the young and beautiful Celia to catch her in his trick — he plays at being impotent but is not — in order to satisfy his lust than to hear Lady Would-be prattle on, even with her occasional malapropism *avant la lettre*, such as confusing the golden mean with "the golden mediocrity" (47). Women are not supposed to have any intellectual pretensions in these two comedies, although Beatriz's youth and beauty may allow her to get away with some of her cultural interests.

Volpone is a great trickster who has met his match in his parasite, Mosca. Their extended jokes and traps are of the most intricate nature, something that Jonson seemed to enjoy as he created another virtuoso performance of that kind in *The Alchemist* (1610). Their plots intertwine and are, near the end of the comedy, at cross-purposes. Mosca has taken over control of the tricks and speaks of his "Fox-trap" (V.v.18). Volpone's death is faked in order to fool the others but he, too, even in his disguises, is being fooled. The servant, Mosca, is becoming the master, while Volpone is becoming his servant. Duped by Mosca, Voltore says to him: "Well, flesh-fly, it is summer with you now; / Your winter will come on" (V.ix.1-2). There will be a reversal — a chill on the parasite's comic dance. During the trial, in an aside, Volpone begins to feel that his traps have trapped him: "I'm caught / In mine own noose —" (V.x.13-14). The plot of this comedy is, as the Second Avocatore observes of the situation, "a labyrinth" (V.x.42). In the street, Volpone admits that he has caught himself: "To make a snare for mine own neck! and run / My head into it, wilfully! with laughter!" (V.xi.1-2). For Voltore, Volpone comes back from the dead and begins his counter-plot against Mosca.

When Mosca enters as a Clarissimo, the fourth Avocatore, clearly hoping for another kind of happy ending, says in an aside: "A proper man! and were Volpone dead, / A fit match for my daughter" (V.xii.50-51). Mosca then "buries" Volpone, who is disguised and trying to bargain with him in the courtroom, which revives the fourth Avocatore's hopes for a match for his daughter (63).

Mosca will not take the half that Volpone offers him in an aside. The fourth Avocatore begins his bargaining with Mosca as "Volpone" is to be led off and whipped (84-85). This negotiation is a satire on love matches. The recognition is literal as Volpone puts off his disguise (86). He has his own sense of honour, even if it is among thieves, and he uncovers all in order to block Mosca and expose those who would feed on their own to have Volpone's fortune. The fourth Avocatore remains silent as the first three bring justice to the situation, the first Avocatore claiming this revelation a miracle and the second saying that "Nothing can be more clear" (96). Bonario agrees on the divine nature of this anagnorisis (97).

The punishments begin, which makes sense in satirical comedy but not in romantic or pastoral comedy. The second Avocatore asks that Mosca be disrobed; Celia pleads for mercy for her husband, Corvino. Celia and Bonario are vindicated. Mosca, whom the first Avocatore calls "the chiefest minister, if not plotter, / In all these lewd impostures" (108-09), is to be whipped and given life in a galley, partly because he has had the nerve to impersonate a Venetian noble. Volpone thanks the court for Mosca, who says to his master, "Bane to thy wolfish nature" (115), and is led out. The ultimate joke is the like unto like, eye for an eye, sentence the court hands to Volpone, who is a noble and cannot be given the severe sentence that Mosca received. As Volpone feigned sickness to receive wealth from those who hoped to be his heir, his fortune will be given "To the hospital of the Incurabili" (120), and he will be imprisoned in irons until he is lame and sick. Volpone's response reinforces the moral: "This is called the mortifying of a Fox" (126). Voltore is banished to a monastery to die well as he has not lived well, and all his property passes to his son. Corvino will be led through the canals with asses ears and in a pillory, "And to expiate / Thy wrongs done to thy wife, thou art to send her / Home to her father with her dowry trebled" (142-44). The first Avocatore caps the ending with a moral, so that the audience can learn from the end of *Volpone*: "Let all that see these vices thus rewarded / Take heart, and love to study 'em. Mischiefs feed / Like beasts, till they be fat, and then they bleed" (149-51). The only happy ending in this comedy is for Bonario and Celia, but with their families riven, despite the poetic justice that rights the wrongs done to them. The great characters of Mosca and Volpone, even if they are vices and must have a fall, make the end potentially tragic, as if the ghost of the rejection of Falstaff has endured.

The epilogic six lines play on this stress, between the morality of poetic justice and the great representations of vice in satire. Volpone is alone on stage and, like Rosalind, is in and out of character. Jonson plays on the convention of the character asking for applause, but he does not send out Bonario. Instead, he sends the actor who played the role Volpone. The protagonist/antagonist for whom the comedy is named has suffered an unhappy ending but he asks that the audience applaud if they are happy with the play. The first and sixth lines request applause. Volpone says that although the law has punished the Fox, he hopes that he has not done anything to make the audience suffer, that is, tricked them or let them down in the entertainment. If he has, censure him; if not, applaud. Thus, Volpone is resurrected by the audience who has to wonder whether it is not simply applauding a good representation of vice but the Vice himself. Is this a trick, where the frame qualifies the punishment of Volpone and the words that would make him an example, which the first Avocatore pointed out in the previous lines? Volpone is not in leg irons and although the "epilogue" serves to break the illusion and usher the audience back into the world, it also re-affirms that the trickster is free. Perhaps, after all, there is a happy ending to *Volpone* for the eponymous character as much as for Bonario. Whatever the audience decides, there is a fascinating stress between the judgement of Volpone at the end of the comedy and his resurrection in this "epilogue."

Molière's *Le Tartuffe ou L'Imposteur* (1664) is also a satirical comedy and thus tends towards irony and tragic scapegoating rather than to the comic ending of marriage and dance. The exposure and punishment of Tartuffe, who is the centre of attention, allows for the return to harmony in the marriage of Organ and Elmire. But the tricks and hypocrisy of Tartuffe become so dramatic and gather so much force of character that many in the audience cannot help but admire the daring scene or internal play that Tartuffe is directing. Even if Tartuffe is not morally admirable, he is one of Molière's most admirable creations. This ambivalence also occurs with Falstaff and Volpone. The centuries of controversy over the rejection of Falstaff demonstrate that the audience has a hard time to part with such an extraordinary comic character (see Hart, *Theater and World*, esp. 125-26). There is, then, a friction between characterological magnitude and the need to make an example of the great character. The blast of Juvenalian savage indignation and the frost of Horatian ironic satire try to contain the blaze of comic carnival. The tricks have to stop somewhere, and the hypocrite who doesn't play by the rules of conventional morality has to be scapegoated and punished. At the end of *2 Henry IV*, the Epilogue promises that Falstaff will reappear in a sequel but when Shakespeare does write *Henry V*, he kills Falstaff early, offstage, and in a report, as if the appearance and speech of this white-bearded Satan of comedy would demand his return and his usurpation and rupture of the history play into a full comedy. Louis XIV himself asked that Molière's Tartuffe and the eponymous comedy be resurrected. In the Troisième Placet Présenté Au Roi Le Février 1669, Molière asks: "Oserais-je demander encore cette grâce à VOTRE MAJESTÉ le propre jour de la grande résurrection de *Tartuffe*, ressuscité par vos bontés?" (1: 635). As with all narrative and drama, the end can become the beginning again, even if the design of the work is not as self-conscious as that in *Finnegans Wake*. In the preface to *Tartuffe*, a defence which Molière attached to the printed version in 1669, he says that those who were the objects of his comedy, from marquis to doctor, suffered mildly when they were represented and even pretended to be amused, with everyone else, by the portraits of them. But not the hypocrites, Molière says, for they, being what they are, decided to hide behind a protest that alleged the impiety of the play rather than to look into their souls. He maintains that in this comedy he distinguished between the religious person and the hypocrite (1: 628-29). Against those who assert that the theatre should not talk about religious matters, Molière points to the religious origins of comedy, which Jane Harrison (as well as Murray, Cornford, and Frye) would have insisted on. Of these critics, he says:

> et, sans doute, il ne serait pas difficile de leur faire voir que la comédie, chez les anciens, a pris son originale de la religion, et faisait partie de leurs mystères; que les Espagnols, nos voisins, ne célèbrent guère de fêtes où la comédie ne soit mêlée, et que même, parmi nous, elle doit sa naissance aux soins d'une confrérie à qui appartient encore aujourd'hui l'hôtel de Bourgogne; que c'est un lieu qui fut donné pour y représenter les plus importantes mystères de notre foi; qu'on en voit encore des comédies imprimées en lettres gothiques, sous le nom d'un docteur de Sorbonne et, sans aller chercher si loin que l'on a joué, de notre temps, des pièces saintes de M. de Corneille, qui ont été l'admiration de toute la France. (1: 629)

Perhaps in his defence of comedy, Molière overemphasizes these religious origins, but it is sensible to stress the seriousness of comedy without making it solemn. He himself argues for something that supports my argument. He associates comedy with satire, which involves irony and a dark side, such as scapegoating, which makes the "happy" ending of comedy more complex: "Si l'emploi de la comédie est de corriger les vices des hommes, je ne vois pas par quelle raison il y en aura de privilégiés" (1: 629). Molière says that virtuous theatre is founded on its ability to correct faults in people through satire because nothing achieves that correction more that a portrait of their vices. The reason he gives is that "On veut bien être méchant; mais on ne veut point être ridicule" (1: 630). The exposure of the ridiculous is the aim of comedy, at least Molière's satiric comedy, and the purging of sin is connected with the pleasures and successes of satire, that is, according to Molière and in accordance with my argument, satire is more powerful in achieving this end than are "Les plus beaux traits d'une sérieuse morale" (1: 630). Even as some of Molière's opponents, those who occasioned the preface, howled and plotted as much as Tartuffe did, it may be, that in the long run, the very attractive repulsion or repulsive attraction of the character, Tartuffe, like Volpone before him, makes the audience see the glory of vice, in this case hypocrisy. The end of Tartuffe at the end of the comedy brings applause, and without his gargantuan vice, the play itself would not exist. The very pleasure the audience gains throughout the play and at its end is not simply one of a katascopic or god's eye moral superiority as Molière suggests but also the dangerous pleasures of satiric comedy, that one is part of a grand ruse or game. The pleasures of dramatic irony, which is especially apparent in the gap between public virtue and private vice in hypocrites, have to end but perhaps the audience is less glad at their conclusion.

The happy end of comedy may be more mixed than Molière can admit publicly. He is like all of us who defend education and the arts publicly, in that we may be caught in our own rationalizations and hypocrisy. We have to put forward the ideal image of what we do and hope that society will leave us alone and think what we do beneficial, moral, and useful, because the more we know our subject or job, the more doubts we have. And Molière, one of the greatest of satirists, would have been much aware of this delicate position and that all satire is a satire against ourselves, including the author. At some time or another, we all appear ridiculous. In a polemical battle, however, ambiguities and compromises are left beyond the margins. In the preface, Molière represents the objections of his detractors. Perhaps for the wrong reasons, they have hit on something when they concentrate on the character of Tartuffe. They are naive to equate his words with Molière's, and they have forced Molière on too narrow ground in wanting to say that the playwright has made Tartuffe's ideas dangerous by representing them in the theatre and impressing them on the souls of the audience (1: 630). There is some truth in this accusation if one sticks strictly to a moral argument, but the aesthetic dimension — the fact that this comedy is a fiction— complicates this matter. Molière is not Pascal or La Rochefoucauld writing *pensées* or maxims, but a playwright representing characters in a situation who speak of ideas in a kind of dramatic dialectic. The danger that Molière's opponents raise, however, is not easily dismissed even by those, like me, who admire his comedies.

For Molière, to condemn *Tartuffe* is to condemn all comedy. It is not really a matter of condemnation, but of understanding the stress between form and message at the end of the play. In the preface, Molière, like Corneille in the preface to *Théodore*, admits that some of the Church Fathers were not fond of

drama: "c'est qu'ils ont pris la comédie différemment, et que les uns l'ont
considerée dans sa pureté, lorsque les autres l'ont regardée dans sa corruption,
et confondue avec tous ces vilains spectacles qu'on a eu raison de nommer des
spectacles de turpitude" (1: 630; see Barish). Molière appeals to the important
place Greece and Rome, at its height and not in its decline, accorded for comedy
and the theatre (1: 630-31). Although he admits that comedy, like all things, has
in some periods known corruption and its good has been turned to bad ends, he
maintains that we must not confuse the bounty of things ("la bonté des choses")
with the malice of its corrupters. If Rome banished medicine and Athens
philosophy, it is not right to banish them in all times, and the same is true of
comedy (1: 631). Molière will allow that comedy should be condemned for not
regarding God directly, but only if all other such human activities are also
condemned. He sees comedy as the most innocent diversion that people can have
when they take a break from worship. Molière alludes to le prince de Condé, and
reports how he replies to the king's question about why Molière's comedy
scandalizes people but not the comedy *Scaramouche*, in which a hermit dressed
as a monk spends the night by the window of a married woman, saying from
time to time, that his visits to the window are for mortifying his flesh (1: 921).
The prince says that *Scaramouche* represents heaven and religion, which the
scandalized people do not care about, but Molière's comedies represent these
people, and that is what they cannot bear (1: 632). In outlining the ends of
comedy, Molière calls upon the king and the prince as a means of invoking
authority, to show how powerful his allies are, and to remind others that he has
the king's favour, which they seek as the ultimate form of arbitration in the
matter. It is easy to see why some critics want to emphasize the political nature
of comedy.

In the preface Molière defends comedy by emphasizing its unequivocal
nature and by appeal to the world of things, as distinct from the paradoxical
realm of language:

> Et, en effet, puisqu'on doit discourir des choses et non pas les mots et que la
> plupart des contrariétés viennent de ne pas entendre et d'envelopper dans un
> même mot des choses opposées, il me faut qu'ôter le voile de l'équivoque, et
> regarder ce qu'est la comédie en soi, pour voir si elle est condamnable. (1:
> 630)

Here, the playwright is defending the morality of comedy, not by stressing the
anagogical or allegorical morals that it represents through story but by talking
about its essence and, by implication, rendering his "moralist opponents"
Sophists, who accuse in a confusion of words. The ends of comedy are literal:

Molière's defence would leave little, if any, room for interpretation. How much of this stance is a politics of necessary literalism, where the writer finds himself, yet again, in the position of saying — "I know what this work means because I made it, and it is clearly moral and will teach us all to be good" — remains to be seen. The preface is not the play, as the prefaces of Bernard Shaw illustrate. There may be a large gap between Molière's position (unless it is ironic or a courtesy to the king) and the post-Saussurian revolution in literary theory where many post-structuralists and postmodernists take an opposite and more rhetorical view of *mots et choses*. The ends of comedy are as much a matter of interpretative assumptions as of the words with which the playwright ends the play.

Molière's satirical comedy must show clearly the satirical targets, and it is true that satire is more pointed and apparently clear than many other literary forms. None the less, the shifts of point of view, as we have seen in *Volpone*, complicate how satire is to be taken. Is the audience to be corrected or ridiculed as well? Are Volpone and Tartuffe so magnificent as characters that they are larger than life and therefore not ironic because the audience cannot look down upon them with a feeling of superiority? Are there substantial differences between Tartuffe and Volpone, explaining why the one is more resurrected than the other?

Molière begins the Premier Placet Présenté au Roi Sur la comédie du *Tartuffe* with "Le devoir de la comédie étant de corriger les hommes en les divertissant, j'ai cru que, dans l'emploi où je me trouve, je n'avais rien de mieux à faire que d'attaquer par des peintures ridicules les vices de mon siècle" (1: 632). The most dangerous vice, he continues, is hypocrisy, and he thought that he was doing a service to all the honest people in the kingdom (and thus to the king) to attack these hypocrites and to expose "toutes les grimaces étudiées de ces gens de bien à outrance, toutes des friponneries couvertes de ces faux monnayeurs en dévotion, qui veulent attraper les hommes avec un zèle contrefait et une charité sophistique" (1: 632). Molière claims to expose the sophistical words and feigning gestures of a hypocrite as a warning to the honest people of France. His equates comedy and satire, and this implicit move is not surprising considering the ritual satire of Aristophanic comedy. But, between correction and entertainment, the instruction and delight that Horace recommends, there lies an opening. Certainly, entertainment can make the instruction more palatable, but it can also divert the audience from the moral or make the duty of comedy seem less full and rich as the representation itself. *Tartuffe* is not a treatise on religious hypocrisy but a play.

Elsewhere, Molière makes this point that a comedy is not comic theory. He understands the complexity and difference of representation. Having discussed this matter elsewhere, I shall mention it only briefly here (see Hart, "Narrative" 149-51). Even if Molière is less given to theory than is Corneille, he likes to state his views. In the preface to *Les Précieuses ridicules* (1659), Molière sets out ideas that he expresses throughout his career: comedy is a worthy genre; the public is the absolute judge of plays; the representation of the play is more important than learned, if not pedantic, criticism of drama (2: 193-94). He satirizes critics and criticism, as in the "Avertissement" to *Les Fâcheux* (1662), he says that he is not concerned with the rules of laughter and that one day he will publish remarks on his plays where he will cite Aristotle and Horace. In *La Critique de l'École des femmes* (1663), Dorante defends the playwright's work against Lysidas's claim that Aristotle and Horace would condemn Molière (see vol. 2), however. Amidst the controversy between Molière and his opponents, he celebrates the comic spirit in *L'Impromptu de Versailles* (1663) and makes himself one of his characters in a royal performance for Louis XIV, who will empower and protect them. Particularly in the last speech of this comedy, the king becomes part of the story: here, Molière tells Bejart of the king's good grace towards them. This is a king blessing their comedic marriage and the end/s of their comedy. The distance between Louis XIV and the Molières as actors and as people is collapsed as much as possible. Here the playwright speaks to the godfather of his child as much as to his king.

As Molière represents *Tartuffe* to the king, it is a play that depends on his grace as much as the Tartuffe in the comedy and the Tartuffes of this world do. Despite the blessing of Louis XIV and that of his legate and prelates, a priest has written that Molière is a demon and a libertine. Molière puts himself in the hands of his king, who, like God, knows best, and he awaits his judgement (1: 633). The Second Placet is also presented to Louis XIV, "*Dans son camp devant la ville de Lille en Flandre*" in August 1667 (1: 634). *Tartuffe* placed Molière in a difficult situation, so that, at the end of the comedy, he wished for the grace of the monarch to set things right. Even as he wanted to distance himself from the equivocal fictionality of his play by stressing its clear relation to the world, his opponents showed how equivocal interpretation is by taking up the opposite side — that Molière's comedy was simply immoral and impious. Here are two ends to Tartuffe and the eponymous play, both insisting on the truth, plain and simple. The ends of comedy, then, have also to do with reception. When addressing the king, Molière takes his case to the battlefield — the literary war shifts to the site of an actual war:

C'est une chose bien téméraire à moi que de venir importuner un grand monarque au milieu de ses glorieuses conquêtes; mais, dans l'état où je me vois, où trouver, SIRE, une protection qu'au lieu où je la viens chercher? et qui puis-je solliciter contre l'autorité de la puissance qui m'accable, que la source de la puissance et de la puissance et de l'autorité, que le juste dispensateur des ordres absolus, que le souverain juge et le maître de toutes choses? (1: 634)

The playwright wants the king to become the ultimate arbiter of the play. Interpretation becomes a matter of patronage and authority. The king should have the final word.

This Second Placet shows the lengths to which Molière says he has gone to placate his critics. He tells the king that in vain he has produced the comedy under the title, *L'Imposture*, disguised his character as a man of the world, and cut with care "tous ce que j'ai jugé capable de fournir l'ombre d'un prétexte aux célèbres originaux du portrait que je voulais faire: tout cela n'a de rien servi" (1: 634). Molière, who in his preface of 1664 had insisted on the clarity and morality of his play, has now succumbed to his critics' censorship. Even though he is now playing by their rules, he is not winning the game: "La cabale s'est réveillée aux simples conjectures qu'ils ont pu avoir de la chose" (1: 634). "La chose" is not as simple as Molière had said. There is more than one kind of politics of interpretation, even in comedy. Molière, like characters in Shakespeare's *Tempest*, says he finds himself in a storm ("cette tempête"). This time the magician is caught in a tempest that is and is not of his own making. Owing to clerical pressure, he closed his theatre for seven weeks (1: 921). Now the playwright is confounded as to why he should ask his opponents' permission when the king had granted his:

Daignent vos bontés, SIRE, me donner une protection contre leur rage envenimeé; et puissé-je, au retour d'une campagne si glorieuse, délasser VOTRE MAJESTÉ des fatigues de ses conquêtes, lui donner d'innocents plaisirs après de si nobles travaux, et faire rire le monarche qui fait trembler toute Europe! (1: 635)

The place of comedy in the social sphere rests with the king's authority, his ability to direct a battle implicitly akin to his ability to direct the diversionary tactics of a play, or at least its reception. During Alexander the Great's eastward campaign, he read Homer's epics, a copy of which Aristotle had apparently prepared for him (Breisach 28); rather than epic inspiration, Molière offers Louis XIV comic relief from the campaign.

Molière's opponents took *Tartuffe* seriously, so that on 5 February 1669, he was again defending his comedy in a Troisième Placet. With wit and satire, Molière seeks the king's grace to resurrect his comedy in order to be reconciled with the devout and with doctors, both of whom he has satirized (1: 635). The end of *Tartuffe* also exerts the king's authority, which through L'Exempt, descends *ex machina*. L'Exempt comes to deliver Tartuffe to prison rather than to respond to his cries for deliverance. After the comic enormity of Tartuffe, such an order may seem like the appeal Edgar, Kent, and Albany make after the great gap of Lear's death (V.iii.313-27). Molière felt the public pressure of his opponents and owed a debt to the king for supporting public performances of *Tartuffe*, so that the reversal here has political dimensions. Like Volpone, Tartuffe must be imprisoned, but he, too, can be resurrected by the grace of the audience, in this case, of the very king whose authority must send him to prison.

Poetic justice is also served by the end of *Tartuffe*. After L'Exempt has emphasized and exercised the authority of the prince and after Dorine, Madame Pernelle, Elmire, Mariane, and Organ have made their brief and approving exclamations about the king's power to punish Tartuffe, Cléante and then Organ provide amplification. The first expresses the hope that Tartuffe will return to virtue, correct his life while detesting his vice, and face the mild justice of the great prince, while the second seconds those words and celebrates hymen and love (V.vii.1897-1962). The stresses between Tartuffe's serial game of duping and the brief reversal that enforces moral order and closure express the ambivalence of comedy in which the holiday mood sweeps the audience away and the tricksters dazzle with traps and ploys, but in which the ethical anxieties of the world wait at the exit. It may also be that, for some, art is a supplement or world of wishes, where virtue is rewarded and vice is punished, precisely because in the world they live in, it is so often not not the case.[6] *Tartuffe* is a satirical comedy, and while satire must punish the vicious and reward the virtuous, comedy is a festival that celebrates desires and dreams without end.

III

The pastoral or romantic comedy tends to achieve order through marriage, whereas the satiric comedy through a pattern of poetic justice. These are different poles of comedy and often contain elements of the other but to varying degrees. Jaques and Malvolio bring in the satiric and tragic possibilities into pastoral and romantic worlds, whereas Volpone and Tartuffe need correction for the enormity of their tricks. The strength of these characters threatens to bend the comic logic of the plot out of shape. There are also thematic concerns, such as the role of women in the comic world, that make it even more difficult for an audience in the 1990s to accept the structural movement towards harmony. Stresses occur, then, between the romantic and satirical aspects of comedy, what may be called the celebratory and cursing functions, between the form and the content. These elements cannot be separated, and so feeling and thought meet, and modify the French proverb in my epigraph. The ends of comedy include thought and feeling both in the movement of comedy, which involves convention but with an infinite variety. In the very problems or stresses lie the energy of comedy, and so the generations return again and again to great comedies with different emphases on these stresses.

ROBERT RAWDON WILSON AND EDWARD MILOWICKI

Troilus and Cressida: Voices in the Darkness of Troy

As a literary genre, epic, studied both early and long, may seem comparatively narrow. There has been so much agreement about epic over the centuries that it must seem eminently knowable. Knowledge about epic has always operated on two distinct levels: as a genre, epic entails a number of precisely understood conventions (too many disparate conventions and the text will become a romance or, uncertainly, a "romance-epic"); as a way of telling stories, epic incorporates a number of recognizable moral virtues, such as courage and piety, and emotional states, such as anger and honour. Hence, discussions about epic tend to focus upon the hero, the actor in the single action that, since Aristotle, readers of literature have sought in epic. In the hero, the different (though never extensive) epic elements combine. Shakespeare was quite aware of the "epic elements," those heroic conventions and values, that permeate western literature. His treatment of Hotspur, Hal, and Falstaff in the *Henriad* illustrates his profound grasp of the epic tradition. In particular, the epic elements in *Henry V* are well known and have been much discussed.[1]

Shakespeare also inherited another set of narrative conventions which had developed in a series of narratives over several centuries, a distinctive, powerful rhetoric. As a narrative mode, distinguished from epic by its open-endedness and (potential) interminability, romance tends to emphasize different values. Romance, typically (though not necessarily) developed upon a quest, entails a narrative founded upon a structure of "deepening complication" (Parker, *Spenser Encyclopedia* 618) and may incorporate an in(de)finite spectrum of discontinuous motifs (unlike the epic concentration upon a single action and a limited range of synergetic motifs).[2] In romance, love is, and has always been, as such works as Chrétien de Troyes's *Lancelot* suggest, counterpoised against honour.

Shakespeare returns frequently to the distinct conventions of epic and romance: this return shows an interest, perhaps deep but certainly continuing, in how different conventions work to create distinct narratives and radically dissimilar fictional worlds. Not only the Romances but also the Comedies display the interest in exploring the conventions of romance; certain plays, *A Midsummer Night's Dream* or *Cymbeline*, are virtually concise encyclopedias of romance conventions. Even the tragedies, notably *Romeo and Juliet* but also, if far less obviously, *Hamlet* (think of the quest motif, the mysterious country with intransitive boundaries, the night sea voyage, the theme of metamorphosis), show the continuing experimentation with romance conventions. One may suppose that Shakespeare found the creation of a mixed discourse interesting, but that he also enjoyed creating fictional worlds that were split, bifurcated between opposed values, and exhibited the traces of distinct conventional matrices. Nowhere is this more evident than in the highly problematic (and even downright enigmatic) *Troilus and Cressida*. Shakespeare's retelling of an old tale, *Troilus* examines and redefines both love and honour, in the process dissecting the rhetoric of epic and of romance.[3]

Troilus slants sharply into the fictional world of ancient Troy at a late moment in its intricate story: that world is extremely shadowy and dark (it is difficult to see clearly in Troy, whether one is a character or merely an observer), bloody, and inescapably doomed. The play announces its beginning *in medias res* in the Prologue's words, explicitly invoking a narrative epic convention as an initial move. (*Richard II* also begins in the middle of an action, though it does not explicitly call attention to this move, and the Chorus of *Henry V*, who identifies himself as "Prologue-like," seems to ask that the action be imagined from its middle, both as the single course of the hero's life and as a representation of a single heroic endeavour.)[4] It is the way that Troy normally seems in Renaissance writing and the way that Shakespeare always makes it seem. The entire action of *Troilus* must be viewed, borrowing a phrase from Thomas McAlindon, in "retrospective contrast" (24) since the ultimate destruction of Troy, its inhabitants and its civilization, was well-known and an inevitable part of the way the play, as any story about Troy, would have been understood.[5] However, the future, though large, appears only in brief narratives within the play, in terse expressions and splintered hopes. The characters cannot know what the audience knows all too well. Cassandra's seven line proleptic narrative about Hector's death ("O, farewell, dear Hector") evokes one of the major episodes of the Trojan war, if not precisely its downward turning-point, then at least the representation of its futility and vast loss, and it does so with maximum economy (5.3.80-87). The Prologue manages to indicate the course of the war, from Greece to the landing at Tenedos to the plains before Troy, describes the city, hints at the early battles, and then drives directly to "what may be digested in a play" (Pro. 29), the twinned stories of Hector's and Troilus's defeats. Troy evoked a sombre story for Renaissance writers, the main line of which, well-known and rehearsed, served as the strings of a narrative instrument. Troy was both a story-matrix and a machine for narrative effect. The Renaissance seems always to have found in Troy, and above all in the figure of Hecuba, an emblem of human sorrow. The myth, the Matter of Troy, is, always and already, the "classical topos, the set piece, the commonplace, the cliché, the name that has become a concept" (Freund 21), Spenser's Sir Paridell laments,

> Troy, that art now nought, but an idle name,
> And in thine ashes buried low dost lie,
> Though whilome far much greater than thy fame,
> Before that angry Gods, and cruell skye
> Upon thee heapt a direfull destinie.... (FQ III.9.33)

In *Virgil's Gnat*, Spenser's narrator exclaims,

> O who would not recount the strong divorces
> Of that great warre, which Troianes oft behelde,
> And oft beheld the warlike greekish forces,
> When *Teucrian* soyle with bloodie rivers swelde,
> And wide *Sigœan* shores were spred with corses,
> And *Simois* and *Xanthus* blood outwelde,
> Whilst *Hector* raged with outragious minde,
> Flames, weapons, wounds in *Greeks* fleete to have tynde. (497-504)

Spenser's reflections are typical. Troy provided the matrix for the oldest tale, and one that was still the most complex, the most extended, the most retellable.[6] Shakespeare's uses of the Troy-theme outside of *Troilus* are always intricate and highly reflexive, drawing upon the contemporary memory of both classical and medieval literature.[7] We shall never get *Troilus* right, Tillyard observes, "unless we think of a Shakespeare steeped as a youth in the antique and venerable and quaint world of Lydgate's Troy" (*Shakespeare's Problem Plays* 41). Above all, Shakespeare's understanding of the potential for narrative effect in retelling the story of Troy seems to have centred upon the feeling of sorrow.

The ekphrastic moment in *The Rape of Lucrece* (when Lucrece evokes the final moments of Troy's independent existence as it falls to the Greeks' deception and military power) depicts violence, death, and sorrow in graphic detail. Lucrece has chosen the painting of Troy's death to be an exterior correspondence of her inner feelings of rage and suicidal self-disgust. In *Hamlet*, Troy reappears in the short narrative that Hamlet and the Player King share. Like the representation in *Lucrece*, it is dark and bloody, drenched in violence, anger, revenge, and sorrow. Indeed, it is sorrow once again (the dominant element in the ekphrasis in *Lucrece*) that holds the highest register. The Player King weeps for the image of Hecuba, a clout upon her head, herself weeping, and only indirectly, if at all, for Troy. Of course, it is impossible to infer what Shakespeare may have thought about Troy, or what it "really" may have meant to him, but it does seem that it must have meant (at least) loss, disappearance, finality, unswept stone. A narrative boundary divides the action in Priam's palace from the world of *Hamlet*. This second boundary also divides the action in Priam's palace from a larger story, which is not the story of *Hamlet*. The fifty-seven lines of the narrative are a fragment of, or perhaps a small peephole into, the vast story of Troy. Every schoolboy knew well the matter of Troy which, Harry Levin observes, "Caxton had popularized, which English ballads celebrated, which poets and artists could draw upon as freely as the matter of England itself" (*The Question of* Hamlet 146). The Renaissance, Thomas M. Greene writes,

> discovered its cultural paths by the light behind it of a vast holocaust, and used this mythical light as the principle of its own energy. It made its way through ruins by the effulgence cast in their destruction, finding in privation the secret of renewal, just as Aeneas, sailing westward from the ashes of his city, carried with him the flame that had consumed it burning before his Penates. (*Light in Troy* 3)

Aeneas's tale to Dido breaks into the action of *Hamlet* in an extremely exact manner, shifting the focus of the action to the distant elsewhen and elsewhere, but once attention has been transferred, then, like a bubble suspended in shadows, it becomes enveloped within a surrounding story-matrix. It is, to borrow a phrase from Roman Ingarden, as if a beam of light illuminated a part of a region, while everything else "disappears in an indeterminate cloud but is still there in its indeterminacy" (218). The story-matrix, the shadowy, indeterminate cloud of potential narrative, is the matter of Troy, the tentacular accounts of Bronze Age Heroes, the nested networks of legendary materials.

Troy may also have meant (and one senses a slipping confidence) a wonderful story, a matrix of stories that had been, and could still be, told and retold with immense effect. Of all the many stories that might be retold, none (except perhaps that story of origins that begins the Judeo-Christian narrative) possessed the resonance that Troy could still let sound. Elizabeth Freund refers to Shakespeare's "plight" as a "belated writer who knows all the stories have already been told" (34). When one reads the Troy passages in *Lucrece* and in

Hamlet, it does not seem quite as if Shakespeare had been writing out of his "plight," but rather more as if the opportunity to retell, to find a new significance in an extremely old matrix, was glorious. The world of Troy, glimpsed in the ekphrasis in *Lucrece* as well as in *Troilus* or in the Player King's narrative in *Hamlet*, invites entrance through many textual slivers. Whenever a text alludes to it, as happens so commonly (but always incompletely) in Renaissance literature, the historical world of Troy, repeatedly refracted through legend, myth, and prior literary texts, springs back into being. Shakespeare repeatedly draws upon this fundamental gestational potential, but no where more fully than in *Troilus*.

Troilus is a complex intellectual undertaking which causes the play to suggest a probing, questioning dialectic. In what appears at first impact to be an examination of the relationships between love and honour, the poet, Shakespeare, redefines both western bywords. This was not, in itself, novel: Chrétien in his *Yvain*, and Chaucer in his *Franklin's Tale*, had presented views of honour other than those traditionally held by the narrative voice in epic, interposing a view that suggested women were relatively important not only in the fields of love, but also in those of honour. In his redefinition, Shakespeare follows the reductive approach to the heroic which Ovid developed in the *Metamorphoses*.[8] He seems also to be familiar with the rethinking of the war which had developed in the Middle Ages inspired by Ovid's quasi-epic and Virgil's *Aeneid*, a view that made the Greeks the villains and the Trojans the heroes. He is, however, doing a great deal more.

To begin: the unbelievable Babel of "voices" in the play, with their difficult and inexhaustible wordplay, suggests that the play is an examination of the uses of language to persuade, to argue, and to make points. It is an examination of various "rhetorics." The two most prominent rhetorics in the play outline the history of literature in the west: the rhetoric of love and the rhetoric of honour, the former evolving out of and with romance narrative, the latter out of and with heroic narrative. The central tensions in the play, indeed, turn upon the struggle between love and honour as it is exemplified in Achilles's abandonment of the battlefield, and Troilus's occasional martial lapses because of his love for Cressida. This dialogue between love and honour usually ended in earlier texts with some redefinition or realignment, but seldom or never with total deconstruction. In *Troilus*, this movement towards redefinition is, in the final act, displaced by the failings of Achilles and Cressida, as the fruitlessness of the idealization of either love or honour as a means of motivation, or of determining human value, is underscored.

It is even possible to schematize the roles of the principal characters in relation to love and honour: Hector, with his impractical, idealistic behaviour on the battlefield (Troilus criticizes his lack of the killer instinct), elevates the heroic because he creates the suggestion that war need not preclude humane behaviour; Achilles, on the other hand, in remaining the anger-obsessed hero of the *Iliad*, suggests that there is no room for sentiment on the battlefield, killing Hector in a dishonourable fashion. In the matter of love, Troilus's idealistic passion for Cressida is starkly contrasted to Diomedes's and to her "realistic" and "practical" view of love, unconstrained, like Achilles's anger, by considerations of "honour." Every idealization, each possible hierarchy of values, is itself undermined quite thoroughly in the play: the most resonating voice at critical moments is not that of Hector or Ulysses, but that of the menippean Thersites. And Shakespeare, using another rhetoric, the rhetoric of satire (especially in its virulent menippean mode) has given the completely deflated and defeated Thersites of the epic a "valorized voice" upon the stage, that of the clown. Thersites's cowardliness at the close of the play does not weaken the savagery of his pronouncements on love and honour, since he has all along professed his distaste for both love (which he calls lechery) and honour. That is to say, he cannot be held accountable for not abiding by ideals for which he has no use whatever. Thersites is another version of the "all-licens'd Fool" (*KL* 1.4.201), but he also embodies a distinct fictional type, the menippean satiric voice, harsh, rasping, systematically undercutting, carnivalesque.[9]

It is not a coincidence that, in a play so pervasively discursive, Thersites has the chief role in the last act's central scene (5.4). It might even be considered among the most dramatic in all of Shakespeare: three levels of drama, and an intricate interplay among all three levels, are present in the scene where Cressida flirts with Diomedes while Troilus comments in rage and Ulysses seeks to restrain him, while even further in the background (a daring director might place him in the audience) Thersites makes comments that are spatially, and hence thematically, inclusive and definitive. Furthermore, in the scene, his is the only point of view that is not "qualified" by interaction with another character, or by a response to another person, as with Cressida and Diomedes, Ulysses and Troilus. Troilus, for example, may have good reason to be upset, but he uses language to deflect Ulysses even as Diomedes and Cressida are using it to their own ends. Finally, the judgments Troilus lavishes on Cressida are further "judged" by Thersites, who talks to no one and, thus, to everyone. The dramatic conception, especially in the manipulation of point of view, is astonishing. One climbs a hierarchy of knowledge only to find a clown, not a guru, at the top.[10] Yet Thersites is a different sort of clown. This can be seen most clearly by considering the character of Falstaff who, in his range of carnivalesque language and behaviour, resembles Thersites in significant respects. Unlike Thersites, however, Falstaff pretends to be that which he is not. Falstaff surrounds himself with a discursive zone, the dominant chord in which is pretence. ("Ah, whoreson caterpillars! Bacon-fed knaves! they hate us youth" [*1H4* 2.2.84-85].) Thersites, in true menippean fashion, has no pretence about him, no make-believe that he projects upon the world. He does not call all into doubt, like the deconstructive Feste of *Twelfth Night*; he never indicates, neither in playful jest nor in direct comment, that what he is saying is make-believe, merely pretence, however significant or meaningful or just. His attitude is consistently serious with a singularly cynical bitterness and disillusionment more suggestive of Timon, or of Hamlet prior to the final act, and of no character elsewhere in Shakespeare. (Thersites comes from an entirely different species than Iago, Jachimo, or Don John, of course; he is not, except accidentally, a malcontent.) In sheer bitterness he resembles Coriolanus, the broken hero of the third play in Shakespeare's classical trilogy of disillusionment (*Troilus*, *Timon*, and *Coriolanus*), but his linguistic play, this range of disgusting images, his pervasive verbal downkeying, sets him apart from both Timon and Coriolanus, neither of whom, for all their bitterness, is menippean. It is as if Thersites has not always been a clown, as if the Thersites that we meet in the play is what remains after his suppression in the epic.[11]

Little, if anything, in Shakespeare's canon up to this point in time compares with the intense scrutiny reason, will, appetites, and emotions receive in the play, notable even for Shakespeare (for instance, 2.2 and 3.2). Consider Troilus as he anticipates his first sexual encounter with Cressida:

> I am giddy; expectation whirls me round;
> Th'imaginary relish is so sweet
> That it enchants my sense; what will it be,
> When that the wat'ry palates taste indeed
> Love's thrice-repured nectar? Death, I fear me,
> Sounding destruction, or some joy too fine,
> Too subtile, potent, tun'd too sharp in sweetness
> For the capacity of my ruder powers.
> I fear it much, and I do fear besides
> That I shall lose distinction in my joys,
> As doth a battle, when they charge on heaps
> The enemy flying. (3.2.18-29)

A few lines later, Pandarus now having led Cressida to him, Troilus introduces the notion of monstrosity. There is, he affirms to calm Cressida, no monster in "all Cupid's pageant" (74-75). There is only the "monstruosity" in love that the will "is infinite and execution confin'd, that the desire is boundless and the act a slave to limit" (81-83). This examination of the will and its seduction by appetites extends throughout the play. A dialectical, even deeply dialogic, process, it draws support from a cluster of images concerning blood that is striking. The word "blood," and all the mental and physical states suggested by the word, occurs as often, or even more so, as in the bloodiest of the tragedies. Another powerful image has to do with eating, tasting, feeding, and so forth. This cluster of images suggests "appetite" as a pendant to the "emotion" of the blood images. Whatever Shakespeare's specific aims were, the play is a telling inventory of human depravity. He creates this inventory utilizing the voices of both epic and romance narrative traditions.

Consider the *Iliad*. Achilles in his wrath, and after having left the windy plains of Troy littered with innumerable parts of countless Trojans, wants to devour Hector because killing the great Trojan hero has been an inadequate revenge. Anger constitutes one of the epic elements. It is a motivator to action, a spur to accomplishment and honour. This presents the first question, as does much of the *Iliad* in general: if anger is needed to propel young heroes into battle, how is it controlled or directed or suppressed when it is no longer needed? And how is it kept aimed, as it were, at the enemy, and not at one's own people? A related question also comes up: if one encourages or adulates or honours anger, will this not cause some difficulties in time of peace? One unhappy solution would be to extend the definition of honour to include just about any and every violent act, to bring more kinds of violence within the parameters of acceptability. Ovid saw this potential in Homer's honour-hungry Achilles and, in the *Metamorphoses*, had the hero's angry shade demand in the name of honour the blood of Hecuba's last child, Polyxena, thereby driving the old queen mad. She turns, according to Ovid, upon the Thracian king who has performed the sacrifice, tearing his eyes out in an action still belonging to the darkness of Troy,

... et digitos in perfida lumina condit
expellitque genis oculos.... (Bk. 13.561-62)

From the Homeric epic through Virgil to the vernacular epics of the Middle Ages the most driving motivation is the need for individual honour. Heroes may seem to seek national or cultural honour, but it is sought through the attainment of individual honour. This second motivator has been most effective: a history of honour (which, like other important concepts, such as play or disgust, has not yet been written) would take one from the *Iliad* through Faulkner and beyond in literature, and through much of the violence of western civilization.[12] It has been both ubiquitous and powerful. Yet honour presented a definite paradox and problem that Homer grappled with: If honour determines one's relative worth in the culture, how is it to be measured? The Funeral Games and awarding of prizes by Achilles is precisely about this. Most of the characters in the *Iliad* appear to have no problem on this score since honour is taken as quantitative, literally a score: one simply counts the tripods, horses, women, and assorted goods. The one with the most prizes wins the most honour. Achilles, however, seems to have other standards, or at least to be reaching for them.[13]

Both paradoxes, of honour and of anger, appear to be insoluble: anger is an emotion and therefore highly subjective, not always easily directed by a society; in the case of the other motivator, honour, a situation arises where objective values have been used to stimulate a subjective reaction. But objective social values cannot mirror subjective perceptions. There can be no absolute meshing of objective values with subjective perceptions. That is, the objective cultural values cannot remain objective but must be assimilated into each subjective world, each hero's apprehension, and must therefore dissolve into a multitude of interpretations and, conversely, reappear in a multitude of voices. So it is in the *Iliad*, when Achilles seems to be considering an honour apart from that held by the three members of the embassy, Odysseus, Phoinix, and Aias, whose views of honour may be essentially similar, but show some variations.

If Homer was examining the roles of anger and honour in culture (an ideal culture), he nonetheless presents an explicit paean to both. At a deeper level, he may even have been questioning the unquestionable. But such doubting never becomes explicit in the *Iliad*, and potential problems that would undermine the accepted values, such as Thersites, are summarily dealt with: Thersites is lashed both verbally and physically (with Agamemnon's staff of office, no less) and his "counter-voice" is rendered ineffective, silenced by Odysseus. But even prior to his encounter with Odysseus before the Greek army, he is "disarmed" before Homer's audience by the poet's physical description of him, unusual in the epic, which paints him as excruciatingly ugly and, therefore, presumably an unacceptable source of any serious counter-argument. After Homer, down through the ages, writers confronted honour and attempted, quite explicitly at times, to create counter-voices, to redefine honour: Chrétien de Troyes, for one, who used love to lever honour off the centre of the culture in his *Knight of the Cart*.

Although one thinks of romance, in contrast to the epic, as lacking structure, an in(de)finitely continuing collocation of episodes (anticipating the novel's structureless structures), the deeper rhetoric of romance follows a pattern. The archetypal design of romance can be represented with a single parabolic line traced from the beginning of the narrative to its end. Underneath that single arc, which includes the beginning and the end of the romance, would be included a series of smaller arcs, each of which would represent a particular episode in the romance. These smaller arcs would best be drawn as beginning on the horizontal, then descending to represent the knight's encounter with various threats, returning to the horizontal as he triumphs at the close of each episode: a reversed half-turn of the Wheel of Fortune! This pattern might be called the "rhythm of reassurance." Each episode, however harrowing, ends positively, thus reassuring the audience that the knight's destiny has been provided for, that there is a providential hand in the proceedings. The ultimate manifestation of this providential hand comes with the close of the tale, when the major quest, which binds the tale together structurally, is successfully completed, confirming for the reader or audience what has been implicitly established by the recurring rhythm of minor triumphs in the episodes, that God is in his heaven and all is right with the world. The French master of this form is Chrétien de Troyes; the English master, Spenser. Malory adapted it to achieve an almost infinite variation both on theme and on structure. Cervantes demolished it. Shakespeare, obviously, conforms to this structural rhetoric in several of his comedies; in *Troilus and Cressida*, however, he confronts the romance convention of a reassuring closure: even in the Greek romances, and certainly in the medieval romances, the closed and usually satisfying endings (evils overcome and punished, good in triumph and rewarded) were doubtless a reflection of religious concerns, with the theology of Providence providing an imitable paradigm. A pagan or Christian God works good out of evil. Disturbingly enough, *Troilus* ends with nothing closed, nothing resolved, nothing "defined," with good turned instead to evil on several occasions, and with more evils to come, suggesting the ominous endings of such epics as the *Iliad* and *Beowulf*.[14]

Troilus* is, thus, an examination of human motivation within the spheres of both honour and love. Shakespeare invokes the conventions of both epic and romance for complex effects, but among these are the creation of distinct voices, speaking the values of honour as well as love, and a clear, even outrageous, counter-voice in Thersites. The examination takes place within the conceptual framework of the traditional hierarchy of human powers: reason at the top, will (the faculty of choice) next below, and then followed by, in a descending scale, the emotions and the appetites. Ideally, will should remain under the direction of reason, and resist the promptings of the emotions and appetites. But in the play, will is a slave to the lower urges, while reason itself is prostituted to serve the baser instincts. (This is so thoroughly the case in *Troilus* that sonnet 129 could provide a terse conceptual map for the play's action.) Humans not only have base drives but also, as Shakespeare pursues the matter, inadequate methods of managing those drives. The anger that drives Achilles to glory in the *Iliad* is here presented as what it normally is: the prelude to treacherous and cowardly murder. The love that is intended to inspire to great deeds in virtually all romance narratives is unmasked as base passion or trivial lust. When love fails Troilus, he reverts to anger, to epic values.

It would be wrong, then, to see Troilus as untouched by the play's biting examination. What is suggested in the scene of Cressida's betrayal is that Troilus, were he to live, would probably become another Ulysses (his momentary mentor), older and wiser, yet twisted by the world's ways. This allusion ahead may save Troilus, provided one sees Ulysses favourably. The allusion ahead for Cressida is that she will become another Helen, but outside the epic context, without Helen's style, reduced. She will become what she is in Henryson's *The Testament of Cresseid*, "the wanton of tradition" (Knights 154). Beyond Homer, but before Shakespeare, she will become "shallow, hard, and lascivious" (Tillyard, *Problem Plays* 85), a woman who, finally, will "inhabit with obtuse and unreflecting singleness of purpose the world of the senses" (77). In Shakespeare's *Troilus*, she is witty, charming, desirable, weak, vulnerable, trapped by history and by her gender. She is the quick self-confident young woman who lies

> Upon my back, to defend my belly, upon my wit, to defend my wiles, upon my secrecy, to defend mine honesty, my mask to defend my beauty, and you [Pandarus] to defend all these; and at all these wards I lie, at a thousand watches. (1.2.260-64)

For all of these confident actions, she is also the young woman trapped by circumstances, and compelled by forces she cannot control into the unequal banter, its up-shot foreseen, with Diomedes that Troilus, Ulysses, and Thersites overhear. Shakespeare recuperates Cressida by showing her vulnerability, her powerlessness within her particular circumstances. (He uses this technique of balancing weakness against external compulsion in other female characters to great effect: Ophelia, even more than Desdemona, seems like the most striking example from the tragedies, but Lady Anne in *Richard III* and even Cleopatra are also important instances.) Shakespeare's Cressida is a revolutionary character that alludes ahead to the tradition that she will become even while denying that tradition.[15] Neither Troilus nor Pandarus, who both invoke their own proleptic allusiveness, are as strikingly revolutionary in their conception as Cressida.

Nothing more particularizes Cressida than her moment with Diomedes except, perhaps, her highly reflective and reflexive exchange with Troilus, essentially a preamble to her betrayal. (Similarly, nothing more particularizes Achilles than his unbridled enjoyment — reported by Ulysses with ironic scorn — of mimicking Patroclus' reduction of the Greek leaders. And nothing more deflates both.) Self-consciousness in characterization is a two-edged weapon. A convention of characterization that Ovid invents, Shakespeare always handles it well: time and again one encounters characters who express their private axiological worlds and, in so doing, create a discursive zone about themselves.[16] It is two-edged because a self-conscious character can gain sympathy by extending the possibilities for understanding, but such a character may also undercut itself through self-ironization. Hence there would seem to be a trade-off in characterization between sympathy, based upon increased understanding, and distance, brought about through irony. Unlike classical epic or tragedy, which seeks to idealize human suffering, Ovid's reductive techniques produce an art much like satiric comedy, always a downward (or wintry) movement. Irony and the mock heroic are integrally a part of Ovid's literary method, though not necessarily at its centre. This reductive view of the human condition (indeed, of the universe itself) colours one of Ovid's central aims in the *Metamorphoses*: to anatomize force and beauty as inimical to the classic ideal of reason, and in the process to suggest, too, that the ideal itself may need re-examining. A great many Ovidian conventions for creating character, all belonging to the common repertory of Medieval and Renaissance literature, are evident in Shakespeare. *Troilus* illustrates many of them, but none more so than self-consciousness leading to ironic undercutting. This reduction through self-conscious reflexivity reaches a limit-case with the many-faceted Ajax, a construct of characterization at the other end of the spectrum from the simple lumbering Aias of Homer. Such an Ajax as Shakespeare creates early in *Troilus* could not appear in the epic, and does not appear at all later in the play. Shakespeare's Ajax, surrounded by a self-conscious discursive zone, seems to belong to a different genre, the novel.[17]

The excessive self-awareness such characters as Achilles and Ajax indicate is almost Narcissistic, and sets them off from Ulysses, Agamemnon, and Diomedes. Ulysses, for example, refers to

> The great Achilles... [who]
> Having his ear full of his airy fame,
> Grows dainty of his worth and in his tent
> Lies mocking our designs... (1.3.142, 144-46)

Ulysses describes Achilles' proud self-consciousness with a suggestion of the running imagery of food and eating ("full," "dainty") as a surfeit of selfishness.

Moreover, the valorized epic motivator, honour and fame, here takes the hero Achilles from the battlefield, rather than driving him into war.

Ulysses epitomizes this debilitating self-consciousness when he goes on to describe Patroclus's mimicking of the Greek leaders (1.3.146-85) "with ridiculous and awkward action" (149). The caricature of Achilles and Patroclus is that of a couple of drawing room dandies rather than ancient epic warriors. As Ulysses continues, one observes that structuring of overlaid points of view so striking in the scene of Cressida's betrayal of Troilus: Ulysses's description of Patroclus's reduction through caricature of the Greek leaders in turn reduces both Achilles and Patroclus. That is, Ulysses's view of Patroclus's and Achilles's views of the leaders (essentially a dramatic placing or staging) become the audience's view, the normal view. Ulysses, like Thersites in the betrayal scene, must be accepted as a reliable source, much like the narrating voice in a novel. Thus, *Troilus* presents two characters at either end of a psychic spectrum who pronounce on human depravity, the one a perennial voice of reason, the other an embodiment of embittered madness. Though both their voices may be persuasive, even definitive at times, they, too, carry with them the battered baggage of their respective journeys through literary history.[18] They cannot escape the play's dominant reductivism. In *Troilus*, deflation "is the rule" (Tillyard, *Problem Plays* 54).

Achilles's Narcissism and divided mind, both deeply Ovidian, are made apparent by Ulysses:

> ... possess'd he is with greatness,
> And speaks not to himself but with a pride
> That quarrels at self-breath; imagined worth
> Holds in his blood such swoln and hot discourse
> That 'twixt his mental and active parts
> Kingdom'd Achilles in commotion rages
> And batters down himself... (2.3.180-86; cf. 161-79)

Here many of the major motifs come together unhappily. The struggle "'twixt his mental and active parts" recalls, for example, Ulysses' great meditation on degree, and his lament on the division in the Greek camp. Most notable, however, is the corrosive aspect of intense self-consciousness, of a reflexivity become asocial in having created its own society, "Kingdom'd Achilles." The great warrior needs no outer enemies, having enough aplenty within him.

The projection of reflexivity at times suggests the modern novel (Henry James, say), as, for example, in Ajax's reference to Achilles: "Is he so much? Do you think he thinks himself a better man than I am?" (2.3.144-45). Reflexivity is most stunningly evident in a discussion between Ulysses and Achilles, with Ulysses citing a passage from Plato's *Dialogues* with which he has been wrestling:

> A strange fellow here
> Writes me: "That man, how dearly ever parted,
> How much in having, or without or in,
> Cannot make boast to have that which he hath,
> Nor feels not what he owes, but by reflection;
> As when his virtues shining upon others
> Heat them and they retort that heat again
> To the first giver...." (3.3.95-102)

Achilles, in glossing for Ulysses, sees no problem:

> This is not strange, Ulysses.
> The beauty that is borne here in the face
> The bearer knows not, but commends itself
> To others' eyes; nor doth the eye itself,
> That most pure spirit of sense, behold itself,
> Not going from itself; but eye to eye opposed
> Salutes each other with each other's form;
> For speculation turns not to itself,
> Till it hath travell'd and is mirror'd there
> Where it may see itself. This is not strange at all. (3.3.102-11)

Nowhere near the windy plains of Troy, one has been transported to the Athenian Academy, and Achilles's subtlety here is seductive, even if it misses the point. Ulysses retorts:

> I do not strain at the position, —
> It is familiar, — but at the author's drift;
> Who, in his circumstance, expressly proves
> That no man is the lord of any thing,
> Though in and of him there be much consisting,
> Till he communicate his parts to others;
> Nor doth he of himself know them for aught
> Till he behold them form'd in the applause
> Where they're extended.... (3.3.112-20)

Just so. In putting down Achilles's apparently unintended putdown, Ulysses also demonstrates that solipsism has its limitations, but the lesson goes unheard:

Ulysses has suggested that proper pride is justified if it is socially generated, if it comes as a reward for valuable social service. He is almost painfully trying to show Achilles that honour can have a valued social role. Nonetheless, Achilles persists narcissistically in his self-enveloping pride, hinted at in the imagery of reflections and mirrors (his world-view, in effect) associated with him. (Ulysses's associated imagery suggests alchemy.) Ulysses has one perspective which is essentially heroic; Achilles, quite another, that of the romance. The different voices continue to clamour.

There is a fragmentation of voices in *Troilus*, a sense of many voices yet calling for answers or asking unanswerable questions, composing the play's verbal polyphony.[19] Of course, there *are* passages that suggest "shared values" in which an Elizabethan audience might have rejoiced and rejoined, as, for example, Ulysses's often-cited speech on concord and hierarchy (1.3.75-137), and Hector's lucid plea, based on Aristotle, for moral values (2.2.163-93). However, both are oddly isolated, treated comparatively brusquely, and tonal aberrations. Hector, significantly, soon abandons his magnificent argument and takes up Troilus's and Paris's adolescent quest for honour. The passages, though thematically related,[20] are, paradoxically enough, too isolated both from the play's general action and from the interplay of voices. Thus, too, the recurrence of "refining" or "purifying" images, as though the characters and their world might in a "last resort" be alchemically elevated, seems isolated, tonally aberrant. What seems closer to the grain of the play is the dialectic between narratives, particularly between epic and romance values. This is not surprising, given the play's inscribed self-consciousness of its literary antecedents, its "parasitism" among other literary tests (Freund 34). Given, too, the play's pervasive concerns, love and honour, "collisions" between epic and romance are inevitable. Contention between the ideals of love and honour necessarily suggests a contention between the narrative forms that were most closely associated with those ideas, romance and epic. For example, the second scene of Act III is charged with the conventions of love so common to the medieval romance as the affair is brought to a joyous consummation: all the "surface characteristics" are present, from love at first sight to the dangerous lady. From the go-between, here less than appealing, to the suggestion of a refined, spiritual love, the rhetoric of the romance resounds. However, there is also the "national" will, the intractable epic concerns with identity and destiny, and the running images of blood and feeding and tasting which undercut all.

The persistence of the confrontation of heroic and romance narrative values with a relentlessly mock-heroic mode is striking. The perennial ideals of the heroic narrative, *fortitudo et sapientia*,[21] courage and wisdom, for example, which were to coexist in each hero, if not always in perfect complementarity (Achilles would have more of the former, Ulysses of the latter, but both heroes should possess both qualities) become in the play a means for identifying opposing parties, as Ulysses notes how the representatives of *fortitudo*, Achilles and Ajax, scorn those who embody *sapientia*, Ulysses and Nestor, the two prominent "wise warriors" of the *Iliad* (1.3.197-210). This splitting of the perennial twin ideals was very likely suggested to Shakespeare by Ovid's depiction in the *Metamorphoses* of Ajax as a flawed embodiment of *fortitudo* (his towering epic anger drives him to kill himself) and Ulysses as a *sapientia* closer to cleverness than to wisdom. Indeed, Ovid has both heroes expose each other in their debate over who should wear Achilles's armour. Shakespeare denies to Achilles a whole half of the ideal warriors' composition; significantly, he also has him fall far short of being a magnanimous hero in the one opportunity he has in battle, when he treacherously kills Hector, the single representative in the play of magnanimity (classical) and of chivalry (medieval). All this suggests (among other examples) Shakespeare's preoccupation with the interaction of both individual and generic voices, the way they batten upon each other, supporting and undercutting each other (often synchronously), in creating composite wholes. Shakespeare follows this preoccupation in all his plays, not only in *Troilus and Cressida*, but in this play it is dominant, strikingly in the foreground. What may at first sound like a babel of voices turns out to be, listening more carefully, a quite distinctly self-conscious polyphony.[22]

HARRY LEVIN

Two Tents on Bosworth Field: *Richard III* V.iii, iv, v

Polonius, ever ready to expatiate upon the obvious, would inform us that the dramatic repertory has many different genres; it could encompass such hybrid modalities as the "tragical-comical-historical-pastoral." Tragedy and comedy had set up their classic polarity, but they were not turning out to be mutually exclusive, and the ever-widening middle ground offered room for multiform possibilities. The principal new mode devised by Elizabethans would be canonized — between the two old ones, and along with the playwright who had made it his very own — on the title page of the First Folio: *Mr William Shakespeares Comedies, Histories, & Tragedies.* Now history, in its generic sense, takes the form of story; the same word serves for both in Romance languages; and early English novels have been presented as "histories." Ordinarily, it had been expected to narrate, rather than dramatize, what it attested to have actually taken place somewhere in the public domain. Tudor England had become history-conscious to an unprecedented degree. Its chroniclers evoked the past to sustain the present, to justify and glorify the regime, to consolidate a patriotic attitude within a nationalistic ideology. Among its increasingly eloquent means of expression, the drama was outstandingly in the ascendance, and dramatists were continually faced with the need for popular and spectacular material. Hence, it seems inevitable that those two distinctive forms should have been temporarily conflated into the English history-play.

Temporarily, because its recorded subject-matter, while extensive, was not inexhaustible; nor would its plangent strains appeal so whole-heartedly to the more sophisticated playgoers of the Stuart period. With the upsurging decade launched by England's victory over Spain's Armada in 1588, every preceding epoch in the entire historical cycle, from the legendary Brut to the reigning Elizabeth, was exploited dramaturgically. Adaptation made for loose construction, since there was always so much to be crowded in: sprawling casts and episodic swerves, genealogical roll-calls and walk-on parts for famous figures who could not be left out. But the rules were stricter for controlling the interpretation of events, which would have been decimated by censorship if it did not hew to an accepted political line. Accordingly, when Shakespeare undertook to consider politics in a deeper ethical perspective, he would turn back to ancient Rome and Plutarchan biography for *Julius Caesar, Antony and Cleopatra*, and *Coriolanus*. It also happened that two of his major tragedies were drawn from the matter of Britain — circumstances treated in Raphael Holinshed's *Chronicles* — though *Macbeth* was distanced by its Scottish setting and *King Lear* was shrouded in a prehistoric aura. On the other hand, both *Richard III* and *Richard II*, though they were listed and printed among the histories in the Folio, were likewise accorded the title of tragedies, centring as they did upon a royal protagonist in his wickedness or in his weakness.

The critical distinction that assigned them to the middle section lay in the fact that both were based upon strictly English subjects. Consequently they could be held up to the warrant proclaimed by the alternative title of *Henry VIII: All Is True*. Where tragedy had kept captains and kings at some aesthetic distance, history brought them home to their own citizenry, with a thrust that could chill as well as thrill. Its chronological framework was set by the reign of a given monarch; and if that had restricted him to a rather formalistic part in the background, then his play could not take much more shape than a loosely related series of military pageants and ceremonial episodes. But if he could be psychologized into the fullest characterization, for better or for worse, then the documentation could be unified into genuine drama. "True tragedy" must have sounded like something of a mongrel during the heyday of the chronicle play. But such was the designation of a crude script dealing with Richard III, which seems to have slightly predated Shakespeare's treatment. Its induction featured an allegorical dialogue between personifications of Poetry and of Truth itself, in which the latter promises: "Then will I add bodies to shadows." If there was a borderline, it could be crossed in either direction; truth could become the stuff of poetry, shadows — mere actors — could embody vital actualities, and history could point the way for tragedy.

During the first ten years of his literary career, which coincided so auspiciously with the Armada decade, Shakespeare's chief commitment was to dramatic history. His involvement with it did much to prepare the situation for his emergence as a tragic dramatist. The temporal span of those ten plays was predominantly the fifteenth century, if we allow for *King John* as a retrospective prologue and for the belated *Henry VIII* as a prospective epilogue. The sequence framed domestically by the Wars of the Roses and abroad by the Hundred Years' War comprised eight plays, which can be grouped into two tetralogies; the earlier group (*Henry VI, Parts One, Two,* and *Three,* and *Richard III*) dealt with more recent happenings than its artistically riper sequel (*Richard II, Henry IV, Parts One and Two,* and *Henry V*). Taken all together, they constitute what A.W. Schlegel, invoking still another genre, described as "a national epic." That category has since been distended by Hollywood; and yet the cinema, relying more upon direct action and less upon verbal rumination, would prove an apter medium than the stage for the presentation of history; witness Laurence Olivier's *Richard III* and *Henry V,* so much more successfully adapted than his cinematic *Hamlet*. The epic, celebrating primarily arms and the man, specialized in the narration of warfare. Dramatization would be more difficult; for its agon had to be mainly elocution, eked out with the stylized assistance of dramaturgic convention.

The novel, succeeding the epic, could adjust itself more sensitively to the increasing complications and devastations of war, both collective and personal. The Napoleonic experience would be narrated in their various ways by Stendhal, Hugo, Thackeray, and Tolstoy — whereas, if it was to be dramatized, it would call for the panoramic scale and the interplanetary outlook of Hardy's *Dynasts*. Individual combatants had stood out, more heroically than their regimented successors, from the armies of medieval days; but most of the Shakespearean battles had occurred when swords and arrows were yielding to guns and cannons; and for theatrical reasons he reverts, whenever he can do so, to single combat. The deployment of troops had to be symbolized by such economical devices as alarums, sound effects from a tolling bell in the open theater's turret, and excursions, parties of three sword-bearing extras (Ben Jonson) or maybe four or five (Shakespeare) rushing across the stage from both directions in the respective colours of York or of Lancaster. Christopher Marlowe had developed the stratagem of letting grandiose oratory stand in for physical conflict, taunts, and vaunts before and after the not too observable battle; and Shakespeare's warriors, including the younger Richard (as Gloucester), reecho the Marlovian phrase "to play the orator" (*3HVI* III.ii.188);[1] Jonson, dismissing the history play in the prologue to *Every Man in His Humour,* particularly disapproved of its "foot-and-half-foot words," echoing the dismissive example of Horace, "*sesquipedalia verba*."

Shakespeare, however, in full control of his medium, offered a frank apologia for the obvious disparities between an actual display of monarchic grandeur and "this cockpit," "this unworthy scaffold," "this wooden O." The Chorus of his climactic and most epical history, *Henry V,* calls upon the playgoer to transcend such limitations by taking the word for the deed, by equating rhetorical declamation with martial prowess. Setting the scene as it shifts from

England to France and filling in the action as it leaps from court to battlefield, the choric interlocutor invites us to suspend our disbeliefs and to lend our imaginations. The physical imperfections of a performance can, and should, all be pieced together and redeemed in the mind's ear and eye. Not that Shakespeare asks us to idealize the portraiture in his gallery of kings. The only one who qualifies as a hero on the epic plane is Henry V, whose triumphal career would be prematurely cut off, and who had charmed us more in his wayward youth as Prince Hal. To commemorate the triumphs of his line, as Shakespeare did in the second tetralogy, was to compliment the regnant house of Tudor, which claimed the throne by collateral descent from the house of Lancaster. The decline of that family under the lengthy and disastrous kingship of Henry VI, together with the violent interventions and transitory enthronements of the Yorkist faction, had previously furnished themes for the first tetralogy.

Shakespeare's histories were bound to reflect an accumulation of narrative sources, as retold by Holinshed: the official Latin of Polydore Vergil, the Tudor apologetics of Edward Hall, the fragmentary but corrosive *Life of Richard III* by Sir Thomas More. These set forth a Lancastrian party-line, which would be challenged in later centuries; Horace Walpole would raise *Historic Doubts*, transferring the malevolence from Richard to his enemies; and today there are professed Richardians who would exculpate — nay, venerate — him as a martyr to adverse propaganda. Without sharing their devotion, we might well concede that the legend, by the time it reached Shakespeare, had transformed a man into a monster. This by no means diminished his histrionic potentialities. Villanies were as apposite as heroics to the rough dialectic of the history-plays, and no one could pose more suggestively for the very model of an arch-villain. Fabulous deformities had clustered around his physique from his traumatic birth; the crooked back, the withered arm, the limping gait, the motivation of an ugly cripple seeking revenge upon the hale and the handsome — even the heraldic boar that could be reviled as a hog. His notoriety as "a deep dissembler, not of affection only, but of religion," would be attested by Milton, among others. Shakespeare's Richard, publicly pretending to be "a plain man," has secretly vowed to exhibit more shapes than the mythical Proteus (I.iii.51). Taking a cynical pride in deception, he covers up by quoting scripture:

> And thus I clothe my naked villany
> With odd old ends stol'n forth of holy writ,
> And seem a saint, when most I play the devil. (I.iii.335-37)

Of course he overshoots the saintly mark. Lessing would write him off as unabashedly diabolical, contrasted with the fairer-spoken devilry of Edmund in

King Lear. Yet every villain, in being himself while seeming to be a more decent human being, is cast in a dual role. It is not for nothing that hypocrisy has its metaphor in playacting, that *hupokrítes* was the Greek term for actor. Shakespeare's earliest and most overt malefactor, Aaron the Moor in *Titus Andronicus*, has a face as black as his soul. But the dark-skinned Othello, Moor of Venice, moving through an atmosphere of greater tragic complexity, has a noble heart, and is tricked into wrongdoing by that villainous comrade who figures as "honest, honest Iago." Malice is never wholly unmitigated in Shakespeare; usually it is motivated by grievance of some sort; and even that remorseless hatemonger, Aaron, discloses a tender feeling for the mulatto baby he has sired. The energetic zest of Richard's malefactions, the "habitual jocularity" that endeared him to Charles Lamb, could be all too easily flattened out into caricature. He could be the archetypal Wicked Uncle, licensing the blithe brutalities of Mr. Punch or Mr. Quilp, not to mention the off-hand decapitations of Lewis Carroll's Red Queen. Yet those "odd old ends" of traditional piety, though they are quoted only to be flouted, still convey their moral implications. God is invoked a hundred times in this play.

Macbeth would not be a hypocrite by nature; his temperament is more active than reflective; and, when he soliloquizes, it is in order to bring out the compunctious resistance of his thoughts to his deeds. Though Richard harbours no such innate compunctions, his congenital duplicity — as well as the playwright's obligation to keep us informed about his plans — makes him a past master of the stage-villain's twin verbal conventions, the soliloquy and the aside. Rich in both ranging monologues and crackling one-liners, onstage two-thirds of the time, his is the second largest Shakespearean part; Hamlet has 1507 lines to Richard's 1145, and *Richard III* is the play next longest to *Hamlet.* Although many of Shakespeare's plays stand much higher in the critical reckoning, few of them have had so very popular a stage-history. It was the first (1750), and for many years the most frequent, to be performed in the United States. Could it have been that so dire a depiction of monarchy held a particular fascination for republican audiences? It was equally prominent in the British repertory, and its quartos were more reprinted than *Hamlet*'s. Reaction had been registered from the outset through allusion. Contemporary anecdotes recall that Richard III was popularly identified with his originating performer, Richard Burbage. A Cambridge satire mouthed the opening speech as a shibboleth of the London theater. All the attestations of the play's success bear witness to its unbridled theatricality.

Its main attraction was the protean scope of its leading role, whose continual challenge was taken up by a majestic succession of star actors. Richard's exaggerations were maximized in the stridently reductive adaptation by Colley Cibber, the vehicle of David Garrick's début, which held the stage — eclipsing Shakespeare's original version — throughout the eighteenth century and the first half of the nineteenth. Viewing Charles Kean's performance, according to Coleridge, was "like reading Shakespeare by flashes of lightning." After the sublimity of classical drama, in Victor Hugo's terms, Shakespeare has infused a romantic strain of grotesquerie; and none of his grotesques could out-Herod Richard. The intrinsic duality of the part was redoubled by its alternation of actor's masks. He can "counterfeit the deep tragedian," when occasions arise, even better than his stage-manager, the Duke of Buckingham (III.v.5). But Richard names his most congenial mask when, caught in an equivocation, he likens himself to "the formal Vice, Iniquity," mischief-maker and commentator in the moralities, sardonic as well as demonic, who relishes the fun while he lures the sinners to the everlasting bonfire (III.i.82). "Earth gapes, hell burns, fiends roar, saints pray," and other metaphorical omens foretell the revenges that moral outrage has been storing up (IV.iv.75). His ironic perception of himself is notably vice-like when he plays — not once but twice — the "jolly thriving wooer," courting in each case a woman doubly bereft by his murders (IV.iii.43).

Richard as the deep tragedian had an academic prototype in the Senecan tyrant of a Latin tragedy, *Ricardus Tertius* by Thomas Legge. Closer to Shakespeare's point were those tragedies in the medieval vein — monologues narrating the falls of princes or the exemplary fates of other worthies humbled by the vagaries of Lady Fortune — which had been collected, augmented, and widely circulated in *A Mirror for Magistrates*. Ten of these poetic plaints were grounded on characters, starting with Buckingham and including himself, who would be involved in Richard's career. In transposing them to the theater, and adjusting them to the broader perspectives of the Renaissance, Shakespeare was influenced by the current impact of his most brilliant rival, Marlowe. Marlowe's rhetoric, with overwhelming bravura, pitted will against fortune and stressed the self-made rise that led toward a fall. Where he was temperamentally an outdoer, Shakespeare outdid him; Machiavelli makes a personal appearance as prologue to *The Jew of Malta*, but Richard undertakes to give him lessons, "to set the murtherous Machevil to school" (*3HVI* III.ii.193). Except for *Edward II*, which may show some reciprocal Shakespearean influence, Marlovian tragedy tends toward monodrama, dominated by its driving protagonists. Its dramatic action is initiated, characteristically, by the self-exploratory exposition of Barabas the Jew or Doctor Faustus. Shakespeare had learned that lesson when he provided Richard with his opening soliloquy, sketching the exposition through its interconnected antitheses: summer/winter, peace/war, proportion/deformity, sunlight/shadow, lover/villain.

The introductory trope is a pun; "this son of York" is Richard's newly crowned brother, the philandering Edward IV; and the shining sun has been emblematic of kingship from the Pharaohs to Louis XIV, *le Roi soleil* (I.i.2). As the invidious comparison develops, the image of lengthening shadow becomes an emblem for Richard. This neatly balanced speech is essentially a recapitulation of the earlier monologue — Shakespeare's longest — wherein the young Richard Crookback emerges from the prior trilogy as Duke of Gloucester, bugbear, potential usurper, ultimate Yorkist, and heaviest of theatrical heavies:

> Then since the earth affords no joy to me
> But to command, to check, to o'erbear such
> As are of better person than myself,
> I'll make my heaven to dream upon the crown. (*3HVI* III.ii.165-68)

Here the tone, the resolve, and the key-word strike us as distinctly Marlovian. So does the rhetorical figure, *epiphora*: "crown" is repeated at the end of three subsequent lines and resounds again in the terminal couplet. To compare the two monologues is to realize that *Richard III* has become more typically Shakespearean in its succinct formulation, its structural equilibrium, and its psychological modality. The mature Richard confidently establishes himself in the sequel: "I am determined to prove a villain..." (I.i.30). Then, having brazenly wooed and won the Lancastrian widow, and having exchanged insults with two queens, he steps aside for an interlude that facilitates his ascent and portends his downfall. The tragic spokesman here is the Duke of Clarence, the brother who stands between Richard and the dying King, consequently imprisoned in the Tower of London and about to be assassinated. Clarence's recital begins with the archaic verb for reporting a dream: "Methoughts..." (I.iv.9). His report to the Keeper parallels the general "Induction" of Thomas Sackville to the *Mirror for Magistrates*: the fearful sensations of drowning after a shove from Richard, leading into a journey through the underworld, where he encounters the reproachful shades of those whom he has injured. His own murder, that fatal submersion in a butt of malmsey, is volubly but inadequately resisted by the Second Murderer, tardily troubled with "certain dregs of conscience" (I.iv.121f.).

Clarence's dream was not mentioned in the accounts of the chronicles. Shakespeare seems to have introduced it as a point of departure for the portentous configuration of dreamwork that runs through the play. It foreshadows, and is complemented by, the most notorious of the Tower murders, that of Richard's two nephews, Edward's heirs. These episodes are linked through the survival of Clarence's son and daughter, another pair of stage children whose innocent precocity puts to shame the worldly corruption of their conniving elders. But the horrific misdeed is itself glossed over, perhaps because infanticide had so long been the best known charge in Richard's criminal record, and its pathos had so frequently been exploited. Holinshed gives a detailed account at first hand *coram populo*. But Shakespeare hands the confession on to Tyrrel, the hired assassin, who has hired two other assassins to do the dirty work off-stage. His brief, albeit sympathetic, announcement derives from theirs at second hand; and they in turn have been reluctant killers, whose mission has been penitently salted "with conscience and remorse" (III.iii.20). This is a far cry from Richard — Lord Protector forsooth! The fate of the youthful princes hangs, like a suspenseful cloud, over the municipal scenes aloft that Buckingham has been staging in the city. There, while he is manipulating the Mayor and the Citizens, Richard feigns diffidence, and has to be coaxed away from his prayers and his spiritual advisers to assume the pomp of majesty.

The decisive business of the histories — civic, conspiratorial, military — falls within the unrelenting conflicts of man's world. Yet Richard has a surprising way with women, as he demonstrates in his hectic courtship of Lady Anne, an episode of Shakespeare's own invention. Clearly he enjoys "this keen encounter of our wits," welcomes further bouts of ungallant repartee, and inexorably manages to get in the last stichomythic word (I.i.115). As the roll of his victims continues to swell, their wives and mothers form a mourning chorus, antiphonally lamenting husbands, fathers, sons, and brothers. *Ubi sunt...?* Edward's widowed queen, joined by Richard's mother, the dowager Duchess of York, asks the aged virago, widowed queen of Henry VI ("she-wolf of France"; *3HVI* I.iii.111), to lead the litany:

> O thou well skill'd in curses, stay awhile
> And teach me how to curse mine enemies! (V.iv.116)

Gradually their imprecations and denunciations give way to prophecies and forewarnings; these feminine retreats, in the battle of the sexes, prefigure Richard's defeat in the masculine battle that lies ahead. The emotional contrariety heightens the formal agon, structuring the antagonistic positions into what M.C. Bradbrook would term "Shakespeare's most patterned play." Its overarching pattern can be traced by two complementary principles, which Wolfgang Clemen stresses in his discerning commentary: contrast and symmetry. These had been crudely outlined in the morality play, where good and evil stood in Manichaean opposition, and nearly every part was offset by its adverse counterpart. An underlying dualism fits in with all the double-talk and the duplicitous gestures of Richard's villainy. If at heart he remains single-minded, like Marlowe's immoralists, his immorality will be counterbalanced by an enlarging frame of social reference. Setting the one-sidedness of strong characters into relief, Shakespeare surpasses Marlowe by reanimating our sympathies for the other side.

Though the other side has been vocal in its sorrows, it must undergo the conventional wait until the fifth act for its forcible retaliation and official vindication. The future Henry VII, at this stage Earl of Richmond, inheritor of the Lancastrians and founder of the Tudor dynasty, has meanwhile been waiting in the wings. His claim to the throne has been validated by a laying on of hands, when he was saluted in his youth as "England's hope" by the moribund Henry VI (*3HVI* IV.vi.68). Richmond is not a colourful deuteragonist, but we may have had too much colour with Richard; it is enough for his foil to be sober, sincere, conscientious, genuinely religious, and finally triumphant. Heralded by conflicting reports, his entrance in the second scene of Act V is preceded by Buckingham's farewell: a repentance worthy of the *Mirror for Magistrates*, ominously dated on All Souls Day, his "body's doomsday," when the dead return to remind us of our own sins (V.i.12). As the most confidential of Richard's retainers, Buckingham has been personally responsible — up until the moment he balked at infantile regicide — for the previous beheadings. "Off with his head!" Richard's peremptory command, which has become a *mot de caractère*, is uttered with slight variation thrice, and would be reechoed into a virtual refrain by Cibber's travesty (III.i.193; iv, 76; V.iii, 344). It would be hard to think of another dramatic interjection which, in four monosyllables, could occasion such a Brechtian *Verfremdungseffekt*.

We have already arrived at the long concluding scene, for the Folio indicates no breaks after "*Scena Secunda*"; nor do the quartos, though they supply a somewhat more satisfactory text for the last 357 lines of the play. At all events, the scenic designations would not have meant much for Elizabethan staging, where *exeunt omnes* took the place of a curtain. Where the announced locality was a battlefield ("even here in Bosworth field"; V.iii.1), uniformed actors walking on and off created a *liaison des scènes*. Scenes ii, iii, and iv — the last 429 lines — flow into one another continuously, and build up into a culminating set-piece. The dénouement is always a compensation for the suspense, and both should be intensive at this juncture, catastrophic in the broadest meaning of the old theatrical term. The running title from the Folio appeals to built-up expectations: *The Life and Death of Richard the Third*. So does the balanced emphasis of the full title: *The Tragedy of Richard the Third: with the Landing of Earle Richmond, and the Battell at Bosworth Field*. That historic field, within Shakespeare's playhouse, had to be a wooden platform less than sixteen yards square; and his whole troupe, with some doubling, could do no more than suggest those clashing armies. But it is suggestion that actors work with, after all, as the Chorus in *Henry V* declares, when pleading with his hearers for their imaginative collaboration.

Given such collaboration, Shakespeare's histories could function more effectively in a formalized arena — with an open stage, side entries, central balcony, and an all-but-surrounding audience — than against the changing pictorial scenery of more modern theatres. These spatial arrangements almost seem laid out to correspond with the symmetries and contrasts of *Richard III* — or rather, to put it more broadly, the dramatic habitat seems to have conditioned the interplay of its inhabitants, as they move from posturing tableaux to dynamic clashes. The spectacle could be ordered diagrammatically, with the opposing parties on opposite sides, as the issues converge in a vibrant climax. The rebel forces, by the Duke of Norfolk's estimate, number six or seven thousand soldiers; the royal army "trebles that account," by Richard's claim, though the defection of Lord Stanley's troops will reduce the odds (11). Historians would considerably enlarge the numbers for both camps, while augmenting the underdog's proportion. These rival hosts, presumably miles apart, are now to be exhibited simultaneously, each encampment represented by its commander's tent, stage left at war with stage right. The tents should not be imaginary but portable properties, carried in and pitched to set the scene (though this stage business is referred to only in Richard's dialogue). Standing there, so near to and yet so far from one another, they hark back to the multiple stages of medieval drama, where the pilgrimage of life proceeded from one symbolic mansion to another.

"Here will I lie tonight — " says Richard, while his tent is going up. "But where to-morrow?" (6f). Businesslike, he shrugs off the uncertainty: "For, lords, to-morrow is a busy day" (18). Rallying one of them on his sad expression, Richard leads them out to survey the terrain. Thereupon Richmond enters to set up his headquarters, charging his officers with fuller preliminary instructions, and undertaking to draw up a "form and model" for the next day's campaign (24). His first remark, which sees promise in the golden sunset, takes up the solar theme that has been associated with kingship, and initiates the sequence of incidental remarks that will tell the hours from eve to morn: "nine o'clock" (47), "dead midnight" (180), cock-crow (209f.), "the stroke of four" (235), "*The clock striketh*" (275f.). Just as theatrical space can be foreshortened, so theatrical time can be compressed. It ran out through the course of a valedictory monologue, during the last hour of Doctor Faustus. Acted in broad daylight, Elizabethan plays utilized allusions to convey a nocturnal effect. Benighted images cluster about Richard, as he perpetrates his deeds of darkness. "Subjects follow him," the

Queen has mourned, "To his new kingdom of ne'er-changing night" (II.ii.46). And he himself threatens the Stanleys with a fall "Into the blind cave of eternal night" (V.iii.62). Clarence has indeed been sent there; his premonitory vision had transported him "Unto the kingdom of perpetual night" (I.iv.47). Endless night means death.

After the withdrawal of the Tudor staff into Richmond's tent, the Yorkist leaders reenter their locale. It is supper-time, but Richard is not hungry; conscious of being less alert or cheerful than usual, he calls for a bowl of wine, together with ink and paper. Crisply he gives messages for his allies and orders for early rising to his most trusted followers, Catesby and Ratcliffe. He is concerned that his helmet, armour, and weapons be ready, and especially his favourite horse: "Saddle white Surrey for the field tomorrow" (64). Left alone on his pallet, he falls asleep at once. The switch to Richmond's quarters brings in his stepfather, Stanley, grimly arrested between loyalty to his stepson and fear for his own son, whom Richard has taken hostage. When Stanley notes a further passage of time, his anxieties are figuratively linked with Richard's night and his hopes with Richmond's dawn: "The silent hours steal on, / And flaky darkness breaks within the east" (86). After the mixed emotions of this leave-taking, Richmond bids goodnight to his aides: "I'll strive with troubled thoughts to take a nap" (104). Yet, before he goes to sleep, he confirms the recurrent contrast with Richard by kneeling and saying his prayers. In commending his soul to heaven, he envisions himself as God's captain and his army as an instrument of divine retribution — "ministers of chastisement" delegated to crush "the usurping helmets" of their adversaries (112f.).

What happens for the next sixty lines, while the antagonists and their assembled cohorts sleep, is Shakespeare's apocalyptic showpiece (117-76). Richard's sleepless queen has spoken of his insomnia, to which he was being awakened by "timorous dreams" (IV.i.84). These were attributed to the ever-increasing burden of his guilt by the moralizing historians, who took note of the peculiarly sinister dream that had agitated him at Bosworth Field. It was a "straunge vision," according to Hall, beset with "diverse ymages like terrible develles" — and therefore not unlike the images to which Richard himself is compared. Apart from those not unfamiliar devils, the "many dreadfull and busy Imaginacions" remain unspecified, leaving Shakespeare to fill in the horrors. This he accomplished by recreating a mirror, not of magistrates brought low by fortune, but of those who had been victimized by the malignity of Richard's ambitions. Successively their ghosts now cross the stage, each of them appearing first to him and then to Richmond, both asleep. There are eleven in all, presenting themselves in chronological order, beginning with two shades who met their deaths in *3 Henry VI*, the crown prince Edward, and the titular monarch himself. Then we hear from Clarence, from the three courtiers who tried to save the doomed princes, and from the two princes in person. After them comes Hastings, the accomplice who hesitated, and after him one woman, Lady Anne. And finally, ironically, Buckingham, victim of the train of conspiracy he had fostered.

There are eight visitations, six of them passing one by one, with Rivers, Grey, and Vaughan coming on as a trio, soon shadowed by the princelings, paired forever and speaking in unison. In the Elizabethan staging, each of the visitants would have entered at one side-door, addressed the slumbering king in malediction, stalked across to the other door in tense pantomime, and made an exit after blessing the dormant adversary. Later productions utilized trap-doors, through which the apparitions could rise and sink; since this could put some strain upon squeaking machinery, they also cut down on the number of ghostly reappearances. Later audiences, at all events, would not expect so itemized a rehearsal of the case against Richard. Eerie music accompanied the mute crossing-over from one tent to the other: Edwin Booth's prompt-book specifies drum-rolls, trumpet-calls, and tremolo orchestration. The spectral speeches are brief and, except for a word of self-identification, almost liturgically repetitive. Prince Edward's opening, "Let me sit heavy on thy soul to-morrow!," is twice reechoed (118, 131, 139), while the consistent byword of admonition to Richard — echoing the valediction of Faustus — is "Despair and die!" (120, 126, 135, 140, 143, 149, 158). The antithetical watchword for Richmond is "Live and flourish!" (130, 138, 143). These dead Yorkists vie with one another in their well-wishing approbation for this ascendant "offspring of the house of Lancaster" (136). The session is rounded out by the final speaker, Buckingham, who delivers the closing couplets. To Richard:

> Dream on, dream on, of bloody deeds and death;
> Fainting, despair; despairing, yield thy breath. (171f.)

And then, to Richmond, with the tragic paradigm:

> God and good angels fight on Richmond's side,
> And Richard falls in height of all his pride. (175f.)

What is the psychic status of the supernatural pageantry that we have just witnessed — or, to look at it in a more psychological light, the vision that we have been watching vicariously through the minds of tomorrow's opponents? Shakespeare employs his ghosts theatrically as the expressionistic manifestations of subjective mental states, like Macbeth's "dagger of the mind." Banquo's ghost is not objectively visible to anyone else, nor can the shade of Hamlet's father be seen by Gertrude. But *Richard III* does not ask us to believe in such phantoms, even as supernatural hypotheses, since they are merely dreamed about, though the phantasmagoria is divided between the two opposed dreamers. Human experience is richly intertwined with the process of dreaming for Shakespeare; drama is "a dream of passion" for Hamlet; and life itself is "such stuff as dreams are made on" for Prospero. It glides through *The Tempest* "as in a dream"; romance thrives upon that dreamlike reluctance to distinguish between sleeping and waking; and comedy can readily turn into *A Midsummer Night's Dream*. Tragedy, somewhat more superstitiously, looks upon nightmares as portents, warning signals emanating from fate or providence. Romeo's foreboding is dismissed by Mercutio, who blames it upon the "vain fantasy" of Queen Mab, and reduces pleasurable dreams to exercises in wish-fulfilment. This is an anticipation of Freudian analysis; but Freud would likewise interpret darker dreams as expressions of anxiety; and Romeo and Mercutio both suffer for disregarding an omen.

Similarly, Julius Caesar, ignoring his wife's premonitions and accepting a misinterpreted augury, goes forth to his assassination. Thus in *Richard III*, when Stanley, by dreaming of a rampant boar, is forewarned to seek safety, Hastings refuses "to trust the mock'ry of unquiet slumbers," and pays the price for doubting with his head (III.ii.27). Shakespearean history operates through a network of cosmic design, to which we are alerted not only by backward glances but by predictions and oracles of the future. Richard apprehends such disclosures well enough to abuse them, sceptically laying his plots with "inductions dangerous ... drunken prophecies, libels, and dreams" (I.i.12f.). *Dream*, the word itself with its cognates, is enunciated twenty-five times — surprisingly more than in any of Shakespeare's other plays, where dreams are very frequently recounted but seldom acted out. The ghosts that haunt the masque-like slumbers of Posthumus, in *Cymbeline*, present another exception, which had its precursor in *Richard III*. That earlier and earthier presentation had gone beyond its narrative source by resurrecting the murdered *dramatis personae*, as well as by extending the dreamwork to Richmond. Hall had even voiced some doubt as to whether Richard was asleep at that hour: "I thynke this was no dreame, but a punccion and pricke of hys synfull conscyence." But Shakespeare's stage direction is unambiguous: "*He starteth up out of a dream.*" And Richard's spontaneous reaction, still between sleeping and waking, yet presaging his imminent catastrophe, is to cry:

Give me another horse! Bind up my wounds!
Have mercy, Jesu! Soft, I did not dream. (V.iii.177)

His combative impulse is aroused, but with the apprehension of being injured and the reversion of invoking Christ. Now fully awakened, Richard brushes his somnolent fancies aside, though he will end the soliloquy by returning — with the formulaic "methought" — to those souls who visited his tent and threatened forthcoming vengeance (204ff.). The workings of conscience, admitted for the first time, are rejected as symptoms of cowardice. Yet at this dead midnight "the lights burn blue" — a sign of ghostly phenomena — while Richard stands trembling in an uncharacteristic cold sweat (180). Can he be himself? Then who is he? He has fulfilled the overpowering commitment to egoism that he announced in *3 Henry VI*: "I am myself alone" (V.vi.83). Self-interrogation, probing deeper than before, now brings home his self-wrought isolation and its ensuing desolation for all those around him: "Richard loves Richard, that is, I am I" (V.iii.183). Arguing with himself, he oscillates between self-love and self-hatred, between villainy and revenge. A new note of ambivalence is sounded; though he sticks to his own selfish side, he recognizes the moral alternative. Conscience arises to the surface again, and with it the realization of homecoming sins that exclaim: "Guilty! guilty!" (199). Confession drags him toward those depths of despair envisaged by his accusers. He is badly shaken when interrupted by Ratcliffe's arrival to wake him, and to deflect him from his "fearful dream" to the confrontation that lies before him (212).

When the focus shifts to Richmond's unhurried arousal from "the sweetest sleep... / That ever enter'd in a drowsy head," there is a difference in tempo as well as in tone (227f.). The compound "Methought," when it is he who employs it, can summon up the "fairest-boding dreams"; and hence, he tells his attending lords, his "soul is very jocund" (230, 232). When they tell him that it is four o'clock in the morning, he springs into action, arming himself and addressing a formal "*oration to his soldiers*," so entitled in the text. This, with some trimming and shaping, broadly matches the argument of the chronicled address. Richmond's troops are conceived as God's agents, backed by "The prayers of holy saints and wronged souls" (241). Richard, "A bloody tyrant and a homicide," is doubly damned as "God's enemy" (246, 252f.). The distich,

If you do sweat to put a tyrant down,
You sleep in peace, the tyrant being slain,

introduces a drastic series of four more conditional clauses, each followed by a line predicating the happy outcome (255f.). If — and the air is still full of uncertainty — these conditions are met, then your country will reward you, then your wives will be there to welcome you home, then your children will extend your families, and finally every one of you will share my victory. The peroration, with a spoken cue for drum and trumpets, is a battle-cry in the name of God and Saint George. But both commanders would naturally advance their respective claims by invoking England's spiritual patron, and Richard will sharpen his invocation by alluding to the knightly champion's monstrous opposition: "the spleen of fiery dragons" (350). If he has a tutelary saint, it must be the Apostle Paul, whom he regularly calls upon, originally while interrupting the funeral procession of Henry VI, whose corpse was being transported from Saint Paul's Cathedral (I.ii.36, 4l; iii.45; III.iv.76; V.iii.216). If Richard has any scriptural affinity, it is with that apostle before his conversion, the unregenerate Saul, who "made havoc of the church, entering into every house and, haling men and women, committed them to prison" (*Acts* viii.3).

With the departure of Richmond's battalions, leaving the last words before the battle to be uttered in Richard's camp, Shakespeare reversed the sequence of the historical narrators, for whom the ascendancy of Richmond would be the climax. But Richard is more than ever the dramatic protagonist, if not the culture hero, and his edifying downfall must make full amends for his terrifying climb to power. His uneasy mood is further dampened by the bleakness of the day: "The sky doth frown and lower upon our army" (282). However, that is just another omen to be dismissed; the sun that beams on royalty is neutralized today; and ambiguous clouds will darken the same battleground for both Richmond and himself. Snapping his lieutenants to attention, Richard lays out his plan of campaign: "Come, bustle, bustle! Caparison my horse!" (289). Norfolk's supportive arrival is not as reassuring as it might have been, since he has just picked up an anonymous screed predicting defeat. Richard, having fought off "babbling dreams," and rejected conscience as "but a word that cowards use," is ready to dismiss such discouragements (308f.). His oration is much less dignified than Richmond's. It snarls with vituperation against "vagabonds, rascals, and runaways ... scum..." (316f.). Richmond, put down without being named, is "a paltry fellow,... A milksop" (323, 325). Richard's uncertain *if* leads into a desperate predicate:

> If we be conquered, let men conquer us,
> And not these bastard Britains, whom our fathers
> Have in their own land beaten, bobb'd, and thump'd.... (333ff.)

Hastings had been denounced and condemned for questioning his master's word with a conditional clause: "Talk'st thou to me of 'ifs'?" (III.iv.75). The crudity of Richard's language now lays bare its ineffectuality; the failure of eloquence coincides with the decline of authority. Harsh commands are quickened by the sound of the enemy's drums, as a messenger brings in the news of Stanley's pivotal defection. And this time Richard's standard reprisal, "Off with his son George's head!," has to be postponed and will never happen (V.iii.344).

Though "Scene IV" is an editorial demarcation, it seems evident that this long-drawn-out night, with its sessions of introspection and retrospection, is over at last; that tents have been struck, preparations bustled, and the full stage cleared for the Battle of Bosworth Field. Nearly all of the fighting, except for a short but crucial pantomime, will take place offstage and be verbally relayed. The alarum-bell clangs; the York and Tudor excursions rush back and forth on their choreographic sorties; and one breathless lull amid the Yorkist ranks is animated by thirteen lines of dialogue. Catesby calls upon Norfolk to come to the rescue of Richard, whose horse has been shot out from under him. The dismounted King has been braving all dangers afoot, seeking out his opposite number and slaying several warriors dressed in Richmond's uniform — a confusing tactic also practised by Shakespeare's Henry IV. Enter Richard himself at this turning point, ready to stake his life on one final cast of the dice and repeating that hollow ejaculation for which he will always be remembered: "A horse, a horse! my kingdom for a horse!" (iv.7, 13). Having lost his equestrian seating, he will be losing his throne. History would inform us that his plea could not have been granted; so would the conditions of Shakespeare's stage; for living steeds were not among its physical resources. Again we must heed the Chorus of *Henry V*, teaching the spectators how to observe the conventions:

> Think, when we talk of horses, that you see them
> Printing their proud hoofs i' th' receiving earth.

Given this conspicuous limitation, plus the equine presence so ubiquitous in Shakespeare's chivalric material, he handled the problem with a special ingenuity. Not only are those unseen horses conjured up by talkative messengers and others reporting, but characters talk much about mounting or dismounting when they make their exits and their entrances. The joke that runs through *1 Henry IV* is based on forcing the "uncolted" Falstaff — that habitual "horseback-breaker" — to walk through his highway robbery at Gadshill. Shakespeare made a comparable virtue of the same theatrical necessity when he dramatized Richard's proverbial horselessness. He had cleared the way with the King's announcement that the advance guard would consist "equally of horse and foot" (iii.294). In practice it is the infantry who are visible, and the cavalry whom we hear about. Later, more extravagant, and more literal-minded productions would sometimes make use of animal acts. Richard's plight was celebrated at Astley's Victorian hippodrome by covering the stage with dead or dying horses. The versions of Booth and Sir Henry Irving, sharply focussed upon the star, omitted the concluding scene. But the unhorsed Richard must ultimately encounter the veritable Richmond, and they must mime their hand-to-hand combat on foot. Shakespeare provides no eulogy nor epitaph of any kind for the vanquished. Richmond simply announces: "The day is over, the bloody dog is dead" (v.2). And the mediating Stanley, having plucked the crown from the usurper's corpse, places it upon the victor's brow.

The aftermath is so conformably official that we can understand its being cut; yet it was needed, especially when these matters were still topical, to steer the argument toward a dialectical resolution. Richmond, now Henry VII, must authoritatively and generously take charge, confirming young Stanley's deliverance, inquiring about the slain nobles, promising pardon for his repentant foes, and reviewing the condition of England. Favoured by God's blessing, his marriage to the late King Edward's daughter "will unite the White Rose and the Red," assuring a peaceful dynastic succession "with smiling plenty, and fair prosperous days!" (19, 35). Anxious reminiscences of treason are counteracted by the hopeful prospects ahead. Father and son will no longer shed one another's blood — as they have done so allegorically in *3 Henry VI*. And, with this declaration from the new King Henry, baronial strife has run its course; the Tudor epoch has dawned. Closing couplets pronounce a benediction:

> Now civil wounds are stopp'd, peace lives again;
> That she may long live here, God say amen! (40f.)

Justice, both retributive and poetic, has been affirmed, though not until the negation of humane values has done its worst. And yet "the worst is not," we may go on to learn from *King Lear*, "So long as we can say 'This is the worst'." History, in its darker aspects, can fascinate us with the evil that men do, with machination and manipulation. Such behaviour provokes countervailing activities which are also humanly contrived; but Richmond's part is that of a revenger, the predestined agent of a higher eventuality, whether contingent or providential; and that is why his agonistic interaction with Richard partakes of melodrama, if not of a *deus ex machina*. In tragedy, although various strings may be pulled by an Edmund or an Iago, the fundamental predicaments seem to be moulded at least as much by cosmic circumstance as by human initiative.

Pity has been less prevalent than terror in *Richard III*, despite the grieving queens — though it might have worked out otherwise, if we had been allowed to witness the child-murders more directly. As a rule, the pity ends by purging the fear, by exorcising our terrors. Tragedy has had a mandate to probe the inner nature of guilt, to examine the cross-purposes that account for suffering; whereas melodrama, calculating those evils from outside, has a knack for piling them up, with sabre-rattlings, shock tactics, and terroristic menaces. That may interpose a touch of sado-masochism in the relations between the spectator and the dramatist; but drama is privileged to celebrate the exceptions, the sensations, the extremities; and who could be more exceptional than Richard, the "cadodemon"? what could be more sensational than his demonic trajectory? and what extreme could go beyond the pandemonium that he brought about? (I.iii.143). Old Queen Margaret voices its self-conscious theatricalism, when she speaks of "this frantic play" (IV.iv.68). Insofar as it takes leave of an old order, now fallen into cataclysmic disorder, it might be viewed as Shakespeare's *Götterdämmerung*. Certainly it is his major contribution to that development of our own problematic century which Antonin Artaud would style "the Theater of Cruelty." And it is not hard to appreciate the comment of Bertolt Brecht, whose own work was bringing drama and epic together again, when he singled out the scene at Bosworth Field: "A theater full of alienation-effects!"

KEIR ELAM

As They Did in the Golden World: Romantic Rapture and Semantic Rupture in *As You Like It*

As You Like It is a play full of irreverent literary allusions, many of them overt, some of them less certain and to be dug out with philological or archaeological patience.[1] One of the more hidden, and certainly one of the more irreverent, of these possible references is to be found in the servant Adam's warning to Orlando just before they set out for the forest of Arden: "this night," warns the aged Adam, referring to Orlando's tyrannical brother Oliver, "he means / To burn the *lodging* where you used to lie" (2.3.22-3). Adam's use of the term "lodging" at this point in the play may be more than a casual instance of banal dramatic topology. *As You Like It*, as is well known, is the comedy in which Shakespeare is most consistently and substantially indebted to a narrative source, the prose romance *Rosalynde*, and Adam's lexical choice might be seen as an acknowledgement of sorts of this debt to the author of the source text, Thomas Lodge Esquire (2.158-256).[2] Indeed, "lodging" is exactly, in a sense, what Shakespeare does in composing the play whose *fabula*, and a good deal of whose plot, are lifted unashamedly out of the source. While "burning" the lodging, in Adam's phrase, namely omitting or completely recasting the source material, is an operation that the dramatist carries out at the other levels of the play, especially at the level of discourse.

Lodge himself might be suspected of repeated and somewhat narcissistic self-name-dropping in the course of his anything but witless narration. His romance opens with the death of Sir John of Bourdeaux, who exhorts his sons: "keep my precepts as memorialls of your fathers counsailles, and let them be *lodged* in the secrete of your hearts" (163). As soon as they arrive in Arden, Rosalynde and Alinda encounter the shepherds Coridon and Montanus, with whom they converse "until Montanus and he *lodged* their sheep for the night" (189). They conduct the disguised ladies to their "course *lodging*" (191). Similarly, Rosader in Arden bids goodnight to a forester: "and so till tomorrow you to your Foldes, and I will to my *Lodge*" (with capital L; 214) and so on.

Rosalynde is a romance of the pastoral species, and its author's name is itself eminently pastoral, at least in one of its various dictionary senses: that of the "small country house or cabin." Sidney's *Arcadia* is full of lodges, and Shakespeare furnishes his own "greenworld" plays with them ("I will visit you at the lodge," *Love's Labour's Lost* 1.2.126 etc.). And it is precisely on this aspect of Shakespeare's relationship with Lodge, and with literary and dramatic history in general, that I wish to reflect in this paper, since romance and pastoral are related, although not identical, modes of literary representation of a mythical or otherwise lost world, and Shakespeare's treatment of the two sets of conventions in *As You Like It* tells us a good deal about his special way with nostalgia, or perhaps, as we will see, without nostalgia.[3]

The relationship between romance and pastoral is, as it were, one of family resemblance, even if, as in most families, there are certain more or less deep-rooted tensions in the kinship. Despite their common origins in myth and magic, the two modes develop along distinct and in some ways antithetical lines. This troubled fraternity can be seen quite clearly in the relations between Lodge's *Rosalynde* and its source, the pseudo-Chaucerian verse romance *The Tale of Gamelyn*, which relates precisely the story of a troubled fraternity. The medieval poem is given over altogether to virile and vigorous blood-spilling action in the Robin Hood mould, with its emphasis placed unmistakeably on a seam-bursting and muscle-bound *fabula* made up of a succession of nasty family vendettas, and culminating in the unsurprising triumph of the good-hearted outlaw Gamelyn. Here the woodland setting has a purely ideological and axiological role in marking out a zone that is negative, i.e. illegitimate, in terms of the abusive political powers in force, but positive, i.e. legitimating, in terms of the simple moral values encoded in the poem. There is no attempt to paint a bucolic idyll distinct from the corrupt domain of feudal feuds; on the contrary, the forest is the point from which the forces of good are able, when not involved in the anticlerical persecution of passing monks, to intervene directly in, and indeed subvert, the rank baronial power-mongering embodied in Gamelyn's tyrannical elder brother.

Lodge's *Rosalynde* respects and reflects much of the *fabula* pattern of the medieval source: from the fraternal squabbling to the flight into the forest to the violent dénouement. But in his prose narrative, the emphasis shifts markedly from the actual *events* to their setting, to their ordering, and above all to the language of their acting out. Lodge's energies are given over substantially, not to the creation of an irresistible sweep of manly episodes, but to the depiction of a distinct woodland world dedicated to delicate conversing and intense ecloguing, to which end he invents important bits of *fabula* regarding disguised ladies and poetical shepherds. A choice which, naturally, is dictated by the most elementary canons of pastoral, which has little to do with fratricidal violence and everything to do with circumstantial evocation and conversational recreation. This is the first point of encounter and contrast: romance is a *fabula* mode, having to do with the kinds of action shown forth; pastoral is a mode of *plot* and *discourse*, having to do with spatiotemporal circumstance and with linguistic registers. So that the notion of "pastoral romance" of the kind attempted by Lodge is not in itself a contradiction in literary terms: a romance *fabula* can be suitably decked out in the environmental trappings and dainty discourse of pastoral with the happy results expressed in a venerable tradition of successful coexistence, from *Daphnis and Chloe* to Montemayor's *Diana* to *Arcadia* to *Rosalynde* itself.

This difference in levels produces other areas of contrast, however. One is of a structural order. Romance, with its orientation towards *fabula* and its embodiment of anthropologically deep-rooted symbolism, tends to be ternary in structure (in *Gamelyn*, for example, we find three sons, a three-phase syntax of action [feud — outlawing — return] etc.). Pastoral, on the other hand, with its orientation towards circumstance and dialogic discourse, usually involving the exploration of antithetical worlds, of contrasting environments, of moral oppositions in ritual debate, is unquestionably binary in its structural and thematic disposition: nature versus culture, country versus court, the language of innocent communion versus the used coinage of communal decay. Again there is no radical incompatibility between the numbers three and two, which can always be added or multiplied together, as the history of folk literature demonstrates, and Lodge's solution is simply to "dress up" the ternary as the binary, which he steps up almost to the point of mania by adopting the fashionably antithetical language of euphuism ("Ah *Saladyne*, though I seeme simple, yet I am more subtile than to swallow the hook because it hath a painted bait: as men are wilie so women are warie, especially if they have that wit by others harmes to beware ..." [236]). Although the old romance patterns do show through (there are still three sons and three action phases), they are all but smothered by the overwhelming sense of syntactic and propositional balance on the narrational surface.

The one area of radical conflict between the two, however, is of an epistemic order, and raises the whole question of the "other" world characteristic of each. To hazard an outrageous generalization, one might claim that romance narrates a world of fantastic happenings, governed by the autonomous logic of the marvellous, subject to the unanswerable laws of magic: in brief, founded on a closed code of values with an internally coherent and exclusive frame of reference. Pastoral, instead, *looks back* to an irretrievably past world of innocent engagement with created nature, which it attempts to re-evoke through the edenic illusion of uninhibited play and the suggestive powers of bucolic poesy. One might label this distinction provisionally as the opposition between the poetics of the *green world* and the poetics of the *golden world*: the one vigorously present, though undisguisedly fantastic, the other sensed as woefully distant, though infinitely desirable. The difference is registered above all in terms of the relationship with the here and now of our own all-too-grey "actual" world. Romance is a mode of licensed engagement with the "otherness" — the marvellous, mythical, and oneiric potentials — of this world; pastoral is a form of codified nostalgia for a time and place — or better, for a timeless place and place-less time — that are by definition inaccessible from the brazen *hic et nunc*.

There's the rub: of the two modes, it is pastoral that spells nostalgia. The reconstructed golden worlds of Theocritus and of Tasso and of Sidney, potentially repellent in their insistent and often insipid shepherdly poeticizing, take on an irresistible seductive force from the fact that they are offered as impossible *alternatives* — the more remote, the more appealing — to the even more intolerable decadence of the present moment. And if the pastoral has demonstrated a formidably *longue durée* within our culture, this is surely because the present moment is *always* perceived as being especially decadent. Thus the poetics of pastoral become, with its development over a good many centuries into and beyond the Renaissance, the poetics of melancholy indulgence, of communal self-pity, of ritual elegy for lost origins that are no longer mythical but conventionally literary.

Let us return for a moment to the matter of emblematic names. No name is more resonant for cultivators of nostalgic pastoralism than that of the original gardener, Adam himself. Both *Gamelyn* and *Rosalynde* have an Adam, and so, as we have already seen, does *As You Like It*. Indeed, the three Adams are, at least in actantial terms, the same Adam, selfless helper of the outlawed protagonist; but at the same time Adam's career from the late Middle Ages to the late Renaissance across the three texts is quite revealing. *Gamelyn's* Adam the spencer is perfectly at home in the *fabula* of a masculine and muscular romance, brimming as he is with corporeal energy and offering as he does efficacious assistance to the hero in the trying business of handling the opposition:

> Adam felde tweyne, and Gamelyn felde thre.
> The other setten feete on erthe, and begonne fle. (Lodge 144)

An Adam worthy of his Biblical namesake in his simple high-protein physicality. In Lodge, Adam the spencer becomes Adam Spencer: he has been cognomenized, and thus, in a sense, modernized, as well as anglicized ("an English man, who had been an olde and trustie servant to sir John of Bourdeaux" [173]: when Adam delved and Eve span, who was then the Englishman?), and in his passage to the modern era, he bears the signs or symptoms of the world's decay, "the penalty of Adam." He paints himself as the veritable icon of decrepitude: "Thou art old, *Adam*," he auto-apostro-phizes, "and thy haires wax white, the Palme tree is alreadie full of bloomes, and in the furrows of thy face appeares the kalenders of death?" (195). During their flight to Arden, the old man faints. The only help he can offer the protagonist now is moral support, and that of a decidedly melancholy tone:

> Ah *Rosader*, could I helpe thee, my griefe were the lesse, and happie should my death be, if it might be the beginning of they reliefe: but seeing we perish both in one extreame, it is a double sorrowe.... What cheere master? though all faile, let not the heart faint: the courage of man is shewed in the resolution of his death. At these words Rosader lifted up his eye, and looking on *Adam Spencer* began to weepe. (195)

Understandably. For the rest, and appropriately for a spectacularly decayed Adam, his discourse is all oriented towards the past, towards the heroic or epic epoch of the dead Sir John: "When I remember the worships of his house, the honour of his fathers, and the vertues of himselfe..." (195).

As You Like It takes off precisely at this backward-looking point: "As I remember, Adam," begins Orlando's opening speech, seeming to cast a sorrowful retrospective glance over the whole of world history, and seeming to promise a feast of wistful indulgence to come. Orlando proceeds, or recedes, to express a temporally marked woe — "there begins my sadness" (1.1.4) — while at the same time taking the dramaturgic opportunity to recount the *fabula* so far, which is, naturally, the same slice of *fabula* that Lodge took over from *Gamelyn* and that Shakespeare now appropriates as he likes it for his own text. So that the melancholy sense of the universal and pre-dramatic past in the play's *incipit* comes to coincide with an oblique look back to the comedy's own literary antecedents, as much as to say that such eloquent present-despising nostalgia is itself a borrowed topic. Certainly it is a topic that Shakespeare elaborates with some insistence here as in the openings of other comedies. Adam is allowed several mournful references to the all but holy memory of Sir Rowland de Boys ("for your father's remembrance, be at accord"; "God be with my old master," etc.).

The strongest parallel to this sanctification, or one might say orification, of the pre-dramatic past is found in the first act of *All's Well That Ends Well*, in which the mourned *aurea aetas* is the miraculous era of the recently dead and all but divinely gifted Count of Rossillion and Gerard de Narbon: "This young gentlewoman had a father — O that 'had,' how sad a passage 'tis! — whose skill was almost as great as his honesty; had it stretch'd so far, would have made nature immortal, and death should have play for lack of work..." (1.1.16-20). Again, the present is seen as a modern and thus decadent fall from this magical state of grace: "*Lafew.* They say miracles are past; and we have our philosophical persons to make modern and familiar, things supernatural and causeless" (2.3.1-3).

There is, however, a radical difference between the straight-faced earnestness of *All's Well*, whose opening mood of post-diluvial pathos and corruption is maintained virtually throughout until Helena restores *in extremis* the lost values of the past, and the determined gaiety of *As You Like It*, whose doleful *incipit* is anything but a portent of things to come. And this difference is symptomatic also of Shakespeare's treatment of the comedy's intertextual debts, both in the guise of its specific source material and in the form of the literary and dramatic conventions it reworks.

A reliable clue to Shakespeare's re-elaboration of his pastoral romance material (one might say his change of lodging) is to be found precisely in his presentation of Adam. The old servant — no longer Adam the spencer or Adam Spencer but just plain naked Adam — retains in part his emblematic role as embodiment of a lost past and thus as the measure or touchstone of modern decay: "O good old man," exclaims Orlando, "how well in thee appears / The constant service of the antique world" (2.3.56-57), and adds "thou art not for the fashion of these times" (59). He has, indeed, aged even further in the process of his journey into drama, now boasting "almost fourscore" years (71). And though verbally he vaunts the kind of manly powers displayed by the younger and more carefree Adam of *Gamelyn* — "though I look old, yet I am strong and lusty" (2.3.47) — in the event he shows the same frailty as Lodge's Adam, collapsing on arrival in Arden ("I can go no further"; 2.6.1). What is interesting to observe, however, is the rhetorical vitality Shakespeare's character exhibits in his clash with the tyrannical Oliver. Where *Gamelyn's* Adam simply lays low the lackeys of the despot, and where Lodge's Adam contents himself with silent subversion against the sinister Saladyne, Shakespeare's dramatic Adam is allowed a brief but effective say in his own right by way of protest:

> *Oliver.* Get you with him, you old dog.
> *Adam.* Is old dog my reward? Most true, I have lost my teeth
> in your service. God be with my old master! — he
> would not have spoke such a word. (11.81-84)

Adam produces a quiet *asteismus* or "merry scoff," literalizing his master's metaphor and turning it against him. Adam's humble but witty figure is a case of the ingenious disguised as the ingenuous, and as such, signals Shakespeare's main mode of elaborating his inherited material, namely that of liberating it from all its accumulated earnestness through strategic and ironic semantic play.

Pastoral, bound as it is to elegantly elegiac longing, is not the natural home either of irony or of semantic ambiguity. As William Empson — great connoisseur of pastoral and of ambiguity alike — observes, in order for the pastoralizing style with all its artifices to "work in the right way (not become funny) the writer must keep up a firm pretence that he was unconscious of it" (12). Shakespeare does just the opposite. Taking the predominantly ambientational emphases of pastoral convention, he subjects each circumstantial coordinate to some species of ironizing semantic abuse, thereby laying bare the rules of woodland game as such. Thus, on the spatial axis, the forest itself — automatic point of reference for any would-be (or wood-be) pastoralizer — becomes a pretext for free punning; the dutifully topological an excuse for the atrociously tropological:

> *Orlando.* Where dwell you pretty youth?
> *Rosalind.* With this shepherdess my sister;
> here in the skirts of the forest, like fringe upon a
> petticoat. (3.2.328-30)

The convention of atemporality, similarly, i.e. the fanciful notion that within the confines of the edenic "other" world time leaves no trace, is continuously lexicalized and more or less maltreated throughout the Arden scenes, from the Duke's ambiguous "Here feel we not the penalty of Adam" (2.1.5) to the lengthy pseudo-pastoral debate on the subject between Orlando and Rosalind:

> *Rosalind.* I pray you, what is't o'clock?
> *Orlando.* You should ask me what time o' day; there's no clock in the forest.
> *Rosalind.* Then there is no true lover in the forest, else sighing every minute and groaning every hour would detect the lazy foot of Time, as well as a lock.
> *Orlando.* And why not the swift foot of Time? Had not that been as proper?
> *Rosalind.* By no means sir. Time travels in divers places with divers persons.... (3.2.294ff.)

Various other elements of Shakespeare's strategic reworking of the genre emerge here. First, his irreverence towards the binary discursive mode so precious to

Lodge and others. Shakespeare's main exponent of the pastoral antithesis is the clown Touchstone, who reduces to a breathless display of monologic self-contradiction the commonplace of the court/country culture/nature dialectic:

> Corin.   And how like you this shepherd's life, Master Touchstone?
> Touchstone. Truly shepherd, in respect of itself, it is a good life; but in
>   respect that it is a shepherd's life, it is naught. In respect that it
>   is solitary, I like it very well; but in respect that it is private, it
>   is a very vile life. Now in respect it is in the fields, it pleaseth
>   me well; but in respect it is not in the court, it is tedious.
>   (3.2.11-19)

It is to Touchstone, likewise, that Shakespeare delegates his one brief and less than flattering nod towards the manic propositional balancing acts of his euphuistic source:

> A man may, if he were of a fearful heart, stagger in this attempt; for here we
> have no temple but the wood, no assembly but horn-breasts.... As horns are
> odious, they are necessary. It is said, many a man knows no end of his goods.
> Right, many a man has good horns and knows no end of them. The forehead
> of a married man more honourable than the bare brow of a bachelor; and by
> how much defence is better than no skill, by so much is a horn more precious
> than to want. (3.3.42-57)

In Rosalind's tyrannical womanhandling of time as topic, another essential ingredient of the pastoral mixture, or of what we might christen the shepherd's pie, is exposed: namely the dedication of arcadian discourse to the expression of pure passion, especially of the painful or pathetic variety: "sighing every minute and groaning every hour," as Rosalind puts it. The passionality of pastoral is synonymous with its edenic pretences, since an uncorrupted language entails a direct and uninhibited communication of sentiment (the same notion is present today in a good deal of utopian psychotherapy of the Californian encounter school). As Empson says, "The essential trick of the old pastoral ... was to make people express strong feelings (felt as the most universal subject, something fundamentally true about everybody), in learned and fashionable language" (11). The classic model here is Orpheus lamenting the death of Eurydice. Lodge's narrative is substantially and suitably made up, in effect, of a series of monodic performances in which each character gives decorous vent to some potent passional impulse, and he even gives little titles to each outburst: "Rosalynds Passion," "Saladynes Complaint," "Rosalynd Passionate Alone," etc. And equally suitably, the predominant passion is pathos or pity, especially self-pity: "Having therefore death in his lookes to moove them to pitie," he narrates of John of Bourdeaux, "and tears in his eyes to paint out the depth of his passions" (Lodge 161). This might indeed be the poetic motto of pastoral in general: to paint out the depth of one's passions, i.e. to create a pretty speaking picture depicting the sufferings of modern man masquerading as pipe-wielding ante-diluvial pastor.

This is not, of course, the kind of spectacle that Shakespeare's shepherds make of themselves. Indeed, it might be said that if the constructive principle of pastoralism is sentimental directness, the governing tenet of *As You Like It* is expressive obliqueness. This is virtually announced in the first act with Orlando's passional silence in the presence of Rosalind:

> *Orlando.* What passion hangs these weights upon my tongue?
> I cannot speak to her, yet she urg'd conference. (1.2.247-48)

Where Lodge's Rosader issues a carefully composed communiqué or press release on his enamoured state, Orlando's love remains tacit. The point is underlined in the following scene in which, at the point where Lodge's Rosalynde gives way to pretty lamentation, Shakespeare's Rosalind explicitly refrains from expressing her sorrow at her father's banishment ("not a word? / Not one to throw at a dog"; 1.3.2-3). Only when lovers' passions can be playfully *delegated* are they actually verbalized in the comedy: in the forest, Orlando and Rosalind *pretend* to be Orlando and Rosalind reciprocally expressing their feelings while doing so. This ironical theatricalizing of sentiment through play-acting overcomes any risk of ingenuous expressionism. The strategy is characteristically parodied by Touchstone, the play's rhetorical touchstone indeed, in his account of *his* first passional expressions, delegated to various inanimate objects:

> I remember when I was in love I broke my sword upon a stone, and bid him take that for coming a-night to Jane Smile ... and I remember the wooing of a peascod instead of her, from whom I took two cods, and giving her them again, said with weeping tears, "Wear these for my sake." (2.4.43-51)

Otherwise, the delegation of passion involves the play's only conventionally pastoral characters, the native nymphs and shepherds of Arden whose ancestry is the eclogue tradition. Silvius in particular is allowed all the naïve sentimental directness that the main-plot characters so knowingly avoid:

> *Silvius.* Or if thou hast not broke from company
> Abruptly as my passion now makes me,

> Thou hast not lov'd.
> O Phebe, Phebe, Phebe! (2.4.37-40)

But the true shepherds' passional exchanges are framed precisely as pretty speaking pictures by the more worldly characters ("If you will see a pageant truly play'd / Between the pale complexion of true love / And the red glow of scorn and proud disdain, / Go hence a little, and I shall conduct you / If you will mark it"; 3.5.48-52). And they are ready targets for Rosalind's unforgiving irony: "Jove, Jove! this shepherd's passion / Is much upon my fashion." So that the play's token ecloguing, so important in the source, becomes another of its embedded or lodged objects of literary burlesque.

For the rest, what the comedy offers in place of the explication of passion is the anatomy of passion along the lines of the psychological treatises of the day (such as Thomas Wright's *The Passions of the Minde* [London, 1601]). The inevitable Rosalind conducts an acute semiological analysis of the signs or symptoms of enamourment, in order to demonstrate ironically Orlando's lack of any such condition:

> A lean cheek, which you have not; a blue eye and sunken, which you have not; an unquestionable spirit, which you have not; a beard neglected, which you have not.... Then your hose should be ungartered, your bonnet unbanded, your sleeve unbuttoned, your shoe untied, and everything about you demonstrating a careless desolation. (3.2.363-71)

Just as that other canny observer and semiologue, Jaques, presents a cultural typology of the exemplary pastoral passion or humour he supposedly incarnates, melancholy:

> I have neither the scholar's melancholy, which is emulation; nor the musician's, which is fantastical; nor the courtier's, which is proud; nor the soldier's, which is ambitious; nor the lawyer's, which is politic; nor the lady's, which is nice; nor the lover's, which is all of these. (4.1.10-15)

Such electing of behavioural codes as objects of discourse, rather than as objects of direct dramatization, is an important aspect of the comedy's tendency to topicalize those elements of its literary antecedents that it cannot use directly, as if to mark out the very distance it maintains from an over-serious engagement with such leaden stuff.

In a word, to the romantic rapture — *raptura*, a *carrying* away — typical of the pastoral mode, Shakespeare opposes semantic rupture, *ruptura*, a *breaking* away not only from inherited literary canons but from the linguistic and stylistic fixity they presuppose. In place of straight-faced would-be-edenic verbal innocence, he offers determined and this-worldly word-corruption. Instead of static speaking pictures, he creates a shifting parade of literary and pictorial burlesque, transforming the earnestly iconic into the exuberantly ironic. All of which plainly works against the interests of that nostalgia-mongering that Lodge and his predecessors exploit so well.

And yet — and this is the extraordinary achievement of Shakespeare's genuinely (as opposed to decoratively) dialectical comedy — this ironical rupture, this breaking with the codified and sclerotic aspects of pastoralizing rhetoric, far from killing off the poetics of the golden world altogether, *liberates* it and renews it, allowing it to recuperate its original kinship with the greenworld poetics of romance. This is already hinted at in the play's opening scene, in which the hapless wrestler Charles imagines life in Arden, not in terms of the literary arcadianism of the day, but in the more archaic terms of the medieval popular romance tradition à la *Gamelyn*: "They say he is already in the Forest of Arden, and a many merry men with him; and there they live like the old Robin Hood of England. They say many young gentlemen flock to him every day, and fleet the time carelessly as they did in the golden world" (1.1.114-19). And it is emphatically confirmed in the closing scene with the comedy's masque finale, which looks so unmistakeably forward to Shakespeare's late romances.

This ending, stage-managed by Rosalind as a kind of directorial *dea in machina*, and pre-announced by the heroine herself as a display of natural magic ("I am a magician," she boasts [5.2.70-71]), has on the whole embarrassed critics, who have tended to underplay or repress altogether its presence. Indeed, Helen Gardner, for all her promisingly romantic pastoral name, goes so far as to state flatly that "The Forest of Arden ... is not ruled by magic" (17-32), while the still more bucolically named Sylvan Barnet finds the play's conclusion "strange" and "improbable" (119-31). And one can see why the direct intervention of Hymen might seem an arbitrary and unconvincing way to put a stop to so much irony and burlesque, especially since she is conjured up by the eiron-in-chief, Rosalind herself. But this, it appears to me, is to mistake the comedy's brilliantly ironical discursivity for a species of sceptical modernity, a kind of deconstructive undoing of the epistemic principles of the "other" world, whereas, on the contrary, the final effect of Shakespeare's toying with golden-world codes is to strengthen the sense of greenworld "otherness."

Because the function of all the verbal play and all the stylistic parody with which the Arden scenes are replete is to free the forest itself of the literally *deadly* seriousness of conventional pastoralism. The arcadias of Politian and of Tasso and of Sidney and of Guarini are in the end doleful in their very efforts to represent carefreeness, just as nothing is more melancholy in Monteverdi's *Orfeo* than the music of the first act given over to communal felicity and dainty dancing. It is indeed the tragic fate of the magical shepherd Orpheus that conditions much of the pastoral, whereby the innocent dedication to Eros seems always simultaneously to announce the arrival of the sport-spoiling Thanatos, who stakes out a special and peremptory territorial claim in Arcadia: not the *et in arcadia ego* of the *memento mori* commonplace, but a simpler and more disturbing *in arcadia ego*. Every forest frolic or garden gambol becomes a ruse to bide or buy time in a supposedly timeless zone dominated, instead, by that awareness of the impending triumph of Thanatos that underlies nostalgia in all its forms.

Shakespeare's Arden is in contrast fully and authentically erotic, given order to a mode of open dialectical play or *serio ludere* that has nothing to do with arcadian deadliness or deathliness. The comedy rigorously relegates Thanatos to the world of political malpractice within the formal main plot (or what we might call the polis drama) of the usurping and tyrannical brothers. It is this "first" world, the world of the decayed feudal order, that monopolizes ideological and worldly strife, a kind of "first-world" war, leaving the second, "other" world of Arden free to toy with this-worldly intimations of mortality.

And at the same time, Shakespeare, with respect to his source, intensifies in the second, Arden strand of the drama those very aspects of the marvellous, the magical, the non-verisimilitudinous that connote most unequivocally the romance mode. Symptomatic of this strategic change is the much-discussed but little-praised episode of Oliver's arrival in the forest, in which, in vertiginous succession, the elder brother is converted from first-world corruption to second-world benevolence, is saved by his younger brother first from a snake and then from a lioness, and falls requitedly in love on the instant with the disguised Celia. More often than not, this feast of the arbitrary has been judged, according to the criteria of dramaturgic decorum, as a desperate tying up of loose plot ends or endings. But in the light of what follows, namely Rosalind's magical masque dénouement, it surely amounts to an open declaration of the comedy's definitive movement towards the proairetic, epistemic, and poetic canons of the *Gamelyn*.

It is, perhaps paradoxically, this marked shift towards the *fabula* conventions of romance that brings the comedy back into contact with the mythical, magical, and, above all, ludic roots of pastoral itself, freed from the more codified accretions of the literary tradition. "The task of the pastoral imagination," writes Poggioli, "is to overcome the conflict between passion and remorse, to reconcile innocence and happiness, to exalt the pleasure principle at the expense of the reality principle" (159).

Shakespeare's Arden achieves this triumph of the pleasure principle, of freeplay, of the reconciliation of opposing forces precisely through the exorcising of Thanatos, or, if you like, of nostalgia, from the green world, substituting for the constricting canons of the dramaturgic reality principle the liberating laws of the fantastic. The happy consequences of all this for the other structural levels of the comedy can be seen not only in the infinitely pleasurable freedom of its dialogic wit but in the actual *strengthening* of the binary pastoralism of the plot: the three brothers, for example, became virtually two (with a doubling of the third, Jaques de Boys, in the melancholy Jaques of the exiled court; "Oliver" is likewise doubled in Oliver Martext); greater structural use is made of the parallelism between the two journeys into Arden (Celia and Rosalind, Orlando and Adam); greater stress is placed on certain fundamental paradigmatic oppositions, such as Nature vs. Fortune; the comedy concludes ritualistically with four marriages (two plus two), etc. As if to say that it is only the reinforcing of romance, in the guise of the fabulous *fabula*, that licenses the reinvention of pastoral in a dramatically vigorous and persuasive form.

This, then, is the so-called "pastoral romance" of the source decisively recast or relodged, a pastoral romance that presents no longer a yearning for the inaccessible but an *affirmation* of the achievable, namely of the capacity of dramatic theatre itself to create a world at once remote and present, oneiric and pragmatic, magical and ironical. The conclusion of *As You Like It*, in this sense, stands for the recovery of that mythical Orphic magic which, according to Northrop Frye, lies behind not only the romance and pastoral modes but behind the dramatic genre itself:

> drama begins with the renunciation of magic, when ritual acts designed to operate on the order of nature are enclosed by myth when drama renounces magic in this way it gets it back again through the nature of poetic imagery itself, which assimilates the natural to the human order by analogy and identity, simile and metaphor. The traditional symbol of this lost and regained magic in human art is Orpheus. (*Natural Perspective*, 146-47)

The obvious point of comparison and contrast is the epilogue of *The Tempest*, in which Shakespearean pastoral romance, in its most fully achieved and most articulately baroque form, re-renounces the illusionistic Orphism that brought it into being ("Now my charms are all o'erthrown"). In the earlier comedy, there is no suggestion of such retrospective self-undoing.

In a word, then, Shakespeare's way with nostalgia in the play is more of a *doing away* with nostalgia, in favour of a forward-looking assertion of the erotic, the ludic, and the magical potentials of the drama in a freshly re-invented pastoral romance mode. Only the poet, claims Sidney, can create a golden world, and it is in this sense, rather than in any poetics of aureate arcadianism, that Shakespeare follows the Elizabethan master. The dramatist reaffirms playfully and ironically, but — to quote Lodge (not Thomas, but his modern namesake and fellow romance-writer, David) — "with rare eloquence, the old view of nature as cyclical, harmonious, life-giving, self-renewing, susceptible of magical or intuitive control by suitably endowed persons."[4] To show you things "as they did in the golden world," then, may mean not as you *long* for it but simply as you *like* it.

Anticipations

PAUL MORRISON

Noble Deeds and the Secret Singularity: *Hamlet* and *Phèdre*

Hamlet enters the play that bears his name, a play in which Shakespeare is uncharacteristically parsimonious with names,[1] only to tell his mother that he will not act:

> Seemes Maddam, nay it is, I know not seemes,
> Tis not alone my incky cloake good mother
> Nor customary suites of solembe blacke
> Nor windie suspiration of forst breath
> No, nor the fruitfull riuer in the eye,
> Nor the deiected hauior of the visage
> Together with all formes, moodes, shewes of griefe
> That can denote my truely, these indeede seeme,
> For they are actions that a man might play
> But I haue that within which passeth showe
> These but the trappings and the suites of woe. (2.232-42)

"To be" is here implicitly defined as pure interiority, the thoroughly privatized self-possession of "that within which passeth showe." Actions that a man might play, explicitly theatrical and publicly accessible constructions of identity, are dismissed as so much dross. Hamlet conceives of himself — and there is a sense in which the fatherless son is very much attempting to "conceive himself," to originate his own existence — in opposition to the corporeal, the external, the visual, which is also the order of the spectacle, the theatrical.[2] Play and character share a name, then, but reluctantly so, at least from the perspective of character. Not for Hamlet the kinetic consummations, the being-through-action, of theatrical self-definition. Not for Hamlet the publicly accessible surfaces, the "incky cloaks" and "customary suites," of theatrical appearances.

Not for Hamlet and not for us, for there is a sense in which the Prince who would originate his own existence also originates ours:

179

> With Falstaff as with Hamlet (and perhaps with Cleopatra) Shakespearean
> representation is so self-begotten and so influential that we can apprehend it
> only by seeing that it originates us. We cannot judge a mode of representation
> [or, in the case of the passage cited above, a sweeping dismissal of a mode of
> representation] that has overdetermined our ideas of representation. (Bloom 85)

Harold Bloom's celebration of the proleptic power of Shakespearean
representation finds its most compelling example in the figure of Hamlet.
Certainly the Prince has few rivals (and even these, as Bloom suggests, would
be Shakespearean) in terms of the influence he has exerted on the construction
and representation of subjectivity, in determining our position within what
Foucault calls "l'aventure de l'individualité": "Et si depuis le fond du Moyen
Age jusqu'aujourd'hui "l'aventure" est bien le récit de l'individualité, le passage
de l'épique au romanesque, du haut fait à la secrète singularité, des longs exils
à la recherche intérieure de l'enfance..." (*Surveiller et punir* 195). The passage
"de l'épique au romanesque" might here read from drama to novel, as drama, at
least in its Aristotelian form, is predicated on the priority of action to character,
praxis to ethos, "the noble deed" to the "secret singularity":

> For tragedy is an imitation not of men but of a life, an action [praxis], and
> they have moral quality in accordance with their characters [ethe] but are
> happy or unhappy in accordance with their actions; hence they are not active
> in order to imitate their characters, but they include the characters along with
> the actions for the sake of the latter. Thus the structure of events, the plot, is
> the goal of tragedy, and the goal is the greatest thing of all. (Aristotle 1450a,
> 15-24)

Hamlet, who is something of a character in search of a different generic
dispensation, resists these Aristotelian priorities, and thus anticipates, more or
less *avant la lettre*, a novelistic or discursive mode of subjectivity, which the
novel, in its turn, would be only too pleased to grant him. But what the novel
would belatedly grant the Prince, the play itself refuses: against the incipient
modernity of Hamlet's claim to a theatrically inaccessible interiority, *Hamlet*
insists on a properly theatrical life for its eponymous hero. And if this is to make
of Shakespeare something other than a harbinger of our modernity — or to make
of Hamlet something other than the mirror in which we find an idealized
reflection of our interiority — it is precisely the celebration of "Shakespeare-our-
contemporary" that I intend to challenge.

It is a celebration that frequently makes use of the example of Racine, the
better to highlight the modernity of Shakespeare. The comparison, at least outside
the Francophone world, is almost invariably structured as the dispensation of a

large and comprehensive soul, Shakespeare's and all things Shakespearean, over and against the impoverishment of a codified theatrics, Racine's and all things neoclassical. And in what follows, I, too, make use of the familiar comparison: against *Hamlet*, I juxtapose another play that shares a name with its central character, another play, moreover, that is now little more than a showcase for a single performer: *Phèdre*. But where the conventional comparison tends toward the binary — a Shakespeare who is little more than an abundant interiority, a Racine who is little more than the constrictions of form — my own project attempts to mediate between the two, in the manner implied or facilitated by my quotation from Foucault. For if what follows is essentially a study of a generic dispensation, it is informed by a concept of genre that allows both for an analysis of individual texts within the history of literary forms, what Foucault calls "le passage de l'épique au romanesque," and the history of the social construction of subjectivity, what Foucault calls the passage "du haut fait à la secrète singularité." The former, which is for my purposes the passage from drama to the novel, I relate to the founding gesture of genre criticism, Aristotle's *Poetics*. I am concerned with the eclipse of the cultural centrality of drama, its displacement by the novelistic, which is at once a formal dispensation and an historically specific construction of subjectivity. It is this displacement, I argue, that *Hamlet* resists, and that *Phèdre*, in a rather curious sense, awaits.

I have suggested that the literature of psychological complexity was eager to claim Hamlet for its own, but there is a sense in which the Prince always was eager to be claimed. "Be as our selfe in Denmarke" (2.278) enjoins Claudius, but it is precisely because Hamlet will not be "as" the King of shreds and patches, which for Hamlet is "Of nothing," that he implicitly defines "to be" in terms of a theatrically inaccessible interiority. "For the apparrell oft proclaimes the man" (3.485), proclaims Polonius, to which Hamlet, for whom all the world is not a stage, implicitly responds no. Claudius may prepare a kingly face to meet the faces that he meets, but for Hamlet, the mask, the persona, is not the self. Yet if all the world is not a stage, neither is Claudius's success in a role "that a man might play" all of the theatre, although Hamlet implicitly treats it as if it were. The conflation of what might be characterized as Claudian theatrics, with the theatrical itself, is typical of the scholar-Prince, who tends, like the scholars who will come after him, to translate the particular into the general, the historically specific into the metaphysically ineluctable. Stanley Cavell, for example, is clearly of the party of the Prince and his universalist proclivities:

> Hamlet's extreme sense of theatre I take as his ceaseless perception of theatre, say show, as an inescapable or metaphysical mark of the human condition, together with his endless sense of debarment from accepting the human

condition as his (which is terribly human of him); as if his every breath and gesture disjoin and join him, from and with mankind. (187-88)

The perception of theatre as an inescapable or metaphysical mark of the human condition is indeed Hamlet's, as his sense of being thereby debarred from participating in it. The question remains, however, if the movement, from the perception to its apparently logical consequence, from "all the world is a stage" to the authentic self is estranged from it, is best characterized as "terribly" and therefore ahistorically "human." True, the gap that opens up in Hamlet between the inner life of the subject, experiencing itself as "that within which passeth showe," and an inauthentic exterior, the degraded spectacle of the world's "seemings," seems itself the "inescapable" condition of our own schizophrenic subjectivity: ours is a life both governed and diminished by the oppositions inner/outer, soul/body, private/public. It may be, however, that the oppositions are to be periodized as distinctly modern, not accepted as "terribly human." Francis Barker, for example, argues that in this "opening there begins to insist, however prematurely, the figure that is to dominate and organize bourgeois culture" (35).[3] This is to suggest, however, only that the "inescapable or metaphysical mark" of our own lives is rather more novelistic than theatrical, the realist novel, the novel of psychological depth, being, of course, the definitive literary accomplishment of bourgeois culture.

Now Hamlet does seem a harbinger of this discourse of the secret singularity, and certainly no character in the history of dramatic literature has proved as significant to the development of "well-rounded," "three-dimensional" character of novelistic fame as the melancholy Prince. In Goethe's *Wilhelm Meisters Lehrjahre*, for example, Wilhelm distinguishes between drama and the novel in terms that recall Aristotle's distinction between tragedy and epic, but only to assimilate *Hamlet* to the novelistic:

> Im Roman sollen vorzüglich Gesinnungen und Begebenheiten vorgestellt werden; im Drama Charaktere und Taten. Der Roman muß langsam gehen, und die Gesinnungen der Hauptfigur müssen, es sei auf welche Weise es wolle, das Vordringen des Ganzen zur Entwickelung aufhalten. Das Drama soll eilen, und der Charakter der Hauptfigur muß sich nach dem Ende drängen, und nur aufgehalten werden. Der Romanheld muß leidend, wenigstens nicht im hohen Grade wirkend sein; von dem dramatischen verlangt man Wirkung und Tat. (5: 7, 330)

For Wilhelm, *Hamlet* has something of the expansiveness ("von dem Gedehnten") that is, for Aristotle, both the defining characteristic of the epic and the mark of its inferiority to the tragic. Hamlet himself, moreover, has only "Gesinnungen," and it is only "Begebenheiten" that affects him. "Der Romanheld muß leidend ... sein." The novel hero must be suffering, no doubt from what came to be diagnosed as that most Hamlet-like of afflictions, the burden of an exquisite sensibility. Certainly Hamlet himself seems to suffer from his generic dispensation, although in the opinion of at least one nineteenth-century reviewer it never really was his:

> Yes, Hamlet is truly a man of these present times. It is thou Werther, thou Lara, thou Obermann, it is, above all, thou immortal René, in whom we see the sons and daughters of Hamlet ... It is to our own age that Hamlet belongs; it is our age that has discovered him ... and Hamlet himself has grown to maturity in the midst of the psychological literature in which we have all been nourished.[4]

Thus does the literature of psychological complexity, the culture of the book, claim the Prince for its own.

Northrop Frye speaks of the ordered society in Shakespeare's plays, which is manifestly not our own, as "ecstatic" in Heidegger's sense of the term: "its members are outside themselves, at work in the world, and their being is their function" (*Fools of Time* 29). Heidegger's "ecstatic" society resembles, however, nothing so much as feudal society, and the commercial theatre comes into being in England only as feudal social structures were disintegrating. Certainly there are few characters in the history of drama less "ecstatic" than Hamlet, less, as it were, exogenous. Or, to reverse the perspective, there are few characters in the history of drama more incipiently novelistic, more, as it were, endogenous. For in eschewing any role that a man might play, which is also any positionality, social or familial, that the world as stage avails him, the world as stage imposes upon him, Hamlet effectively defines the conditions under which novelistic characterization will be thought, perhaps even can be thought. That is, the protagonists of nineteenth-century realist fiction will follow Hamlet's lead in defining themselves not "ecstatically," but oppositionally, in relation to the world, however much it may be with them. In a terminology that would not be fully comprehensible to the unhappy Prince, but which he nevertheless anticipates, "psyche" rather than "property," internalized self-possession rather than external attributes, defines the essence of "to be."[5] The condition of novelistic subjectivity is characteristically self-possession, interiority, over and against which the world is experienced as objective. "I could be bounded in a nutshell, and count my selfe a King of infinite space" (7.1186-87): Denmark may be a prison, but the mind can make a heaven, a thoroughly interiorized and privatized heaven, of an objective hell. Such, in any case, is the broad premise of a novelistic construction of subjectivity: freedom from the determination which, in its explicitly aesthetic form, assumes the priority of plot to character, praxis to ethos.

But this is not, of course, the whole story: "I could ... count my selfe a King of infinite space" Hamlet continues, "were it not that I haue bad dreames." And the bad dream that impinges on this thoroughly imaginary freedom is determination by plot, praxis, role, the structural determination that the ghost of an unquiet father imposes on his patronymic son. The man who had previously eschewed any role that a man might play, who had defined himself in opposition to the demands of dramatic self-definition, is suddenly propelled into the most creaking and archaic of revenge plots. And given his cue for action, Hamlet subordinates, in proper Aristotelian fashion, ethos to praxis:

> ... while memory holds a seate
> In this distracted globe, remember thee,
> Yea, from the table of my memory
> Ile wipe away all triuiall fond records,
> All sawes of bookes, all formes, all pressures past
> That youth and obseruation coppied there,
> And thy commandement all alone shall liue. (5.714-20)

Johnson said of Shakespeare that "his story requires Romans or kings, but he thinks only on men."[6] With the second entry of the ghost, however, the story requires a revenger, and Hamlet initially thinks only on the deed, on determination or definition by praxis. Appropriately, then, Hamlet defines himself in opposition to an earlier and implicitly textual self ("Ile wipe away all triuiall fond records, / All sawes of books"), which is also an earlier and radically decorporeal self:

> O that this too too solid flesh would melt,
> Thaw and resolue it selfe into a dewe,
> Or that the euerlasting had not fixt
> His canon gainst sealfe slaughter. (2.285-88)

Had this "too too solid flesh" in fact resolved itself into a dew, Hamlet might have achieved the purely discursive status of novelistic existence: translated from theological to generic terms, Hamlet's first soliloquy begs release from the most fundamental condition of theatrical existence, physical embodiment. The Hamlet who labours under a properly dramatic imperative, however, acknowledges both his own and the world's physicality: this "distracted globe" is at once Hamlet's head (a reference to the body, not the internal operations of consciousness), the theatre in which *Hamlet* was first performed (the motto of the Globe was *totus mundus agit histrionem*, which translates roughly as all the world is a stage), and the world itself (the figure of Hercules shouldering the globe, what Rosencrantz calls "Hercules & his load" [7.1291], was on the flag that signalled performances at the Globe). "Hamlet's extreme sense of theatre" is indeed an "inescapable mark" of the world's condition, and the "condition," the "globe," is "distracted." But far from being debarred from participating in it, as Cavell would have it, Hamlet is under an obligation to it, bound or "borne to set it right" (5.807). The secret singularity that allegedly is Hamlet — allegedly, because in *Hamlet* the name "Hamlet" is not singular, not a unique appellation reserved for the presence of a unique subjectivity — becomes Hamlet the agent of his father's will. The genealogical tangles that characterize Hamlet's first utterances in the play — "A little more then kin, and less then kind" and "I am too much i'th'sonne" — are no longer in evidence. Commitment to the noble deed (and there is no suggestion here that revenge for regicide and patricide is not noble) has as its axis of individualization the ancestral, the genealogical. Hamlet the unique self gives way to Hamlet the patronymic son: *Hamlet* the play, Hamlet père, and Hamlet fils are, for the moment, one.

But again, this is not the whole story: Hamlet's "perception of theatre" as the "inescapable mark" of his own condition, his sense of obligation to the "distracted globe," is rather more problematic than I have acknowledged. For if Hamlet initially resolves to "wipe away all triuall fond records, / All sawes of bookes," he proceeds to lodge the ghost's "commandement ... / Within the booke and volume" of his "braine / Vnmixt with baser matter" (5.714-21). That is, the explicitly theatrical reference to "this distracted globe" becomes the radically textual self of "the booke and volume of my braine": from the corporeal to the discursive or the textual, from the body to the internal operations of consciousness, from the theatrical to the novelistic. Even as Hamlet identifies himself as the agent of a dramatic imperative, his language belies his commitment to the dramatic, to the body, which is punningly reduced to "baser matter." Enjoined to action, Hamlet responds by revising, editing, and expurgating a self conceived of as text.

A self conceived of as text, moreover, in the context of a play that insistently thematizes the discrepancy between text and performance, script and acting. *Hamlet* the play dramatizes Hamlet's theoretical pronouncements on drama, for example, as practical advice to travelling players, although the attitude dramatized is itself antidramatic, antitheatrical, at least given the context of Elizabethan theatrical practice. More specifically, Hamlet advises "those that play your clownes" to "speake no more then is set downe for them" (9.1764-65): the scholar-Prince argues for the priority of *ratio* to *oratio*, text to performance, the better to preserve the integrity of the written word from the accidents and aberrations of performance. And this too is an aspect of the Prince's incipient modernity. For if it is not until the nineteenth century that Hamlet achieves a purely discursive or novelistic existence, there is a sense in which the textual bias of his position finds a more immediate historical fulfilment: the publication of Jonson's *WORKES* in 1616, which was very much an attempt to establish the authority of play-texts, *ratio* uncontaminated by *oratio*, would doubtless have met with the scholar-Prince's approval. Yet the oxymoronic publication of plays as *WORKES* (for it was so experienced by Jonson's contemporaries), specifically literary works, was historically unprecedented. Clearly the cult and culture of the book, with its implicit transference of textual and intellectual authority from the communal structures of the court, theatre, and audience to the private domain of the author, text, and reader, was on the historical horizon.[7] Indeed, for Shakespeare, on the not too distant horizon, his now almost unimaginable indifference to the published fate of his dramatic "works" notwithstanding: the posthumous publication of the Folio of 1623, which was itself modelled on the Jonson Folio of 1616, was clearly a seminal moment in the history of the textualization of the bard. *Hamlet* itself, which is an intensely "bookish" play, full of references to "incky cloaks," texts, tablets, letters, forgeries, and the like, seems to anticipate this historical development, and its central character, who enters one scene "reading on a Booke," seems to want to hasten it. The play that adumbrates or anticipates this historical development, however, remains resistant to it.

Hamlet characterizes "Aeneas tale to Dido," the speech he requests from the players, as "cauiary to the generall" (7.1368-69): aesthetic worth is construed as inversely proportional to popular theatrical success, to performance. ("I heard thee speake me a speech once," Hamlet says, "but it was neuer acted": *oratio*, yes, but hardly performance; the speech Hamlet requests is in fact predominantly narrative, not dramatic.) Appropriately, or at least not unexpectedly, the man who characterizes himself in terms of a privatized and inaccessible interiority also defines himself in opposition to the collective experience and judgement of a theatrical audience. Indeed, the critical bias implicit in Hamlet's fondness for the speech, which is in no way troubled by "some necessary question" of the dramatic integrity of the play from which it is taken (his own theoretical standard), anticipates the critical gesture that will come to lift, say "To be, or not to be" from its larger dramatic context. And thus robbed of dramatic integrity, the great soliloquy, indeed any passage of particular "beauty" or "power," will come to be celebrated as an instance of the "literary" in the modern sense, and thus as an occasion for privatized aesthetic consumption. Yet even Hamlet, who can hardly be characterized as an apologist for the specifically theatrical or performative, recognizes that drama is necessarily a combination of discursive and non-discursive elements: "sute the action to the word, the word to the action" (9.1744-45). Discourse and deed, deed and discourse, are said to form an unbroken circuit. Hamlet's own deeds, however, belie the reciprocity of his purely discursive formulation.

Hamlet the producer of a play, for example, is not Hamlet the theoretician of drama: theatrical practice contradicts theoretical strictures, even as theoretical strictures seek, at least in part, to protect play-texts from contamination by theatrical practice. Thus, although Hamlet the theoretician argues for the priority of text to performance, Hamlet the producer violates the integrity of the former (he inserts "a speech of some dosen or sixteene lines" into "the murther of *Gonzago*") the better to ensure the affective power of the latter. Thus, although Hamlet the theoretician explicitly castigates "inexplicable dumbe showes" (9.1739), Ophelia experiences the "miching Mallico," the dumb show that precedes "The Mousetrap," as in need of explication. Clearly the practices and pragmatics of performance fail to conform to the strictures of theory, at least in the aristocratic, neoclassical form they assume with Hamlet. True, Hamlet's purpose in staging "The Mousetrap" is to expose Claudius's "occulted guilt," and in this he is successful: Claudius's "seeming" is indeed exposed, his guilt given visible and public manifestation. The play catches the conscience of the king, however, by reduplicating appearances, not by penetrating depths. Thus, even that most familiar of definitions, for the "purpose of playing, whose end both at the first, and nowe, was and is, to holde as twere the Mirrour vp to nature" (9.1747-49), tells against Hamlet, as a mirror by definition, knows only "seems." The concealed inside is not, after all, of a different order from the external.

Yet Hamlet refuses to acknowledge or accept the continuity, the lesson implicit in his theatrical success with "The Mousetrap" notwithstanding: "Why looke you now how vnworthy a thing you make of me, you would play vpon mee, you would seeme to knowe my stops, you would plucke out the hart of my mistery" (9.2079-88). Rosencrantz and Guildenstern, who are here acting as Gertrude's "instrument," confront a Hamlet who, immediately after the play within the play, again declares his secret and inaccessible singularity. But as with the earlier declaration, the public and thus oxymoronic insistence on a private interiority, the self-dramatizing and thus oxymoronic denigration of the dramatic, this, too, proves highly problematic. It is difficult to know, for example, how the hollow form of a "pipe," the "being" of which is literally its instrumentality, can suggest the metaphysic of the soul, the plenitude of an internalized self-possession, that Hamlet apparently intends. Indeed, as if fleeing, Claudius-like, the implications of his theatrical success, Hamlet utterly denies the continuity between internal and external, the profound (and thus from the perspective of all things modern, oxymoronic) superficiality that obtains in the world as theatre, the theatre as world. Hamlet denies, however, but the play confirms: in the two carefully juxtaposed scenes that follow shortly after the play within the play, the prayer and closet scenes, the play asserts itself over and against Hamlet's novelistic propensity for excavating depths.

The first of these, the prayer scene, opens with a soliloquy: a now Hamlet-like Claudius, unwitnessed by the character he has temporarily come to resemble, engages in an act of internalized and privatized self-recognition: "O my offence is ranck, it smels to heauen, / It hath the primall eldest curse vppont" (10.2156-57). Claudius, who is characteristically the most public of men, turns inward. The gesture is of the essence of Hamlet, yet here the subject's experience of itself proves continuous with the external:

> My fault is past, but oh what forme of prayer
> Can serue my turne, forgiue me my foule murther,
> That cannot be since I am still possest
> Of those effects for which I did the murther;
> My Crowne, mine owne ambition, and my Queene;
> May one be pardond and retain th'offence? (10.2167-76)

There never can be a purely internalized act of self-recognition or transformation — one cannot be pardoned and retain the material "effects" of the crime — for there is finally no interiority innocent of visible, external, or material manifestation. "In the corrupted currents of this world," where one may smile and smile and be a villain, the truth of the appearance of things may not be immediately apparent. Yet the very man who occasions the crisis in signification, who "corrupts" ocular intelligibility, also comes to acknowledge its ultimate and inevitable rectification: "but tis not so aboue, / There is no shufling, there the action lies / In his true nature, and we our selues compeld / Euen to the teeth and forhead of our faults / To giue in euidence" (10.2176-80). Claudius's final hope, "All my be well" (2188), translates the spatial above, the place "where action lies / In his true nature," into a temporal prospect, the final judgement from which he begs deliverance. But all will not be well. The temporal unfolding of dramatic action will expose action in its true nature, and the truth of the world's appearances will be vindicated. Significance will then be radically corporeal, exogenous. The body, "Euen to the teeth and forhead," will bear, will in fact be, "euidence."

It is precisely the "euidence" of the body, however, that Hamlet, who happens upon the kneeling Claudius, misconstrues: the Prince who "knows not seems" confuses the physical disposition of the praying body with the spiritual efficacy of prayer. And as Hamlet's purpose, which is clearly in excess of the ghost's injunction, is to damn his uncle's soul, not merely dispense with his body, he fails to act. There is a sense, however, in which the spiritual efficacy of prayer cannot be separated from the disposition of physical "effects," the enjoyment of material goods. For prayer fails Claudius, not because of some deficiency of spirit or soul, but because he is unwilling or unable to renounce "Those effects" for which he committed the crime. Here it is property rather than psyche, praxis rather than ethos, that defines the essence of "to be": to be forgiven, to effect an internal transformation, is to renounce possessions, property, external paraphernalia. Thus, the irony reverberates against Hamlet, as the play "reads" the character who fails to "read" aright the "euidence " of the body. In the closet scene, moreover, Hamlet's dramatic "deed," the killing of Polonius, renders ironic his attempt to "read" the recesses of Gertrude's soul.

Once again Hamlet would hold a mirror up to nature, human nature, his mother's: "You goe not till I set you vp a glasse / Where you may see the inmost part of you" (11.2233-34). Here, however, the glass allegedly does penetrate depths, and the nature it takes as its object is patently psycho-sexual: in this scene of compelled self-examination, mimesis assumes an implicitly novelistic, or at least explicitly non-Aristotelian, form. Hamlet's novelistic deployment of the "glass" does find an explicitly dramatic analogue or manifestation, as the psychological sounding of depths, the probing of psychic interiors, becomes a properly dramatic thrust of a sword, the literal penetration of a surface. But because it is a misdirected thrust — Hamlet mistakes Polonius for his better — it is an analogue that belies the claim to psychological probity. And what the thrust of a sword belies, the ghost explicitly interdicts: "this visitation / Is but to whet thy almost blunted purpose" (2315-16). Hamlet's novelistic "purpose," the psychological inquisition that culminates in Gertrude's anguished cry, "Thou turnst mine eyes into my very soule" (2294), is itself turned, redefined in non-psychological, non-novelistic terms, as the ghost enjoins Hamlet to come between his mother and her fighting soul. Appropriately, Hamlet no longer compels introspection; rather, he recommends a course of action, a role that a woman might play, an explicitly theatrical construction of identity:

Assume a vertue if you haue it not.
That monster custome, who all

> sence doth eat
> Of habits deuillish, is angell yet in this
> That to vse of actions faire and good,
> He likewise giues a frock or Liuery
> That aptly is put on.[8]

Hamlet's parting advice to his mother recalls his earlier polemic against "seems," but only to reject its metaphysic of depth, its conflation of being and interiority. Virtue is here precisely "that which does not pass show," which is other than pure interiority. Not the internal transformation of consciousness, but the public deployment of the body, the "fashioning" of virtue that is "aptly" and indeed only "put on" in praxis, in the theatre of the world.

Now there is a sense in which nothing that transpires between Hamlet and Gertrude, indeed between anyone in Claudius's Denmark, remains "within," for there is virtually nothing that escapes surveillance. Paradoxically, however, Denmark is a world of "lawful espials" (8.1570), of eyes behind every arras, in which spying accomplishes nothing. The Polonius who observes Hamlet and Gertrude, for example, learns nothing of significance, least of all where "truth is hid, though it were hid indeede / Within the Center" (7.1089-90); like Rosencrantz and Guildenstern, he cannot pluck out the heart of Hamlet's mystery, if mystery and truth are in fact so located. Polonius is, of course, something of a blunderer, and Rosencrantz and Guildenstern are no match for Hamlet's verbal dexterity. Yet the incompetence of the spies cannot explain the failure of an activity that remains, despite its ubiquity, an epistemological impossibility. For if the truth of the appearance of things cannot be circumvented, as Claudius acknowledges in the prayer scene, neither can things be excavated for their hidden interiority, as Hamlet unwittingly attests to in the same scene. "Inner" and "outer," private and public, are not structurally discontinuous, but only temporarily out of joint. There is, therefore, no possibility of keeping a secret, at least permanently, nor any possibility of discerning a secret, at least prematurely. Hence, the futility, the epistemological impossibility, of spying.

Yet if inner and outer are not structurally discontinuous, there remains an apparent discontinuity within Hamlet himself, a much noted caesura between the figure who is deported and the figure who returns. And it is a discontinuity that troubles, precisely because it lacks obvious psychological motivation or explanation. Rather than "the maturation or development of 'character' that we have been taught to look for in Shakespeare," Barker argues, "there is a quasi-Brechtian discretion" between the pre- and post-England Hamlets (39). And so there is, which is precisely the point. For the "discretion" is not a deficiency in the play's design or execution, but the necessary consequence of transformation that is itself the displacement of "character," at least in the sense of privatized self-possession, from its sovereign position. Because the critical preoccupation with the development of ethos, with the continuity of the self in and through time, betrays a Shakespeare already thoroughly textualized, already fully assimilated to the novelistic, it cannot explain a "discretion" that is itself the assimilation of ethos to praxis:

> there's a speciall prouidence in the fall of a Sparrowe, if
> it be now, tis not to come, if it be not to come, it will be
> now, if it be not now, yet it well come, the readines is
> all, since no man ha's ought of what he leaues, what ist to
> leaue betimes. (19.3433-38)

The unwittingly oxymoronic declarations of the earlier Hamlet — the public insistence on a secret singularity, the self-dramatizing refusal of the dramatic — become the fully conscious paradox of a willed abandonment of the volitional. Character remains an operable category, but henceforth it knows or manifests itself only through praxis, the action to which it consents but does not originate. The axis of individualization, as Hamlet learns from a riddling grave digger, is genealogical, and it implies structural determination, indeed providential determination, by birth, role, plot: "our last king Hamlet o'recame Fortenbrasse" on "the very day that young Hamlet was borne" (18.3112, 3115). One discontinuity, in a sense, resolves another, for if there are now two Hamlets, the Hamlet who is deported and the Hamlet who returns, there is no longer an implicitly novelistic subject, self-defined in opposition to the dramatic, and a properly dramatic imperative to action.

But what Hamlet means by "to come" in the most immediate sense — and to this too he consents, although his heart misgives — is the duel with Laertes. Claudius carefully scripts and stage manages the spectacle, and Hamlet obligingly plays his part. An earlier Hamlet might have attempted to discern hidden stratagems, to plummet hidden depths. Now, however, he plays his part, despite forebodings, in a script of unknown outcome. Or an earlier Hamlet might have attempted to revise the script, to recast, say, *The Murder of Gonzago* as "The Mousetrap." Now, however, he consents to Claudius's plot, to the player king's deadly earnest player duel. Between the two there is again the transformation that is the trip to England, which is also the last of Hamlet's explicitly textual revisions or interventions:

> Being thus benetted round with villainies,
> Or I could make a prologue to my braines,
> They had begunne the play, I sat me downe,
> Deuisd a new commission, wrote it faire,
> I once did hold it as our statists doe,
> A baseness to write faire, and labourd much
> How to forget that learning, but sir now
> It did me yemans seruice. (19.3297-3304)

Hamlet's revisions to Claudius's letter, this not altogether earnest attempt to "forget that learning," recall his initial response to the ghost, the not altogether successful attempt to "wipe away all triuall fond records, / Alle sawes of bookes." Here, however, Hamlet's relation to the textual is explicitly theatrical or performative, not opposed to it, and the text is signed in the name of the father, not the unique self. That is, Hamlet seals the letter that sends Rosencrantz and Guildenstern to their death, a text that is effectively a script, with his father's signet, the possession of which he experiences as providential. The assimilation of ethos to praxis is also the assimilation of words to deeds, texts to performance, the unique self to the patronymic son. What remains for Hamlet is only to consent to what is "to come," the duel with Laertes.

Claudius assures Laertes that Hamlet, who is "Most generous, and free from all contriuing" (17.2912), will not scrutinize the foils. And while this is manifestly not the Hamlet who stages "The Mousetrap," there is a sense in which Claudius is right: Hamlet does not examine the foils because he has abandoned the futile attempt to discern hidden stratagems, to excavate secret depths. And what Hamlet no longer seeks to accomplish or discern by virtue of his own volition, the play accomplishes in and of itself: in the duel in which Hamlet is characterized as "fat" (and I insist that here "fat" means fat),[9] as body rather than consciousness, meaning itself becomes exogenous. The king of shreds and patches stages his most explicitly theatrical event, only to find that the theatrical, which had hitherto sustained him, now betrays him. All plotters are hoist on their own petards, and all the hidden stratagems are revealed in the common light of day. The corpses that litter the stage at the close of *Hamlet* are bodies that have given themselves up "in euidence," as evidence, as a vindication of the truth of theatrical appearances.

Now only one body litters — or, better, graces — the stage at the end of *Phèdre*: Phèdre's own. And death comes to her with the lyric gentleness that she requests from it: "J'ai voulu ... / Par un chemin plus lent descendre chez les morts" (5.7). The body that might have littered the stage, Hippolyte's "corps défiguré" (5.6), appears only in the form of Théramène's *récit*:

> L'intrépide Hippolyte
> Voit voler en éclats tout son char fracassé;
> Dans les rênes lui-même il tombe embarrassé.
> Excusez ma douleur. Cette image cruelle
> Sera pour moi de pleurs une source éternelle.
> J'ai vu, Seigneur, j'ai vu votre malheureux fils
> Traîné par les chevaux que sa main a nourris.
> Il veut les rappeler, et sa voix les effraie;
> Ils courent. Tout son corps n'est bientôt qu'une plaie. (5.6)

The *bienséances* that relegate the body *in extremis*, be it extreme suffering or passion, to this discursivity are clearly non-Shakespearean. Nothing, in fact, more immediately signals the distance from Shakespeare, let alone the spectacular physicality of late Jacobean drama, than the decorums that govern the disposition of the body on the French neoclassical stage. "Cette image cruelle" will be a perpetual source of tears for the Théramène who witnesses Hippolyte's death, and "la sanglante image" (5.7) will forever haunt the Thésée who is responsible for his death. There is a sense, however, in which *Phèdre* itself eludes "la sanglante image," precisely by rendering it discursively.

Phèdre guards itself, then, against the possibility of a monstrous showing, very much in the manner specified by Aristotle:

> Now it is possible for the fearful or pathetic effect to come from the actors' appearance, but it is also possible for it to arise from the very structure of the events, and this is closer to the mark and characteristic of a better poet. Namely, the plot must be so structured, even without benefit of any visual effect, that the one who is hearing the events unroll shudders with fear and feels pity at what happens: which is what one would experience on hearing the plot of *Oedipus*. To set out to achieve this by means of the masks and costumes is less artistic, and requires technical support in the staging. As for those who do not set out to achieve the fearful through masks and costumes, but only the monstrous, they have nothing to do with tragedy at all. (1453b, 1-12)

For Aristotle, any direct recourse to *opsis* or spectacle on the level of content is the mark of an inferior poet: the more immediate the presentation of the fearful or the pathetic, the more "monstrous" the result. The *opsis* that Aristotle bans on the level of content, however, he celebrates as the essence of form: elsewhere in the *Poetics*, he compares a beautiful plot to a "single complete creature" (or as some translations have it, "the picture of a living creature," as Aristotle's term, *zoion*, can mean either a "unified living creature" or a creature's "inorganic structure") that is neither tiny nor huge but is of a size that "can be taken in a single view" (1451a, 5).[10] Aristotle subjects the excessively small to the same censure as the excessively large, but it is clearly the latter, the spatially uncontained, that he experiences as the most urgent of aesthetic threats. It is because of its relative brevity, for example, that tragedy is judged superior to epic: "For the more concentrated is more pleasurable than what is diluted with a great deal of time" (1462b, 3). Drama is not to participate in what Goethe calls the expansiveness of the novel, which, in Aristotle's terms, could only be the mark of its epic rather than dramatic inheritance. The *Poetics* does entertain the possibility of recasting the dramatic in the epic mode — Aristotle speculates on the effect of rewriting *Oedipus* "in as many verses as the *Iliad*" (1462b, 4) — but only as if the absurdity of the idea were self-evident. There is a sense, however, in which Aristotle's own example suggests otherwise.

For there is a curious blindness in Aristotle's celebration of *Oedipus* as the type of "beautiful plot" or "concentrated effect," a blindness to the obvious fact that the play itself is finally about the "breakup of relations that are too closely established," too concentrated (Fry 43).[11] The play may indeed be "of a size to be taken in by the eye," as Aristotle maintains, but the "concentrated effect" also literally costs Oedipus his *kukloi* or (eye) balls, as Aristotle fails to note. Or *Oedipus* may achieve its formal perfection, as Aristotle maintains, by virtue of its conflation of recognition and reversal, which bends sequence back upon itself. The transformation of the linear into the cotemporal, however, which bends the sequence of generations back upon itself, is precisely the source of Oedipus's tragedy, and this, too, Aristotle fails to note. There is a sense, then, in which Aristotle's celebration of form as *opsis* or the spatially contained, which necessarily involves an emphasis on likenesses and affinities, on the praise of the craftsman who has an 'eye for resemblances,' paradoxically tends to "ensure the coming to light of just the sort of unruliness that the observance of proportion is meant to suppress" (Fry 12). Certainly if *Oedipus* were less concentrated, less easily "taken in by the eye," its tragic content could not be so easily conflated with its formal perfection. And what is true of the Aristotelian celebration of form in relation to Sophocles's *Oedipus* is no less true of the neoclassical "règles du poème dramatique" in relation to *Phèdre*. Seventeenth-century French dramatists tended to speak of *la tragédie*, not *le tragique* (a distinction not fully operable in English): tragedy was primarily a matter of form, of a certain elevation of style and characterization, rather than any essence of "tragicalness." There is a sense, however, in which *Phèdre* effaces the distinction between the two. I have argued that *Hamlet* seeks to guard itself against any conflation of being and interiority, despite the fact that the novel, which fully realizes the conflation, claims Hamlet for its own. *Phèdre*, I now want to argue, seeks to guard itself against the threat of a monstrous showing, a monstrous imbrication of form and content (to repeat the familiar example: any direct presentation of Hippolyte's defeat by the dragon-monster of Neptune would itself be monstrous). It succeeds, however, only in identifying its own generic dispensation, its own formal self, as the monstrous.

"Le dessein en est pris," Hippolyte declares in the opening line of *Phèdre*, "je pars, cher Théramène, / Et quitte le séjour de l'aimable Trézène" (1.1). But Hippolyte does not depart. "Madame, avant que de partir, / J'ai cru de votre sort vous devoir avertir" (2.2), Hippolyte tells Aricie after learning of his father's supposed death. And still he lingers. "Théramène, fuyons" (2.6) he enjoins his friend after learning of Phèdre's illicit love. And still he remains. Each of these aborted departures is, of course, open to a psychological reading, and each responds to a specific contingency of plot. All are equally open, however, to the identical formal explanation. For as the first word of the first line of the play suggests, the "dessein" is already fully in place, and "le dessin," in its explicitly aesthetic sense (up until the end of the eighteenth century, *dessein* included the meanings that modern usage specifies in *dessein* and *dessin*)[12] involves the unity of place, which by definition prohibits any Hamlet-like departure for distant shores. Trézène is in fact a prison, much more so than Claudius's Denmark, and there is no exit. Thésée is temporarily absent and presumed dead, but, like the ghost of old Hamlet, he returns, although with disastrous consequences. Hippolyte, like Hamlet, is exiled, but he travels no further than the periphery of Trézène. The exile is his second, and it is telling that it is inefficacious. For if once Phèdre enjoyed a respite from the burden of Hippolyte's presence — she is the agent of his original exile, which, like his death, enters the play only as narrative, not event — *Phèdre* itself admits of no egress from the burden of physical proximity.

No egress from proximity, yet no possibility of physical contact, for if the unity of place begets the former, *les bienséances* prohibit the latter:

Voilà mon coeur. C'est là que ta main doit frapper.
Impatient déjà d'expier son offense,
Au-devant de ton bras je le sens qui s'avance.
Frappe. O si tu le crois indigne de tes coups,
Si ta haine m'envie un supplice si doux,
Ou si d'un sang trop vil ta main serait trempée
Au défaut de ton bras prête-moi ton épée.
Donne. (2.5)

Nowhere is the prohibition against men and women touching each other on stage more palpable than here, in the threat of its violation: in lieu of the hand that Hippolyte withholds, Phèdre grasps the sword that she hopes will become the instrument of her death. The dramaturgical restrictions that govern Racine's stage are fully operable, and they serve him well. In Seneca, for example, who labours under no such restrictions, the encounter degenerates into farce: Phèdre more or less assaults Hippolyte, who demands she remove her wanton hands from his chaste body. In Racine, however, hands never quite touch the body, although the sense of a taboo nearly violated, contact nearly made, accounts for the intense erotic energy of the scene. But the question remains: precisely what taboo? The prohibition against incest, and thus a psycho-sexual taboo? Or the prohibition against touching on stage, and thus a theatrical taboo?

For there is a sense in which the one is homologous with, if not indistinguishable from, the other: both the incest taboo and the neoclassical stage involve a relation of physical proximity and physical prohibition, a nearness that begets desire and a restraint that demands distance. In his Preface to the play, Racine is at pains to assure his "lecteurs" that "les passions n'y sont présentées aux yeux que pour *montrer* tout le désordre dont elles sont cause" (my italics). His purposes are overtly didactic and they presuppose the most rigid of demarcations: the "désordre" that is "shown" on the level of content is not to be confused with the ethical status and efficacy of dramatic showing. It is difficult to separate, however, the "désordre" that the play dramatizes, the tension between Phèdre's desire and her moral restraint, from the conventions that govern dramatization itself. The play's primary figure for "désordre" is the word that appears some eighteen times in the text, *le monstre*. And it is, of course, only the word that does appear, for if Racine is to avoid "monstrous spectacles," a monstrous imbrication of content and form, actual monsters (there is in fact only one) can appear only in the form of *un récit*. But, as with the "désordre" that is the threat of incest or incestuous desire, which tends to blur the distinction between form and content, the monstrous is perhaps best considered, not only as a primary figure in the play, but as a primary figure for the play, the demonic counterpart to Aristotle's "beautiful plot" or "well-proportioned beast." The word *le monstre* is etymologically related to *montrer* — *le monstre* once meant, among other things, a spectacle or representation[13] — and what is finally monstrous about *Phèdre* is the play's own signifying medium, theatrical accessibility itself.

The etymological connection that binds *le monstre* to *montrer*, the monstrous to visuality or visibility, implicitly informs Thésée's response to his son's supposed transgression — for Thésée, Hippolyte is precisely the *monstre qui se montre*: "Perfide, oses-tu bien te *montrer* devant moi? / *Monstre*, qu'a trop longtemps épargné le tonnerre, / Reste impur des brigands dont j'ai purgé la terre" (4.2; my italics). Thésée spends his life purging the world of monsters only to see in his son one more figure of the monstrous. Or, better, Thésée sees in his son's willingness to be seen, to show himself, the very essence of the monstrous. He thus banishes him from his sight, and calls down upon him the monstrous death that will overtake him at the periphery of the play's geographical locale. The hitherto absent father, the monster killer, and the newly exiled son, who will be killed by a monster, exchange positions in the play's radically confined and confining structure of representation. Exchange positions, in fact, twice, for the Thésée who returns only to banish his son, ultimately calls down upon himself an analogous fate. And what Thésée found most monstrous in Hippolyte, his willingness to be seen or show himself, becomes for Thésée the punishment of being seen:

> De l'univers entier je voudrais me bannir.
> Tout semble s'élever contre mon injustice.
> L'éclat de mon nom même augmente mon supplice.
> Moins connu des mortels, je me cacherais mieux. (5.7)

Thésée's punishment is that he will be forever "taken in by the eye": even as he leaves the stage proper, he acknowledges that, henceforth, all the universe will be witness to his injustice.

Prior to taking the stage, however, prior to his return to Trézène, all the universe bore witness to his heroism, to what Hippolyte terms "ses nobles exploits" (1.1):

> Ne pourrai-je, en fuyant un indigne repos,
> D'un sang plus glorieux teindre mes javelots?
> Vous n'aviez pas encore atteint l'âge où je touche,
> Déjà plus d'un tyran, plus d'un monstre farouche
> Avait de votre bras senti la pesanteur;
> Déjà, de l'insolence heureux persécuteur,
> Vous aviez des deux mers assuré les rivages. (3.5)

Hippolyte is here suing for Thésée's permission to quit Trézène, albeit for reasons, among which is Phèdre's confession of love, that he fails to acknowledge. Yet, if one were to take Hippolyte at his word — "Souffrez," he enjoins his father, "si quelque monstre a pu vous échapper, / Que j'apport à vos pieds sa dépouille honorable" (3.5) — there is a sense in which the world no longer affords opportunities for "noble exploits." For Hippolyte, one noble deed, the slaying of even one monster, might excuse all: "Dans mes lâches soupirs d'autant plus méprisable, / Qu'un long amas d'honneurs rend Thésée excusable, / Qu'aucuns monstres par moi domptés jusqu'aujourd'hui / Ne m'ont acquis le droit de faillir comme lui" (1.1). But unlike Thésée's multiple "failings," his wildly profligate life, Hippolyte's single "failing," his forbidden love for Aricie, lacks the justification of an otherwise heroic existence. There is a sense, then, in which the passage from the father, whose fame is "ses nobles exploits," to the son, who is known for what Aricie calls "un courage inflexible" (2.1), is also the exhaustion of a certain form of heroism.

Hippolyte cannot emulate his father's noble deeds, and Racine cannot present them directly: indeed, all praxis or action tends to gain access to Racine's stage only in the form of a "récit de ses nobles exploits," as Hippolyte terms Théramène's stories of his father. Or if action there must be, it is delegated to the servant class, to, say, an Oenone, who, in her effort to protect Phèdre, brings the false accusation against Hippolyte. Racine explains this departure from the source — in Euripides's *Hippolytos*, Phèdre herself makes the accusation — in terms that conflate the ethical and the social:

> J'ai même pris soin de la rendre un peu moins odieuse qu'elle n'est dans les tragédies des Anciens, où elle se résout d'elle-même à accuser Hippolyte. J'ai cru que la calomnie avait quelque chose de trop bas et de trop noir pour la mettre dans la bouche d'une princesse.

But what seems truly incompatible with Phèdre's sublimity is any vulgar jockeying for practical advantage (Auerbach 384), any commitment to the life of action, which, as in Yeats, is best left to servants. And it is here that Racine is both deeply faithful to and deeply in conflict with "les tragédies des Anciens," at least as explicated by Aristotle. Faithful, because for Aristotle "role," be it construed in social or dramatic terms, enjoys priority over "character," and for Racine, the role of Princess, the status of Princess, is itself a full explanation of motives. But also in conflict with "les tragédies des Anciens," because the praxis that is for Aristotle the heart of any plot, the plot that is the heart of any tragedy, becomes in Racine so much getting and doing, an impurity that is to be admitted only as narrative or undertaken only by servants. Both in *Phèdre* and for *Phèdre* the life of heroic action, the histrionics of the noble deed, belong to a not very distant past: the heroes of Racine's older rival, Corneille, like Racine's own Thésée prior to his entry onto the stage, have the universe for their witness in a positive sense, and whatever sacrifice their theatrical visibility entails, it is more than compensated for by the admiring glance that the world returns to them.[14] But not so in *Phèdre*. The Thésée who was once an heroic cynosure quits the stage with the knowledge that henceforth his visibility, his theatrical accessibility, will be the condition of his punishment.

Thésée quits the stage, that is, as Phèdre enters it:

> Que ces vains ornements, que ces voiles me pèsent!
> Quelle importune main, en formant tous ces noeuds,
> À pris soin sur mon front d'assembler mes cheveux?
> Tout m'afflige et me nuit, et conspire à me nuire. (1.3)

This is Phèdre's second sustained utterance in the play, and like Hamlet's polemic against "incky cloaks" and the like, it too is metatheatrical, concerned with the external and explicitly theatrical paraphernalia of identity. Like Hamlet, moreover, Phèdre only reluctantly acquiesces to this paraphernalia, the "voiles" that are the condition of her access to theatrical representation, which, as Oenone complains, she both seeks and eschews:

> Vous-même, rappelant votre force première,
> Vous vouliez vous montrer et revoir la lumière.
> Vous la voyez, Madame, et prête à vous cacher,
> Vous haissez le jour que vous veniez chercher? (1.3)

Phèdre's oscillation between the desire to reveal and conceal herself is ultimately irrelevant, for *Phèdre*, no less than *Hamlet*, admits of no secrets, no hidden interiority. As Hippolyte says, "Le dessein est en pris," and "le dessein" provides no egress from theatrical accessibility. Or as Phèdre might have said, "les noeuds" are ineluctable (*le noeud* is a familiar seventeenth-century term for a complication of plot), and *les noeuds* provide no secret spaces, psychic or social. Hippolyte will imagine "un plus noble dessein" (5.1), marriage with Aricie, and Phèdre will place Hippolyte in her own "dessein" (2.5), the descent into the labyrinth. Phèdre's plan is very much a search for a secret or private place — she proposes to descend with Hippolyte and without her sister's guiding thread, and hence with virtually no possibility of returning — but it succeeds only in exposing her as a "monstre" (2.5) in Hippolyte's eyes. Oenone intervenes to protect Phèdre from a generalized exposure — "Évitez des témoins odieux; / Venez, rentrez, fuyez une honte certaine" (2.5) — but by definition "une honte certaine" cannot be escaped. Phèdre's most characteristic question is "Où me cacher?" but as she herself acknowledges, "tout l'univers est plein de mes aieux" (4.6), which means that the only possible response is nowhere. Indeed, even before she takes the stage, her body, "atteinte d'un mal qu'elle s'obstine à taire" (1.1), bears witness to what Racine's Preface calls "la seule pensée du crime," to an interiority already effectively exposed. Or as Claudius might put it, Phèdre's body is already given up "in eudience," as evidence. For in *Phèdre*, all the universe seems to exist only to observe, and in observing, condemn. There is a sense, however, in which Claudius's term cannot be applied to *Phedre*, for there is a sense in which there are no bodies on Racine's stage, or at least no bodies in possession of specificity or density. Phèdre is no doubt beautiful, but in the manner of what Barthes calls "une bienséance, un trait de class, non une disposition anatomique" (24). Certainly no "fat" or "sweaty" princes grace Racine's stage, although his characters do tend to betray a vestigial physicality: they blush. "Ah! s'il vous faut rougir," Oenone entreats Phèdre, "rougissez d'un silence / Qui de vos maux encore aigrit la violence" (1.3). But as Phèdre well knows, the body has already spoken what the mouth would repress: "la rougeur me couvre le visage: / Je te laisse trop voir mes honteuses douleurs, / Et mes yeux, malgré moi, se remplissent de pleurs" (1.3). And as Phèdre's body in relation to her love for Hippolyte, so Hippolyte's body in relation to his love for Aricie: "Le nom d'amant peut-être offense son courage," Ismène assures Aricie, "Mais il en a les yeux, s'il n'en a le langage" (2.1). In the most Hamlet-like of moments, Thésée bemoans the fact that in Trézène one can smile and smile and be a villain: "Et ne devrait-on pas à des signes certains / Reconnaître le coeur des perfides humains?" (4.2). But the signs are only too "certains," Thésée's obtuseness notwithstanding, and among them is to be counted the utter legibility of the body (a legibility that tends, in fact, to displace the specifically physical, to make of the body a pure sign). It is, then, thoroughly appropriate that the temple of the god who is fatal to perjurers and dissemblers should stand at the periphery of Trézène: *Phèdre* is itself proof against dissembling.

Proof against dissembling, however, not because "la seule pensée du crime y est regardée avec autant d'horreur que le crime même," as Racine's Preface would have it, but because "la seule pensée" simply as *pensée* is the very essence of "le crime," of guilt:

Dans *Phèdre*, les choses ne sont pas cachées parce qu'elles sont coupables (ce serait là une vue prosaïque, celle d'Oenone, par example, pour qui la faute de Phèdre n'est que contingente, liée à la vie de Thésée); les choses sont coupables du moment même où elles sont cachées.... La culpabilité objective de Phèdre (l'adultère, l'inceste) est en somme une construction postiche, destinée à naturaliser la souffrance du secret, à transformer utilement la forme en contenu... L'homme souffre d'une forme. C'est ce que Racine exprime très bien à propos de Phèdre, quand il dit que pour elle le crime même est une punition. Tout l'effort de Phèdre consiste à *remplir* sa faute. (Barthes 122)

For Barthes, "la seule pensée du crime" is culpable, not because of the specific nature of the crime it contemplates, "l'adultère, l'inceste," but because it betrays an interiority that is already and always guilty. The point is well taken, although the rather Dantean remark that Barthes ascribes to Racine, "pour elle [Phèdre] le crime même est une punition," is not exactly Racine's. The final line of the first paragraph of the Preface, which is where Barthes's note sends us, reads "son crime est plutôt une punition des Dieux qu'un mouvement de sa volonté," which is not quite the same thing as the punishment is the crime. Or perhaps Barthes has in mind the passage quoted above, "la seule pensée du crime y est regardée avec autant d'horreur que le crime même," although this, too, is not quite the same thing. Clearly, the Preface worries the relation between "le crime même" and "la seule pensée du crime," praxis and ethos, although its precise nature seems uncertain, both within the Preface itself and between the Preface and play. A crime that is "plutôt une punition des Dieux qu'un mouvement de sa volonté," for example, is a destiny, not a psychology, although if the mere idea of a crime is to be regarded with the same horror as the crime itself, destiny must be bound to psychology. "Le crime même," moreover, proves to be only "une déclaration d'amour," which is hardly praxis in any Aristotelian sense of the term, and even this is a contingent transgression ("liée à la vie de Thésée"), at best tangentially related to ethos. The sublimity of the declaration is, of course, one of the great pleasures of *Phèdre* — Barthes is certainly right in arguing that the play is now received as an ensemble of discrete *tirades* (135), much as *Hamlet* has become a backdrop for the great soliloquies — there is a sense in which it is strictly redundant. For *Phèdre* is best characterized not as a play in which "la seule pensée du crime y est regardée avec autant d'horreur que le crime même," but as a play in which "la seule pensée" is already and always seen. "Importune," Phèdre pleads with Oenone, "peux-tu souhaiter qu'on me voie?" (3.1), but Phèdre has no resources other than to fulfill her transgression, which is to proclaim it, to make it be seen. Barthes is quite right in arguing that *Phèdre* proposes "une identification de l'intériorité à la culpabilité" (122). The very interiority that the play judges culpable, however, it also disallows. Phèdre is condemned for what she does not possess.

"O god Horatio," Hamlet speculates in his dying moments, "what a wounded name / Things standing thvs vnknowne, shall liue behind me?" (19.3565-66). And what in fact does "liue behind" or beyond Hamlet, the discourse of the secret singularity, the culture of the book, is nothing that *Hamlet*, or finally even Hamlet, would acknowledge as its or his own. But there is a sense in which nothing lives beyond or is generated by *Phèdre*, at least not for Racine as a secular dramatist: the rest, as Hamlet says, is silence. There is much to regret in

Racine's silence, and no dearth of explanations for it. The most obvious of these — Racine was granted the post of historiographer royal — may well be the most compelling. Certainly, explanations that impute explicitly aesthetic anxieties or motives to Racine, the most relentlessly careerist of men, seem somehow naive, although it is a naivete that I intend to risk. For, to the extent that the neoclassical aesthetic labours to render representation rigorously adequate to its content, *Phèdre* can hardly be celebrated as the supreme accomplishment of the neoclassical stage. Far from ideally adequating the one with the other, *Phèdre* is a tragedy of form, of genre. For Barthes, this means that "la culpabilité objective de Phèdre ... est en somme une construction postiche, destinée à naturaliser la souffrance du secret, à transformer utilement la forme en contenu." A play that relentlessly transforms form into content, the better to naturalize "la souffrance du secret," may, however, also be a play in which content is in search of a different form, a different generic dispensation. The silence that follows *Phèdre* may, then, be said to await or beckon all that *Hamlet* resists, the discourse and culture of the secret singularity.

RICHARD A. YOUNG

Narrative and Theatre: From Manuel Puig to Lope de Vega

Notwithstanding the deference due Diego de Velázquez and Miguel de Cervantes, it could be readily conceded to the Postmodernists of our day that art has become less about life than about the way in which art represents it. Or, if you prefer, given Postmodernism's proclivity for leaving all possibilities open, the way in which life represents art. Such a conclusion might be argued in light of recent developments in any of the contemporary arts — music, dance, painting, and architecture, for example — but a particularly strong case can be made through certain narrative forms, both verbal and visual, theatre, fiction, film, and (why not?) television, too, perhaps because their diffusion to a mass audience has required conformity to the single most important rule of consumerism and the style it has engendered, namely that the marriage of illusion and reality should not only never be sundered, but include a built-in set of fully illustrated instructions showing how the union is created and sustained.

If meta-theatre and meta-fiction, born anew in recent decades, are among the products of Postmodernism at its most introspective, they have, however, provided ample opportunity for writers to explore the hinterlands of the genres in which they write and for critics to re-examine the traditional forms of literature and their limitations. This activity, however, rather than clarifying our understanding of the differences among the three literary genres, has only muddied the waters further by showing the extent to which differences are frequently transcended. The Aristotelian principle for separating the genres, based on the means of delivery rather than on the character of discourse, is as attractive a criterion as ever, with relatively sound foundations on which to establish a reasonable taxonomy. However, it leaves the critic primarily concerned with the text, the structure of discourse and its contents, in a vulnerable position, made all the more precarious by advances in the semiotics of theatre.[1] This is the case for approaches to texts, such as that adopted here, founded essentially on the rhetorical dimensions of narratology, developed in the light of the formalist and structuralist views of literature by, among others, Gérard Genette, Mieke Bal, and Susan Lanser.

Definitions of the genres founded on the character of the text, based, for example, on the implied rules governing production and consumption, or the particular function of language most emphasized, are fraught with difficulties. With its divisions into acts and scenes, stage directions, predominance of character discourse, and attribution of discourse to speakers, the appearance of the dramatic text conforms to a fairly rigid code that is readily recognizable as such as soon as the reader takes up the book. Experience shows, however, that the predominance of dialogue alone is insufficient to classify a text as a work of theatre. Theatre requires a certain type of dialogue for the advancement of plot and the creation of character, but it is not the only genre to make extensive use of the discourse of figures who populate the world presented through the text. Dialogue may be used just as extensively in the epic, taking this term to refer to both the classical form and its modern descendant. In certain cases, such as the dialogue novel, the reader may experience initial hesitation about the genre to which a work belongs, and, in particular instances, such as Fernando de Rojas's *Tragicomedia de Calisto y Melibea* (1499), more commonly known as *La Celestina*, the use of dialogue is one among several factors that have provoked a protracted discussion about how the work should be classified. Neither the epic nor the drama reserves a particular function of language to itself (Jakobson 209-48), and neither may be separated based on criteria derived from the presence or absence of a narrative voice. Although the dramatic text may be thought of as lacking a primary narrator, this function may be implicitly subsumed by stage directions, which are conveyed in performance through means other than discourse, while, even in performance, narration may fall to the figures presented, as in the classical chorus and its more modern counterparts, or those characters who exercise a kind of intradiegetic narrative role within the drama and narrate part of the story in which they are involved. The differences between text and performance, as well as the potential for narrative in both, are no better illustrated than in the work of the modern Spanish dramatist Antonio Buero Vallejo (1916-). In his *La doble historia del Dr. Valmy* (1976), part of the work is a narrative provided by the principal character's dictation to his secretary, while in *El sueño de la razón* (1970), the representation of the last years spent in Spain by the painter Francisco de Goya requires a particular kind of stage direction and elements of dialogue in the text that disappear in performance, to be replaced by dumbshow, in order to convey a situation presented from the perspective of the deaf painter.

In contrast to the drama and the epic, the lyric, with its emphasis on the expressive function of language, of which the exploitation of tropes is a primary manifestation, would appear to be a separate category. However, the lyric is unable to present any claim to exclusivity in this regard. The figurative qualities of language may be exploited just as readily by the epic or the drama, and the characteristics of the lyric may be adopted by either in their entirety when verse is used as the medium of expression. The trope, in effect, like the story, is just one of the ways in which literature is able to organize and convey its contents. In general terms, the lyric may be distinguished by the emphasis placed on the use of tropes, at the same time as the importance of a diegetic content is reduced, but, as in the case of the drama and the epic, with the predominance of character discourse in the former and narrator discourse in the latter, it is all a matter of emphasis, subject to adjustment by any author in any particular work.

If there is one conclusion to be drawn from the preceding comments, it is that the classification of literature in accordance with the traditional genres is not a simple matter. Whatever criteria are likely to be proposed, they are just as likely to be undermined by transgressions and to be "more honour'd in the breach than the observance." Thus, for the purposes of a discussion of literature oriented towards the kind of discourse exploited by the text, rather than adhering to the concept of genres in the traditional sense, including the innumerable sub-genres into which each may be divided, it seems more appropriate to think in terms of modes or conventions, narrative or dialogic, for example, that transcend the restrictions of genre and manifest themselves in any kind of literary text. This is not to say that all efforts towards a suitable taxonomy based on other criteria should be abandoned, but to imply that a view from the perspective of discourse may be productive in other ways, including contributing to an understanding of the nature of transgression among the genres. It is, after all, the practice of exploiting the modes or conventions of discourse in varying forms that has partly led to the hybrids, the novels that have the textual configurations of theatre or the dramas that exploit narrative as their underlying principle.

To take a case in point, among the characteristics of the Spanish American novel from about the middle of this century is a degree of self-consciousness, entirely compatible with the fashion of Postmodernism, evident in the manner in which, by exploring the scope of narrative, the text is also a reflection of the nature of narrative itself. In the work of the Argentinean writer Manuel Puig (1932-1990), this pattern emerges in a tendency to establish the autonomy of the narrated world by eliminating the basic narrative voice. The quest for autonomy, at least in the Hispanic tradition, is as old as Cervantes, but in Puig's case it is also the likely consequence of an intensification of this tendency in the evolution of the novel between the nineteenth and twentieth centuries where the liberation of narration from the author continues along a logical trajectory that leads to the liberation of the character from the narrator. In one of Puig's earlier works, *La traición de Rita Hayworth* (1968), the effect is achieved through the extended use of character discourse in a variety of forms, none of which is subordinated to a primary voice. Thus, the novel is a composite of different kinds of character discourse, including interior monologue, fragments from a diary, one side of a telephone conversation, and conversations among several characters conveyed without the mediation of a narrator to identify the speakers or comment on what they are saying. In later novels, *El beso de la mujer araña* (1976) and *Maldición eterna a quien lea estas páginas* (1980), in particular, the use of dialogue is extended much further.

El beso de la mujer araña is set in Buenos Aires in 1975 and centres on the relation between two men confined to the same prison cell: Luis Alberto Molina, a homosexual, sentenced to eight years for corruption of a minor, and Valentín Arregui Paz, who is awaiting trial for involvement in guerrilla activities. Although the unmediated dialogue that takes place between the two prisoners in their cell, occupying eleven of the book's sixteen chapters, as well as significant parts of two others, is the core of the work, it is not the only form of discourse contained in the text: three conversations between the prison director and Molina, who has been placed with Valentín in order to obtain information from him about the guerrilla movement, are conveyed in mediated dialogue and have the same format as a conventional theatre script; there is a transcription of one side of the director's telephone conversation with his superiors; there are copies of official records of the two prisoners and of the police report on Molina after his release from prison; and there are a number of footnotes throughout the text that focus principally on the history of scientific and pseudo-scientific enquiry into the origin and nature of homosexuality.

The amount of dialogue in *El beso de la mujer araña* is sufficient to explain the facility with which the work could be dramatised for the stage and subsequently become a successful Hollywood movie, although the producers of the latter may well have been equally impressed by the importance of film itself to the content of the story through the interaction between life and film that is maintained. If, as appears to be the case, the story is now re-cast as a musical, the sequence of metamorphoses from one genre to another will not only be complete, but will provide the possibility, along with any number of other comparisons, for a study of the different kinds of discourse required by each form of presentation. In Aristotelian terms, the stage and the film versions of *El beso de la mujer araña* undoubtedly belong to the dramatic genre, while any eventual musical would just as assuredly be placed somewhere between the dramatic and the lyric. However, the classification of Puig's original text cannot be undertaken with the same degree of assurance. While the association of the stage, film, and musical versions with the dramatic, and the last of these also with the lyric, is confidently made, even with respect to their texts alone, in view of what is known about their intended means of presentation, no comparable claim may be made for the original text. *El beso de la mujer araña*, in its original version, has many of the characteristics of drama, but was not written to be performed and is beyond the scope of conventional performance. At the same time, there is some doubt about classifying it as epic, particularly if this genre is thought of as synonymous with narrative. Since the minimal conditions for a narrative to be considered as such require the presence of a narrator who tells a story in which he may or may not figure, there must be some doubt about the status of *El beso de la mujer araña* as a narrative text. Certainly, a story is told, but it is not possible to be so sure about the presence of a narrator.

To begin with, it should be noted that one of the effects of the Aristotelian principle for the determination of genres is that the source of determination is not necessarily found entirely within the text itself, but may be derived from the author's intention or the circumstances and format of publication. If an author intends a work to be staged, and a reader is aware of that intention, the step towards classification as drama has already been taken and the work will be consumed as such. In this regard, it is enough for the publisher to adopt the format of publication of a particular genre or to include the word "drama," "narrative," "poem," or a synonym of one of these terms on the title page for the reader to adopt a certain frame of mind and to approach the reading of the text from a particular perspective. In the case of *El beso de la mujer araña*, the evidence is lacking that the book published under that title by Seix Barral in 1976 was ever intended to be performed. There is no list of characters, no *dramatis personae*, no division of the text into acts and scenes, and no tell-tale term on the title page. However, the book is published in Barral's series "Nueva Narrativa Hispánica," and Puig is known to be a writer of fiction. Thus, the die is cast and the reader accepts these as sufficient indication of the intention that the book is to be consumed as a narrative.

The fact that *El beso de la mujer araña* is to be consumed as a narrative raises certain immediate expectations in the reader, who automatically looks for the source of narration, as if to ensure that the minimum conditions for narrative are being met. The absence of a primary narrator, the instance to which the discourse of the two interlocutors, Molina and Valentín, might be subordinated, is evident from the first pages of the text in the use of unmediated dialogue and it is not until midway through Chapter III, some sixty pages later, when the first of the footnotes appears, that it becomes possible to think of a hierarchically superior instance to whom the characters' discourse may be subordinated. In the case of a dramatic text, it is theoretically possible to think of a hierarchy of voices, not unlike that conventionally invoked for narrative: the real author (Lope de Vega, for example), conventionally becomes the implied author (the persona of the individual thought of as the source of a particular work, such as *Fuenteovejuna*), who is, in turn, the one who causes a primary voice to speak his own utterances (the stage directions, scant as they may be, and likely in the case of Lope's plays, to be the work of later editors) or those of the characters whose story is presented. In practice, however, we tend not to think in terms of such a hierarchy for dramatic texts but, as if anticipating the performance, when the characters are realized through the actors, to give a degree of autonomy to the text and not to subordinate the discourse of the characters to a superior instance.[2] This is not the case with conventional narrative texts, whereby, if a given discourse cannot be attributed to the narrator, it should be possible to attribute it to a figure introduced within the narrator's discourse. In the dialogue between Molina and Valentín in *El beso de la mujer araña*, this principle is suspended, so that it is not known who is responsible for making them speak or reporting their speech. It is possible that the reader may have a silent narrator or an implied author in mind, but the presence of the latter is really only felt in the text with the appearance of the first footnotes. Only then, as the text proceeds and other forms of discourse are introduced, does it become more readily possible to bring them all under the auspices of an implied author. The primary narrator, however, remains forever silent, or forever absent.

In the preceding paragraph, when speaking of the principle of sub-ordination of the discourse of a character to that of the narrator, the term "conventional" was intentionally applied to the narrative text in order to suggest that there is a general rule but that other possibilities could also arise. Although the principle still holds for particular narratives, it is equally true that modern narrative texts have trained the reader to contend with structures that are transgressive when viewed from the perspective of the past, but are quite common among practices prevailing in the present. For example, the modern reader is more accustomed to polyphony, to the idea that a narrative text may be composed of a number of particular narratives that are connected by the fact that they all contribute to the telling of the same story, but are unconnected by any principle of subordination that places them under the auspices of a primary narrative voice.[3] In this manner, the polyphonic text may liberate characters from a primary narrator and permit them to speak as narrators in their own right. The narrative text, in order to exist as such, still requires that narration take place and a story be told, but this activity may be fragmented among several instances, and the hierarchy of voices responsible may therefore be shortened by converting the role of the primary narrator into an implied role and having it subsumed by that of the implied author.

The story told in *El beso de la mujer araña*, as has already been mentioned, is not derived from a single voice but is the product of various, independent discourses. However, the greater part of the story, effectively containing a number of different stories, is conveyed through the dialogue of the two prisoners, Valentín and Molina, whose conversation amounts to an act of narration. As narrators, the two characters have a varying role that changes according to what they refer to in their speech. In the first instance, they provide a continuing commentary about themselves and each other that refers to actions, thoughts, and feelings experienced as they speak, from which it is possible to reconstruct the story of their daily life in the cell, both their routine activities and particular incidents of their life together. Thus, they speak of iterative events, such as the distribution of food, the provision of water, and visits to the bathroom, and they also speculate on their future after they have been released. Most attention is given, however, to immediate human needs, with the result that the relationship that evolves between the two men is conveyed principally through their discussion about food, health (physical, emotional, and mental), and the desire for companionship and compassion. Whether or not this all amounts to a narrative in any accepted definition of the word may well be disputed. Nevertheless, a story is certainly told and, what is more, is told through the discourse of Molina and Valentín who should not be thought of as figures created through another's discourse, but as narrators who engage to tell their own tale collectively in what might be considered a simultaneous narration fragmented between two speakers, taking the term simultaneous in this instance to refer to a narration that occurs at the same time as the events narrated.[4] However, whatever doubts may linger about Molina and Valentín as the narrators of their daily life in the prison cell, no such reservations need be felt about their narratives concerning their lives before they were committed to prison, when Valentín talks about his existence as a *guerrillero* and his relation with Inés and Marta, or when Molina narrates the story of his relation with his mother and the waiter Gabriel. In these contexts, the two men acquire in turn the status of primary narrators of particular narratives, so that the figures they introduce, including themselves as characters of their own stories, are subordinated to their own discourse. A similar structure is created through the stories taken from films, six of them in total, all narrated by Molina to amuse himself and Valentín. They not only constitute the longest narrative components of the book but, notwithstanding certain peculiarities,[5] allow one of the characters to emerge as a narrator in the fullest sense of the term.

From the preceding commentary there emerge two principal points. First, regardless of the fact that texts may be structured as dialogues and may therefore lack a primary voice, they have ways of constituting themselves as narratives. No one, for example, would dispute the claim that *El beso de la mujer araña* is a novel, a narrative text, even if part of the claim is derived from the tradition in which it is written, albeit a Modern, not to say Postmodernist, one. Second, characters, taking Puig's novel as a guide, may be considered as narrators in three possible ways according to the subject to which they refer: when, in the absence of a primary narrator, their discourse is the sole source of the story and they, as interlocutors in dialogue, become the tellers of a tale that occurs at the same time as their speech describes it; when they narrate the stories of their own lives; when they narrate stories in which they do not figure themselves. In view of these observations, having concluded that dialogues may be thought of as narratives under certain circumstances, it remains to be seen to what extent dramatic texts, which are traditionally in the form of the dialogue and have no apparent pretensions to narrative, nevertheless have an underlying or implied narrative origin or structure. To undertake such a task, however, seems a particularly daunting proposition that would require a more complete theoretical development than the present context will permit, as well as application to a reasonably representative corpus of texts. Since the purpose of this essay is by no means so grandiose, and is intended to provoke speculation rather than propose complex solutions, it will suffice to look at a particular example, namely the Spanish theatre of the sixteenth and seventeenth centuries, giving special attention to *Fuenteovejuna* (1612-14), one of the best known plays of Lope de Vega.

Evidence pointing to certain types of ecclesiastical and secular performances makes it possible to make a case for the existence of a medieval theatre in Spain. However, it cannot be spoken of as a flourishing cultural activity, with characteristics in common with those of either the classical or modern genre. By any definition of the term, the theatre in Spain was born anew when the effects of the Italian Renaissance were felt most fully in the Iberian Peninsula, at the end of the fifteenth and beginning of the sixteenth centuries. Although it is possible to refer to performances and plays of the middle of the sixteenth century that are theatrical in every sense of the term, it was not until the time of Lope de Vega (1567-1635) that the genre became fully acclimatised. Until then, there persisted a degree of uncertainty, reflected in the subjects that were dramatised and in an element of hesitancy with respect to the notion of performance itself, as if theatre were viewed as a particular kind of narrative mode whose identity it was necessary to assert.

The dual origin of Spanish Renaissance theatre from both ecclesiastical and secular sources, culminating in the *comedia* and *auto sacramental* of the seventeenth century, is revealed in the earlier phases of the development of the genre in the kind of stories enacted. Regardless of their source, the stories are essentially a given. The content of many of the secular plays, in both the comic and tragic veins, was frequently received already cast in dramatic form, thanks to the more advanced state of Italian theatre, while the religious plays, although they may have existed previously as drama, were also known to be dramatizations of well known Biblical stories and were taken from narrative forms. Indeed, the early shepherd plays written and performed to celebrate Christmas, even when liberated from an ecclesiastical context, frequently centred around a narrative rather than a re-enactment of the central event. This is the case of pieces by Juan del Encina (1468?-1530?) and Lucas Fernández (1474?-1542), while even in the work of Gil Vicente (c. 1465-1537?), where a Nativity scene is presented, considerable attention is given to description and exegesis, as may be expected of works having a significant catechetical function.[6]

From the preceding remarks, it may be observed that underlying the stories presented in both the religious and secular theatre of the Spanish Renaissance are pre-existing texts, which, in the case of the religious theatre in particular are frequently in narrative form. This is not to say that the early Spanish theatre is completely lacking in anecdotal originality. The incorporation of innovative secular elements into the religious plays of the authors already mentioned is particularly noteworthy, especially in the case of Gil Vicente, and there is a degree of inventiveness in the plots of entirely secular works, such as those by Bartolomé de Torres Naharro (c.1485-c.1520), whose comedies are nevertheless a product of the Italian or Roman style and its Spanish derivatives, especially that most notable hybrid the *Celestina*.[7] As the theatre evolves in the course of the sixteenth century, becoming a more predominantly secular institution through the work of Lope de Rueda (1509?-65), Juan de la Cueva (1550?-1610), and ultimately, Miguel de Cervantes (1547-1616), its content also acquires a more national character, but frequently retains its connection with an underlying text. Although both Cervantes and Juan de la Cueva also produced dramas on subjects not derived from historical sources, their most memorable works in the genre are historical: the *Numancia* (1580-87) of the former is a dramatisation of the resistance to Roman conquest, and the latter's *Los siete infantes de Lara* (1579) is derived from narratives set in the time of the Christian Reconquest of Moslem Spain found in popular ballads and the medieval chronicles. In fact, the kinds of existing narrative texts used in Juan de la Cueva's historical drama established a model assiduously exploited by Lope de Vega, whose plunder of the *romanceros* and the *crónicas* is apparent both in the plots of his many historical plays and in the occasional direct borrowing of lines from a narrative poem. The facility with which the *romanceros* could be quoted is partly the consequence of the polymetric quality of the Spanish *comedia* and use of the traditional ballad form among the different metrical structures it employs, but also has something to do with the nature of the *romance* itself as a highly dramatic form of narrative in which character discourse already had a prominent role. At the same time, by taking one form of narrative text and using it as the basis for presenting the same story in a different medium, Lope and his contemporaries were perpetuating a form of literary mutation already practised among the medieval chroniclers, who are known to have incorporated the verses of the ballads and epics into their prose histories. It therefore comes as no surprise to find that the story told in *Fuenteovejuna*, of the rebellion of a village against an oppressive feudal lord, is developed from an earlier prose narrative. Menéndez y Pelayo, while speculating on the possible existence of a version of the story in ballad form, has long since pointed out the close association between Lope's play and the *Chrónica de las tres Ordenes y Cavallerías de Santiago, Calatrava y Alcántara* of 1527 by Francisco de Rades y Andrada (5: 171-82). When this tendency for literary mutation, as exemplified in *Fuenteovejuna* and found in other historical plays, is extended to include hagiographical plays and plays on mythological subjects or contemporary and ancient history, Lope's *comedia* may be seen as a dramatic form in which derivation from an existing narrative text all but acquires the status of one more convention in an already highly stylized genre. This is to say that, just as the conventionalized plot and characters of the *comedia* undoubtedly created expectations with respect to the kind of text anticipated, so, on account of the practice of dramatizing stories already known from earlier narratives, the content of the plot and the identity of the characters might also be awaited with expectations of familiarity.

From a strictly narratological point of view, the principle invoked above is related to the basic distinction between story and discourse, whereby the latter is a textualization of the former in any of an infinite number of ways. At the same time, it suggests, albeit tentatively, that the derivation of a play from an existing narrative implies the elaboration of an intertextual relationship allowing the play to be perceived as a projection from a context to which the dialogue of the characters may therefore be implicitly subordinated. In some instances, however, the insertion of the play within a narrative frame is made more explicit through the use of a prologue which provides the equivalent of a basic narrative voice. Among the clearest and most complicated examples of this practice in

Hispanic theatre is the combination provided by the first two eclogues of Juan del Encina, which also have the distinction of being the works with which the new theatre in Spain is initiated.

The two eclogues, first published in Juan del Encina's *Cancionero* (Salamanca, 1496), (see n. 6), provide an example of two kinds of prologue. The first, placed at the beginning of *Egloga I* and presumably intended for the reader, is written in prose and contains a brief account of the occasion and circumstances of performance, as well as an introduction to the characters and a summary of their dialogue. A similar paragraph occurs at the beginning of *Egloga II*, in which it is also specified that two of the characters appeared in *Egloga I* and that both eclogues were performed on the same occasion. Prologues of this kind are not found in the later *comedia*, perhaps, in the case of Lope de Vega, in any event, because plays were not written with publication in mind, but they were a common practice throughout the sixteenth century before his time. The 1588 edition of Juan de la Cueva's *Los siete infantes de Lara*, for example, in addition to a summary of content before each act, is also preceded by a paragraph entitled "Argumento de la tragedia" that is followed by a brief reference to the occasion of the first performance in Seville in 1579 (69-70).

The second kind of prologue referred to above in connection with Juan del Encina's two eclogues was intended for the audience and is a more integral part of the dramatic text. In fact, the characteristics of Encina's first eclogue make it appear to be a kind of prologue to the second. As pastoral disguises for the author and his companion, the two characters of *Egloga I*, Juan and Mateo, not only allow the poet Encina to pay the necessary tribute to his patron, but also embody the principle of the transformation of an actor into a character that is carried one stage further in *Egloga II*. There, the two original shepherds are joined by two others, Lucas and Marco, so that all four of them then represent the shepherds of the night of the first Christmas, as well as the four Evangelists who wrote their story, and therefore have the appropriate authority to describe and discuss the events of that night. The use of pastoral disguise as a cloak for writers of both the Old and New Testaments, confirming observations made above about the narrative form that underlies the dramatic text, is common in the religious theatre of the sixteenth century. In the secular theatre, however, the example provided by the work of Bartolomé de Torres Naharro is more representative. The plays published in his *Propalladia*, which first appeared in Naples, in 1517, all include a prologue entitled *Introito y argumento*, each of which is a monologue addressed directly to the audience, spoken in the rustic language of a shepherd, and including topical commentary as well as a summary of the story of the play. Use of the prologue as a curtain-raiser undoubtedly derives from Roman comedy, of which there are additional traces evident in Torres Naharro, but, by affirming the nature of theatre as illusion, it has an effect similar to that created by the relationship between Encina's first two eclogues. In the case of Torres Naharro, through his description of the content of the plot, the speaker of the prologue effectively reduces the autonomy of the play and the discourse of the characters by allowing them to be seen as a projection or elaboration of a story he has already narrated, a structure that once again raises the question of the underlying narrative text, at the same time as it is akin to that implied by the subordination of character discourse to that of a primary narrator in a conventional narrative.

Although prologues of one kind or another continued to appear in the Spanish theatre of the sixteenth century, they are not a feature of the *comedia* and one would be hard pressed to find an example in Lope. The well developed figure of the prologue, combining with that of the chorus, such as in Shakespeare's Gower in *Pericles* or his chorus in *Henry V*, where a more truly narratorial figure is developed, is an avenue that remains essentially unexplored in early Spanish theatre. Aside from the influence of particular traditions in either religious or secular plays, the presence of a prologue and the questions that it raises about the autonomy of the story re-enacted may well reflect some hesitation with respect to the dramatic form. By Lope's time, this has certainly disappeared, but in the endings to his plays he nevertheless preserves vestigial traces of those earlier addresses to an audience. At the end of *Fuenteovejuna*, for example, occur the following two lines, spoken by Frondoso: "Y aquí, discreto senado, / *Fuenteovejuna* da fin" (Vega Carpio 1: 855). In other plays, he is considerably less laconic, as in *Las bizarrías de Belisa*, where the following lines are spoken by one of the characters:

> Belisa.   Senado ilustre: el poeta,
> que ya las Musas dejaba,
> con deseo de serviros
> volvió esta vez a llamarlas
> para que no le olvidéis.
> Y aquí la comedia acaba. (Vega Carpio 2: 1705)

The effect, although it occurs after the fact rather than before it, is similar to that obtained by the prologue, given that the voice responsible for these lines, while belonging in performance to the actor who performed the role, is no longer that of the character. It belongs to a figure able to comment on the world presented by the *comedia* from a position outside of it. Thus, in the light of these comments, the characters of the play and their discourse are reduced to the status of elements within the discourse of another, identified in this case as the poet.

Aside from concluding remarks intended to signify the end of a play, the narrative activity of the characters of a typical *comedia* does not transcend their own world. Conforming to this pattern, *Fuenteovejuna* may be taken as a representative example of a *comedia* with characters that contribute to the telling of the story of which they are part, but from within, without fulfilling any apparent meta-narrative role. Their roles as narrators are not unlike those already described in connection with Molina and Valentín in Puig's novel. In the first instance, the task of conveying the unfolding story is shared by the characters, whose discourse, enunciated in reference to their present situation, amounts to a form of simultaneous narration, in which the notion of simultaneity encompasses the event and the discourse that describes it. The majority of the scenes in the play are based on exchanges of discourse of this kind. A few of these, scenes three and four of the first act, for example, are more thematic in nature and do not advance the action of the play, but are important indicators for the interpretation of plot and the creation of character.[8] Most scenes, however, are dramatic, in the sense that they cause movement to occur and are frequently based on confrontation among characters. They have the kind of dialogue which results in the reputation generally attributed to the *comedia* as a form of theatre in which action is paramount.

The other two types of narrative alluded to in discussion of *El beso de la mujer araña* were distinguished on the basis of the story to which the narrators referred, either events belonging to their own past or to a story from which they are essentially absent. *Fuenteovejuna* contains sporadic reference by characters to their immediate past or the past of others, but there is little sustained first person narrative. Personal retrospection of the kind that Genette would refer to as "external analepsis" is limited in the play and is mostly confined to the early scenes, as, for example when Laurencia includes in her conversation with Pascuala a brief account of the Comendador's pursuit of her (I.iii). The equivalent of "internal analepsis," retrospection encompassing events that have occurred within the time frame of the play, is more frequent, as when the judge returns to Fernando's court (III.xxiv) and relates the outcome of his enquiry in *Fuenteovejuna*, or in the wedding scene (II.xvi) when Mengo recalls the lashing he received from the Comendador's men and the musicians sing of the tyrant's unsuccessful pursuit of Laurencia.

Narration of the past in *Fuenteovejuna* somewhat overlaps, however, with the third of the categories identified in *El beso de la mujer araña*, namely specific engagement in storytelling. This is not to say that any of the characters in Lope's play engage in narrative for its own sake, or that the play incorporates the narration of stories based on events unrelated to the plot developed in the play itself, but there are occasions when characters identify themselves as narrators and their discourse is cast in the verse form traditionally associated with narrative. As Lope writes in his *Arte nuevo de hacer comedias*, concerning the uses of the different forms of versification in the *comedia*, "[l]as relaciones piden los romances" (Vega Carpio 2: 879). *Fuenteovejuna* has six of them, all relatively extended pieces of past narrative, and only one of them, the Comendador's address to the Maestre de Calatrava in the second scene of the play, covers events external to the chronology of incidents unfolding in the *comedia*. The remainder, all internal, include two accounts of the first battle for Ciudad Real (I.v & I.ix), Cimbrano's narration of Fernando's subsequent siege of the city (II.vi), the account of the death of the Comendador given by Flores to the King (III.xi), and Laurencia's tirade before the town council (III.iii), of which a significant part is her indictment of the men of the village for their cowardice. Moreover, all six of these monologues, with the exception of Cimbrano's narration, are prefaced by the speaker's intention to narrate a story, as when the Comendador announces to the Maestre, "Estad atento, y sabréis / la obligación que tenéis" (I.ii), or when Flores begins his narrative of the capture of Ciudad Real with the question, "¿Quién lo dirá como yo / siendo mis ojos testigos?" (I.v).

The *romances* narrated in *Fuenteovejuna* undoubtedly meet the very useful purpose of extending the scope of the play by permitting the inclusion in the story of events that, for all manner of reasons, could not be easily represented in performance. Although this fact alone is sufficient to highlight the importance of narrative to theatre, it should also be noted that the inclusion of the romances is far from gratuitous. They do not serve only to enhance the content, since the very act of narration itself is part of the plot and one of the means of advancing it. Four of the six narratives are exhortations, intended to move the listener to action. The Comendador's address to the Maestre, for example, is both a recent history of the *Order of Calatrava* and the war in Castille and a plea to him to ally himself with Juana and Alonso of Portugal against the Catholic Kings, thereby precipitating the political subplot of the *comedia*. By the same token, Laurencia's incitement of the men of her village to action leads to the death of the Comendador and the climax of the entire sequence of events developed in the play. In both cases, the narratives highlight the fact that drama, especially when looked at as text, is as much about what is said as about what is done.

To view Lope's play as a composite of narratives is to view it no differently from Puig's novel and to point to the fundamental similarity among all literary texts that lies beneath certain intentions and surface differences. An analysis of the two works, undertaken from the point of view of the structure of the stories they present, using a method developed either from the functional model derived from Propp and Bremond or from the actantial model proposed by Greimas, would not lead to significantly different conclusions about the general relation between the two works or among works of literature overall. This is not to say that *Fuenteovejuna* and *El beso de la mujer araña* are comparable works. They are evidently quite different and there is no connection between them, except of the most superficial kind. Yet, although a consideration of both works with respect to the similarity of the narrative strategies they use while inscribing themselves in different literary genres is a helpful, even illuminating, approach, there is, also, a certain irony in the comparison between them that results. If, as is the case, the core of Puig's novel is the meta-fictional device in which figures in a story are given to telling stories while telling the story of which they are part, there is cause to wonder what there is to the Postmodernist endeavour in this aspect of its creative vein that makes it differ from the narrative conventions implemented by the theatre and practised by Lope in one of his *comedias*.

NOTES

Notes to "Reading the Renaissance" by *Jonathan Hart*

1. I am limiting my notes to those works that discuss various European literatures for the sake of space. A good comparative view of gender issues occurs in *Rewriting the Renaissance*. Other important comparative studies of women in the Renaissance are Jones, *Currency of Eros*; Jordan; and Benson.

2. Especially as a coming to terms with the five hundredth anniversary of Columbus' first voyage, there have been such a large number of books and collections on the European first contact with America and its settlement during the Renaissance that it is not a pervasive theme in this volume. All too often these studies are not comparative. Although an interesting and provocative book, Todorov's *La Conquête de l'Amérique* concentrates on the Spanish. Far more needs to be done on the French and Portuguese in this comparative cultural study, but some fine work has been done, especially in regard to the relation of the Spanish to the English. See for instance, Hume and Greenblatt, *Marvelous Possessions*. Anthony Pagden has written a wide-ranging and pan-European study of this encounter from the Renaissance to Romanticism. In 1993, he gave the Carlyle lectures at Oxford that were a comparative study of European views of America in the early modern period. Mary Louise Pratt's comparative work, *Imperial Eyes*, looks at the period from 1750 to the present. On May 3, 5, 10, and 12, 1994, John Elliott delivered the Radcliffe Lectures at University of Warwick, "Worlds Apart: British and Spanish Colonial America." See Hart, "Images of the Native."

3. For discussions of Comparative Literature, see Levin, *Grounds for Comparison*; Culler; Dimić; Greene, "On the Category of the Literary"; Grimm; Hernadi; Lawall; Pratt, "Comparative Literature as a Cultural Practice"; Hart, "Ever-Changing Configurations of Comparative Literature." In the conclusion of *Theater and World*, I tried to place Shakespeare's history plays in a comparative context. For a discussion

of possible and fictional worlds, see Maitre; Bruner; Pavel; Hart, "Comparative Pluralism."

4. Here I have in mind Freud's papers, "Leonardo da Vinci and a Memory of His Childhood" (1910) and "The Moses of Michaelangelo" (1914). See *Freud Reader* 443-81 and 522-39, respectively. Freud's account of Leonardo is controversial; see Schapiro and Elms.

5. On Scève, see Cooper, esp. 21; Charpentier; and Gabe, esp. 201 (in brackets references to Pernette). The connection between Scève and the classical designs of Bernard Salomon for the royal entry into Lyon in 1548 might, in Freccero's terms, be a literal inscription or identification of the classical body; see Sharrett in the same collection.

Notes to "Ritual and Text" by *Thomas M. Greene*

1. Sections of this essay have been taken from my "Ceremonial Play and Parody in the Renaissance."

2. Distinctions between "ceremony" and "ritual" are not easy to make, and my usages of these terms will overlap. In general, the distinction made by Victor Turner is useful: "Ritual is transformative, ceremony confirmatory" (cf. Turner, *Forest of Symbols* 95).

3. In another book, *Praise and Blame in Renaissance Rome*, O'Malley notes the lack of interest in sacramental worship traceable in Renaissance sermons delivered at the papal court. "There is no particular emphasis on the reception of the sacraments as constituting an important element in Christian piety. Although the Eucharist is from time to time eulogized, practically nothing is said by way of direct encouragement to receive or adore it.... Once again, what the preachers fail to speak about is almost as significant as the themes to which they generally recur" (167-68).

4. Montaigne continues, "La ceremonie nous emporte, et laissons la substance des choses" (*Essais* 2: 348).

5. One prince who professed a low opinion of ceremonies was James I, who wrote in his *Basilicon Doron*: "But learne wisely to discerne betwixt points of salvation and indifferent things, betwixt substance and ceremonies" (49). James, to be sure, is speaking here in an ecclesiastical rather than political context.

6.   Saint Jerome's commentary on *Ezekiel 9* implicitly makes a connection
     with the *sphragis* of Christian baptism. "Volo noveritis quia huc usque
     apud Samaritanos tau littera similitudinem crucis habet, quamquam apud
     Hebraeos corrupta sit: ideoque per *tau*, quod interpretatur *signa*,
     intelliguntur illi qui signaculum crucis Christi in fronte et in corde
     ferunt, et per fidem passionis Christi, credunt se salvari posse." The
     phrase "in fronte" in this passage seems to point unmistakably to the
     sphragis of the sacrament of baptism. Jerome's commentary is quoted
     in an article by Sarolli, "Noterella Biblica sui sette P" (see Sarolli note
     1, 221-22). Sarolli remarks in this note that Dante would certainly have
     known Jerome's commentary. Sarolli does not, however, notice the
     allusion to baptism.
7.   This remark concludes a speech devoted to ceremonies by
     Chrysoglottus, who begins by deploring their dominance of most
     Christians' lives: "Si vulgus Christianorum spectes, nonne prora et
     puppis vitae illis in ceremoniis est?"

Notes to "Reading in the French Renaissance" by *Steven Rendall*

1.   See the studies by Saenger; Chartier, "Impact of Writing"; Nelson;
     Stock, *Implications of Literacy* and *Listening for the Text*; Boyarin;
     Howe; Long; Green.
2.   This famous anecdote is found in the Sixth Book of Augustine's
     Confessions (1: 272).
3.   All translations from French texts in this paper are my own. On
     "passetemps" in the Renaissance, see Febvre 189.
4.   For Benjamin, the storyteller is a man who can offer his hearers counsel
     ["ein Mann, der dem Hörer Rat weiss," 442]; he notes that "counsel" is
     less an answer to a question than a proposal concerning the continuation
     of an (even then developing) story ["Rat ist ja minder Antwort auf eine
     Frage als ein Vorschlag, die Fortsetzung einer (eben sich abrollenden)
     Geschichte angehend," 442] (86; I have slightly modified Zohn's
     translation of this passage.) The listener's receptivity — arising out the
     relaxation produced by the rhythm of work, out of "boredom" — allows
     him to incorporate the tales into his own experience in such a way that
     "the gift of retelling them comes to him all by itself" (91). Benjamin
     thus emphasizes the dialogic character of storytelling, its implication of
     a reply and further development on the part of the hearer/reader.

Benjamin's essay is titled "Der Erzähler"; as Green notes, "erzählen" is one of the meanings of "lesen" in Middle High German.

5   In this respect, the *Heptaméron* moves far beyond Boccaccio's *Decameron*, where the listeners' comments on the stories are minimal and usually unanimous. On the dynamics of such processes in modern reading groups, see Long 196-205.

6.   This is not, of course, entirely new; cf., for instance, Ariosto's *Orlando furioso*, X.115, XXIX.50 and *passim*; it is worth noting that *Orlando* is also a very long narrative. Classical rhetoric's warnings against overly long discourse, which were often repeated by medieval and Renaissance writers, are couched in terms of producing *taedium* and *fastidium*, and usually associated with advice to avoid these pitfalls through *brevitas* and *varietas* (Curtius 85, 489). However, these seem to bear chiefly on oratorical argumentation rather than on narrative.

7.   Cf. the line quoted above, which evokes the successful author's books surrounded by buyers at the bookshop: the collective response is here figured as an eagerness to purchase a commodity.

8.   Long argues that this has led scholars to ignore the important role played in the nineteenth and twentieth centuries by women's reading groups, which she sees a significant agent of social change.

9.   It is perhaps worth noting that before long the monks come out of their monastery and conceal themselves nearby in order to hear the stories, thus suggesting that participating in this "textual community" is more attractive than "serious" reading in their cells.

Notes to "Reading *Ultima Verba*" by *Lisa Neal*

1.   See, for example, Friedrich; Starobinski, "Montaigne" and *Montaigne en Mouvement*; Brody; Regosin, *The Matter of My Book* and "Le mirouer vague"; Blum; Boon, "La pensée de Montaigne" and *Montaigne*; Cave, *Cornucopian Text*; Rigolot, "La Loi de l'essai," "Montaigne's Purloined Letters," and "L'amitié intertextuelle"; Butor; Nakam; Villey.

2.   As Steven Rendall has said, "The touchstone of the evolutionary interpretation was, and has remained, the supposed development of Montaigne's attitude towards death" (*Distinguo* 9). For a cogent summary of Montaigne scholarship with respect to the "evolution" of the *Essais*, see Rendall's introduction (1-14).

3. For two astute analyses of the question of reading with respect to the *Essais*, see Bauschatz; Rendall, "*Mus in pice*."

4. Unless otherwise indicated, all references to the *Essais* cite the Thibaudet-Rat edition (1962).

5. On the art of dying, see Tenenti, *La Vie et la mort*; O'Connor; Beaty; Vovelle; Chartier, "Les Arts de mourir"; Macksey. On the importance of this tradition on Montaigne, see Brody's insightful chapter, "Montaigne et l'art de mourir" (99-132).

6. The first quotation dates from the first edition, 1580, and could have been composed as early as 1572, while the second is an addition that comes from the posthumous edition of 1595. These two quotations indicate that Montaigne's preoccupation with death continued throughout his life.

7. Montaigne's attitude toward language has often been referred to as nominalist, a point made, among others, by Friedrich (169-72); Regosin (*The Matter of My Book* 95-105, 200-44); and Compagnon, who argues that it is essential to the logic of Montaigne's writing and that the essayist, in later writings, counters this unlimited nominalism with realist strategies (*Nous*). Compagnon also speaks of nominalism in *La Seconde Main* (288-90). The nominalist standpoint is common in the Renaissance. Montaigne could have read commentaries on the arbitrariness of the word in Sextus Empiricus (2: 18) or other Stoics; the medieval version of nominalism is elaborated by Ockham, with whom Montaigne was probably not familiar. Abélard also contested Plato's notion that Ideas are more real than things.

8. The note in the Pléiade edition incorrectly gives "emport*e*" rather than "emport*a*." After the word, "peinture," there is the addition, deleted before the 1595 edition: "Et si en y a, qu'il..." and then corrected to "Et si en y a, que je recuse, pour les conoistre trop excessivement proclives en ma faveur." Donald Frame points out that Montaigne later crossed out this last section, which seems to apply to Marie de Gournay.

9. There are a number of good studies of friendship in the *Essais*: Weller; Regosin (*The Matter of My Book* 9-20); Gray ("Montaigne's Friends" 203-217); Schlossman; Mehlman; Henry; Desan; MacPhail; Rigolot, "La Loi de l'essai," "Montaigne's Purloined Letters"; and Langer.

10. See also Panofsky; Lee notes the coexistence in the Renaissance of two distinct views on the artist as both copyist but also corrector. "It is not unusual, at least until past the middle of the [sixteenth] century, to find

them disconcertingly side by side — a fact which the reader will agree, does not argue for the philosophical capacities of these writers" (60).

11. Cotgrave's definitions of "place" and "lieu" are nearly identical, suggesting that the shift from one to the other in Montaigne's letter was necessarily semantic in nature.

12. The end of the letter is characterized by both disregard for and attention to detail. We do not know how much time elapsed between La Boétie's last sentence and his death, nor do we know how many times he said Montaigne's name (not something one would imagine a witness forgetting). On the other hand, Montaigne meticulously records the hour, day, and date of his friend's demise and his precise age at death.

13. In reference to Montaigne's letter, Rigolot writes: "The dignified momentum of the scene comes partly from the fact that it is patterned after literary models ranging from Plato's rendition of Socrates's farewell to the *Gospel* account of Christ's *ultima verba* ("Montaigne's Purloined Letters" 145).

14. Asclepius is the Greek god of healing and the cock an offering to him. Socrates's last words imply that death has healed him of life.

15. The paradox I outline here with regard to the exemplarity of *ultima verba* is part of a much broader question on the rhetorical function of the *example*. This subject has been analyzed by Lyons, *The Rhetoric of Example*; Hampton; and Stierle. Literary critics dealing exclusively with the *Essais* in terms of exemplarity include Starobinski, "Montaigne"; Regosin, "Le mirouer vague"; Gutwirth; Blum; Gray, *La Balance de Montaigne*.

16. Socrates says in the *Phaedo*, that those who "rightly engage in philosophy, study only dying and death" (9: 64). Judging by the first sentence of 1: 20, Montaigne must be alluding to Cicero's *Tusculan Disputations*, which he quotes directly in 3: 12: "Tota philosoforum vita commentatio mortis est."

17. This rejection is indeed striking in an era of religious fervour since a slow bed-ridden death was for centuries regarded as a necessary ordeal by which the dying person was granted the time to make peace with God and men. Philippe Ariès refers to the medieval notion of death that is unexpected (*mors subita)* or of death without witnesses as being "a vile and ugly death ... frightening ... a strange and monstrous thing" (10-13). The Renaissance also held the *mors subita* in horror on spiritual grounds (as opposed to the modern era which seems to value death without warning). Although Montaigne does in fact put in

question the commonly accepted value of the ceremonial death, there are well-known precedents for his preference for sudden death in the figures of Salutati, Bellarmine, and Erasmus. Erasmus refers to ancient sources saying that they wrote "not without reason that a sudden death was the greatest blessing that life could bring" (qtd. in Tenenti, *Il Senso della morte* 242-43).

18. For example, Montaigne emphasizes the inseparability of life and death throughout his two-decade writing career: "Vostre mort est une des pieces de l'ordre de l'univers; c'est une piece de la vie du monde ... C'est la condition de vostre creation, c'est une partie de vous que la mort; vous vous fuyez vous mesmes. Cettuy vostre estre, que vous joüyssez, est egalement party à la mort et à la vie" (1: 20, 91, composed between 1572-80); "[la mort] est une partie de nostre estre non moins essentielle que le vivre" (3: 12, 1032, composed between 1580-88); and, "Tout ce que vous vivez, vous le desrobez à la vie; c'est à ses despens. Le continuel ouvrage de vostre vie, c'est bastir la mort. Vous estes en la mort pendant que vous estes en vie" (1: 20, 91, composed between 1588-92). One of the most outspoken opponents of the evolutionist argument, Jules Brody, writes that: "A l'intérieur de ce seul essai [1: 20,] et à travers des trois couches connues de sa composition, on ne relève donc aucune trace de la fameuse évolution qui aurait marqué d'une façon assez particulière la réflexion montaignienne sur la mort." He sees an evolution, however, in the *form* of the message (*Lectures*) See also Bowen; Boon, *Montaigne*; Gray, "The Unity of Montaigne"; Micha.

19. See note 6.

20. Pierre de Brach ends the letter by requesting commemoration for his friend: "Or je sçay, Monsieur, que vous avez eu en beaucoup d'amitié et en beaucoup d'estime feu Monsieur de Montaigne, vous en avez donné des tesmoignages publiques durant sa vie: donnez en aprez sa mort. Nous faisons dresser une piramide pour son cercueil, un plinte sera reservé pour ce que vous dedierez à sa memoire" (Montaigne, *Essais* 1203).

Notes to "Early Modern Italy and France" by *Carla Freccero*

1. There is an extensive feminist literature on the phenomenon of masculine appropriation of female creativity and the phallocratic woman

as male phantasm; for some interesting recent explorations of variations on this theme, see Sofia; Spackman; Schiesari, *Gendering of Melancholia.*

2. See John Freccero, "The Fig Tree and the Laurel"; Vickers, "Diana Described" and "'The Blazon of Sweet Beauty's Best.'" Schiesari notes that "Petrarch's glorification of Laura became the means through which Petrarch attained glory and through which woman as the specular object for erotic self-recuperation became institutionalized. The ecstasy and despair of Petrarch's lyric eroticized lack in terms of a lost object, the bemoaning of whose loss also erected the poetic subject" ("'The Blazon of Sweet Beauty's Best'" 167). Desaive amusingly discusses this phenomenon in France.

3. See also the conclusion drawn by the more recent *A History of Women,* in the article by Dulong: "Indeed, much of the literary production of women before the nineteenth century was of mediocre quality" (410). Wilson's *Women Writers of the Renaissance and Reformation* is an example of one of the relatively recent anthologies attempting to "counteract" or "correct" this view through the important work of "rediscovering," and thus also reconstructing," women writers of the period.

4. Georges Duby and Michelle Perrot, general editors of the series of volumes *A History of Women,* remark: "Our history is 'feminist' in that its outlook is egalitarian" (Davis and Farge ix). I am not sure what this means, but while I do think it is important to examine the history of women as agents, rather than passive "victims" of history (which seems to be the intent and force of the series), I also think that it is relevant to conduct this examination simultaneously upon the particular forms of "inequality" (to remain within their terms) or male domination that systematically structured that history. I use the term "patriarchy" here, therefore, to point to a historical specificity, generalizable as system, of the mode of the inequality of women in early modernity.

5. See, for example, Laqueur, *Making Sex*; Epstein and Straub; Stanton; James Turner; Lomperis and Stanbury; Hendricks and Parker; Buchet; the special issue of *GLQ* on *Premodern Sexualities in Europe* (Fradenburg and Freccero).

6. For a discussion of the grotesque body in Rabelais as already a "displacement upward" of a prior, and gendered, female grotesque, see Spackman.

7. For a critique of these positions see Parker, "Gender Ideology, Gender Change" 337-64.

8. For a detailed and comparative consideration of the meaning of hegemony in Gramsci, see Bocock. For hegemony's usefulness as a concept dealing with the flexibility of power relations and the resistive agency of its subjects, see Graeme Turner 197-215. I take issue with overly optimistic recent assessments by social historians of women's self-determining agency in early modern Europe in "Economy, Woman, and Renaissance Discourse" (Freccero, esp. 192-94). For an excellent study of aspects of women's social positionings in early modern Italy, see Klapisch-Zuber.

9. For a useful survey of official ideologies of woman in the early modern period, see Maclean; Davis and Farge. For a genealogy of western philosophical exclusionary thinking in relation to gender and its persistence within contemporary Anglo-American feminism, see Spelman. Schiesari analyzes the relation between Renaissance Italian ideologies of gender and the situation of women writers ("In Praise of Virtuous Women?" 66-87). See also Freccero, "The Other and the Same" 145-58. For a survey of some of the inherited medical views on women, see Daston and Park, "The Hermaphrodite and the Orders of Nature" 49-68; Jones and Stallybrass 80-111.

10. See Jones, "Surprising Fame" 77; Jordan also discusses Barbaro's treatise (41-47).

11. Scott has also discussed the public/private split in relation to the study of gender in history.

12. See also Freccero, "Economy" 192-208; Jed 114-30.

13. For an interesting discussion of the political anxieties expressed by the courtier through the discourse on the court lady, see Kelly's chapter "Did Women Have a Renaissance?" (19-50). I discuss the politics of *The Courtier* in relation to the discourse on woman in "Politics and Aesthetics in Castiglione's *Il Cortegiano*: Book III and the Discourse on Women" (Freccero, "Politics and Aesthetics" 259-79).

14. See Hertz and the response from Gallagher in *The End of the Line: Essays on Psychoanalysis and the Sublime* (Hertz 161-96). See also Silverman (69-89). For an unusual instance of masculine praise for the "unruly" or "grotesque" in woman, see John Freccero, "Medusa and the Madonna of Forlì" 161-78.

15. See the excellent study of Veronica Franco by Margaret Rosenthal. Schiesari's book suggests an alternative tradition for certain Italian lyric

poets, who reappropriate the Petrarchan tradition and recast loss in terms of a feminine symbolic (*Gendering of Melancholia* 168), articulating a communal and feminine tradition of mourning and grief; she notes, however, that this tradition has not been valorized by literary history: "According to a long-standing tradition of male literary criticism, the women writers of the Italian Renaissance ... have never been or could never be Petrarchan enough" (169). She then goes on to recount the tragic career of the poet Isabella di Morra, figure *par excellence* of the confinement to which women's lives were subject, whose fame is largely cast in biographical, rather than poetic, terms (160-90).

16. See also Jones, "Nets and Bridles" and her more recent work, *The Currency of Eros: Women's Love Lyric in Europe, 1540-1620.*

17. For an excellent study of the symbolics of queenship and its relation to practices of ruling, see Fradenburg.

18. See Jourda's study of Marguerite's life and works; Roelker; Freccero 1989. For a discussion of the consequences of Sorbonne censorship and the king's privilege, see Freccero (*Father Figures* 136-46). Foucault in "What Is an Author?" points to the ways in which the meaning of authorship is connected to statist modes of surveillance and punishment (141-60).

19. Indeed, it would seem that in France, unlike England, female political leadership and literary authorship were rarely combined in the same figure; the contrasting political and literary careers of Marguerite and her daughter, Jeanne d'Albret, are a case in point.

20. "Et pource que les femmes ne se montrent volontiers en publiq seules, je vous ay choisie pour me servir de guide..." (Labé 43).

21. For some of the symbolic valences of prostitution in the Renaissance, see Kuehn; Norberg; Shemek.

22. See especially, in this regard, the discussion of salon cultures by Dulong (395-419).

Notes to "Female Transvestism and Male Self-Fashioning" by *Katy Emck*

1. I am drawing on Stephen Greenblatt's early definition of the term in *Renaissance Self-Fashioning.* However, my understanding of it is somewhat different. Where Greenblatt emphasises the way Renaissance self-fashioning and social mobility involves the submission to authority,

I am concerned with the sense of the transgression of limits (of rank, gender, geography, ideology); an anxious byproduct of self-fashioning, and one refracted through the figure of the transvestite.

2. There are a number of parallels between the cross-dressed heroines and their male counterparts in the two plays under discussion in this paper and those of *Orlando Furioso*, *The Faerie Queene*, *Twelfth Night* and *The Merchant of Venice*. I will here describe the most obvious similarities, though there are even more which bear closer scrutiny.

The warrior maidens Bradamante and Britomart, in *Orlando Furioso* and *The Faerie Queene*, respectively, both rescue their future husbands, Ruggiero and Artegall, from prison. This resembles Rosaura's role in relation to the incarcerated Segismundo. And where Ruggiero is a pagan, and thus socially marginal and suspect, Artegall's royal origins are unknown to himself. In this sense, he is, like Segismundo and Orlando, a "nobody." Moreover, the role of pastoral in establishing the natural — and therefore free from corruption — vigour and virtue of Segismundo and Orlando is similar to Artegall's role as "The Savage Knight" and his pastoral education in combat with wild beasts.

The hero and the heroine's androgynous identity of concerns in *La vida es sueño* and *As You Like It* is also echoed in other works. The twinning in particular of Segismundo and Rosaura, who are constructed as reflections of one another on a number of levels, is echoed in the mutual substitutability of Britomart and Artegall, and of Viola and Sebastian in *Twelfth Night*. Britomart's self-willed cross-dressing is matched by Artegall's enforced wearing of women's clothes in book 5 of *The Faerie Queene*. And Viola and Sebastian, of course, become indistinguishable at the end of *Twelfth Night*. Moreover, Sebastian is marginalised — both because he is absent and because he, like Segismundo and Artegall, has lost his class origins — and Viola functions as an agent on his behalf. She woos Olivia for him.

In *The Merchant of Venice*, the pairing of a socially and economically powerless hero with a cross-dressed heroine whose agency exceeds and finally assures his own is also visible. The disguised Portia rescues Bassanio from being the cause of his best friend's death, and she ultimately provides him with title and financial wherewithal.

3. For commentaries on Elizabethan outrage and anxiety about the transgression of dress codes, see Jardine 141-68; Levine; Rackin; Howard; Garber 25-32.

4. In this respect, Stubbes represents a new emphasis. Lisa Jardine in *Still Harping on Daughters* says that men's fashions became increasingly extravagant in the course of Elizabeth I's reign (154) and suggests that vitriol against women's fashions by commentators such as Stubbes was related to the attendant sense of social disorder. Presumably, as men's fashions got more extreme, so did women's, and anxiety about the issue increased. Sumptuary extravagance only escalated more in James I's reign. *The Roaring Girl* (1611) and *Hic Mulier: Or the Man-Woman* (1620) can be cited as examples of the sense of the woman in masculine clothing as a monstrous and also revolutionary figure/metaphor after Stubbes.

5. Marjorie Garber wittily suggests this connection in her book on cross-dressing, *Vested Interests*: "Was 'self-fashioning' — the 'forming of a self' — that achievement so consistently claimed as one of the chief distinguishing features of the Renaissance, in fact at the mercy of *fashion*, of *clothing*?" (32).

6. Jean Howard writes that cross-dressed women "signal not only the breakdown of the hierarchical gender system, but of the class system as well. She cites the author of *Hic Mulier*, who "calls them 'but[t] ragges of Gentry,' 'the adulterate branches of rich Stocks,' and 'this deformitie all base, all barbarous'" (425). More generally, Lisa Jardine suggests that in the Renaissance anxiety about social change is displaced onto women, once more testifying to the substitutability of class and gender where questions of social order, of hierarchy, are concerned (162).

7. On the rise of patriarchalism in the seventeenth century, with images of family bulwarking political authority and vice versa, see Schochet's "Patriarchalism, Politics and Mass Attitudes in Stuart England" and *Patriarchalism and Political Thought*.

8. For a reading of *As You Like It* as a translation of Orlando's patrimonial dispossession into success as a way of resolving prevalent social anxieties about inheritance laws, see Montrose.

9. Orlando's elder brother as well as Basilio is a figure of repressive patriarchal authority here. Montrose points out that "Oliver is simultaneously a father and a brother to his own natural sibling; he is at once Orlando's brother and his peer. Primogeniture conflates the generations in the person of the elder brother and blocks the generational passage of the younger brother" (36).

10. Jardine explores the strong connections between female independence (or male perceptions of women as independent) and sexual slur (68-77).

Once again, this prompts one to ask the question, why then is female independence, and indeed female transgression of the most flagrant kind, so favourably constructed in much of Renaissance literature? Is it because it reflects a *masculine* spirit of self-invention and even rebellion? See also Montrose.

11. Significantly, Pico della Mirandola seized on Origen's interpretation of the Old Testament line "God created man male and female" as an image of original, Adamic androgyny in his exposition on the self-determinability, and thus self-completeness, of man. For Renaissance humanists, Plato's myth of the androgyne became an acceptable image for universal man. So much so, that the image of the androgyne was incorporated into the iconography of François I.

12. Phyllis Rackin's interesting essay "Androgyny, Mimesis, and the Marriage of the Boy Heroine on the English Renaissance Stage" describes a connection between the move towards an increasingly mimeticist representation in seventeenth century England, and an increasingly negative view of androgyny. She perceives Shakespeare's theatre as being caught in a subversive indeterminacy between the two aesthetic and ideological systems, and I would suggest this goes for Calderon, too.

13. Jean Howard claims that "enormous energies were devoted to revealing the "monstrous" nature of those who moved out of their places" (422) and refers the reader to Barker 31-33.

14. Montrose shows how *As You Like It* "is quite persistent in creating strategies for subordinating the flesh to the spirit, and female powers to male controls." Thus, "fraternity and paternity can be conceived as male relationships unmediated by woman, relationships of the spirit rather than the flesh" (51). Or, to use Simone de Beauvoir's terms for the male-female binary, the transcendence of the exclusively male pre-eminence promulgated at the end of the play supersedes the immanence embodied in the transvestite heroine and her accompanying forms of social disorder. This goes for *La vida es sueño* too, as I hope I have shown.

15. On transvestism as the articulation of a third term, see Garber 11.

Notes to "The Ends of Renaissance Comedy" by *Jonathan Hart*

1. In an essay on comic theory I argue for a recognition of recognition. Comic recognition, or *agnitio* or *cognitio*, became equivalents for Aristotle's anagnorisis, or discovery. Recognition is a central part of comic structure. Although I do not have space here, I think it is important to make this point. Aristotle speaks about anagnorisis in tragedy, but not, in the extant version of *Poetics*, of comic discovery or recognition. Menander is credited with refitting the recognition plot to comedy, and Plautus and Terence provide examples of the use of comic recognition. Like Terence Cave, I am interested in the ways recognition unsettles the boundaries of genre that poetics sets out (see Cave, *Recognitions* 50-54). The recognition most often occurs towards the end of comedies and has tragic origins or at least analogues, so that it complicates the ends of comedy. Donatus, Franciscus Robortellus, Cinthio, Guarini, and Ben Jonson all comment on discovery and peripety (reversal) which bring about catastrophe (see Herrick 106-26). Like Guarini, Northrop Frye tries to defend tragicomedy, and especially romance. He does so by making recognition (sometimes as vision and epiphany) the centre of his defence of romance and, perhaps even, of literature and culture (see Frye, *Anatomy, Secular Scripture*; Hart *Theater and World, Northrop Frye*; Cave, *Recognitions* 190-99). Before Frye's return to recognition, ritual and order in comedy and romance, Cambridge anthropologists and theorists like Francis Cornford had discussed these matters. A subtext of my essay is the shared ritual origins of tragedy and comedy and the implication that this common provenance is one reason why comic ends can be at least partly tragic. Cornford's predecessors and contemporaries often emphasized the asymmetrical and exceptional elements of the end of Old comedy.

    Horace emphasizes how in the Old comedy personal freedom degenerated into excess until a law was passed that silenced the Chorus ("Successit vetus hic Comoedia non sine multa laude: sed in vitium libertas excidit, et vim Dignam lege regi: lex est accepta: chorusque turpiter obsticuit sublato jure nocendi." The stresses that satire causes between social order and criticism is evident in the controversy surrounding *Tartuffe*, which this essay later discusses. In *De Comaedia et Tragaedia*, Donatus draws on the Ciceronian view that comedy is an imitation of life, a mirror of custom, and a reflection of truth, and discusses the ritual origins of comedy and cites Horace on Old comedy.

The *parabasis*, especially as it appears in Aristophanes, provides interesting contrasts with the structure of Renaissance comedy. See Zielinski, *Gliederung d. altattischen Komödie* [Leipzig, 1886], qtd. in Cornford 2, 5. On the structure of Greek comedy, including *parabasis*, see Cornford vii-viii, 1-3; Cornford also credits Jane Harrison as an influence. The Middle Comedy gave up the *parabasis* and what Horace calls the *ius nocendi* or right of injury, such as Aristophanes's taunting of Cleon (Levin, *Playboys and Killjoys* 30-31).

2. I want to thank students in my graduate seminar in Renaissance comedy in the Department of Comparative Literature at University of Alberta for their discussions of genre in a comparative European context. The reason for my comments on the metaphysical *La vida es sueño* (Hart, "Narrative" 16), which some may not think of as a comedy, is that is shows structural affinity to romantic comedy and romance. For that reason, it also appeared in my course.

3. For discussions on cross-dressing, see Jean Howard and Marjorie Garber.

4. In an epilogue to a comedy in 1564, Ronsard uses the trope that Jaques employs as a context: "Le monde est un théâtre, et les hommes les acteurs" (see Curtius 138, 133-44; Hart, *Theater and World* 231-32).

5. It has been years since I began discussing sexual ambiguity in *As You Like It* with my classes. Two instances, however, stand out and may reflect the importance of an understanding of the conventions in experience and literature in the response to this aspect of the comedy. In 1985-86, I lectured on the topic to first year students at Trent University and later discussed it in a seminar with them. Most of them seemed quite uncomfortable with the topic. At Alberta, a few years later, I discussed the same topic with a graduate class on Renaissance comedy, and there appeared to be more interest in sexual ambiguity in *As You Like It* and more tolerance for it.

6. Some critics might not find the ends of *Volpone* and *Tartuffe* to be intricate and problematic. In discussing Molière's *Dom Juan* and Shakespeare's *Troilus and Cressida* as two plays in search of an audience, Nicholas Grene says that the figure of le Ciel in *Dom Juan*, who is a menace who wreaks vengeance on the sinner, presents "a much more serious difficulty than that with *Tartuffe* or *Volpone*, where the arbitrariness of the dénouement could be reconciled with the satiric viewpoint of the whole play" (182).

Notes to "Voices in the Darkness of Troy" by *Robert Rawdon Wilson* and *Edward Milowicki*

1. In *Shakespeare's History Plays*, Tillyard makes the case that *Henry V* is consciously experimental in mixing epic conventions with drama. Hart argues that all of Shakespeare's history plays constitute a "national epic," a view that he traces back, through Tillyard, to A. W. Schlegel (*Theater and World* 207, 219). For a brief discussion of Shakespeare's use of traditional narrative conventions in drama, see Wilson, "Shakespeare's Narrative."

2. For succinct, but highly instructive, discussion of Romance as a genre known to Renaissance writers, see Patricia Parker's article in *The Spenser Encyclopedia* (609-18). Her 1979 *Inescapable Romance*, though heavily focused upon the paradoxical notion of deferral, remains valuable. Her encyclopedia article contains a useful bibliography.

3. The relationship between Shakespeare's play and Chaucer's narrative is at once uncertain and over-discussed. Kenneth Muir's Oxford edition of *Troilus and Cressida* contains an overview of the scholarly debate until the early 1980s (12-19). See also, Donaldson; and Vivian Thomas, esp. 23-60.

4. Hart observes that Shakespeare "begins *Richard II* in the midst of things, causing his characters to refer ambiguously to the past, presenting Richard's reign in crisis" (*Theater and World* 17). However, *Richard II* does not unmistakably invoke the epic genre's fundamental narrative convention. Both *Troilus* and, less explicitly, *Henry V* do.

5. McAlindon's notion of a contrast that becomes evident only in the unfolding of the action is very similar to Greenblatt's rubric, "proleptic irony" (*Shakespearean Negotiations* 54). The elegant world of analogy may be invisible both to those who are explained by it and to those who would benefit most from seeing it. In McAlindon's chief example, Macbeth does not hear, nor never has reported to him, the praise that the bloody sergeant has lavished upon him. That is to say, he never understands fully what he might have been, or the world he might have occupied. Analogy is part of narrative's self-incorporated otherness.

6. For a bibliography of works relevant to the Troy-theme in Renaissance literature, as well as a short but instructive commentary, see Stephen A. Barney's article in *The Spenser Encyclopedia*.

7. On the specifically narrative reflexivity involved in the Player King's "Aeneas' Tale to Dido" (*Ham.* 2.2.445-520), see Wilson "Narrative

Boundaries." On the concept of reflexivity in general as an element in dramatic development, see Wilson, "Narrative Reflexivity."

8.   For a discussion of Ovid's use of reduction, particularly as it appears in his ironic treatment of characters, see Milowicki and Wilson.

9.   The definition of menippean satire is contested. Since a menippean voice is massively undercutting, acerbic, and pointedly negative, it can be considered carnivalesque in the sense that it is mocking, engages, as Bakhtin puts it, in "parodies, travesties, humiliations, profanations, comic crownings and uncrownings" (*Rabelais and His World* 11) and employs bawdy physical imagery. Bakhtin cites Lucian's character Menippus, based upon literary memories of the actual 3rd century B.C.E. satirist, as one of the sources of "the Renaissance philosophy of laughter" (69). Bakhtin stresses the physicality of carnival which, as he argues, creates a "grotesque realism": the "lowering of all that is high, spiritual, ideal, abstract; it is a transfer to the material level, to the sphere of earth and body in their indissoluble unity" (19-20). The emphasis upon the human body, the "absolute lower stratum" which, Bakhtin observes, is "always laughing" (22), upon copulation, defecation, disease, death, and decay, especially "strikes the eye in archaic grotesque" (26). Hence, remembering that Bakhtin has in mind transformations of classical grotesque in Medieval and Renaissance carnival, it is certainly possible to see Thersites as both a "fool" and as something more archaic, the bodying forth of classical grotesque. On the other hand, it can be argued that menippean satire is essentially intellectual, learned, and erudite. Thersites's humour, the steady carping and undermining, the exaggerated wordplay, must seem extremely (even stunningly so) intellectual. Bakhtin's discussion of menippean satire as a precursive discourse of the novel, voices intercutting one another, transforming and modifying one another in exchange, might identify *Troilus*, because of its "parodic-travestying discourse," as a menippean precursor of the newly-born novel (*Dialogic Imagination* 51-68). Given its verbal intricacy, it may be more correct to think of *Troilus* as more like a metaphysical poem than either a tragedy or a comedy. Or, yet again, it may seem more centrally narrative than dramatic and hence not merely a precursor of the novel but, like a contemporaneous (menippean) text, *Don Quixote*, actually a novel. On the varieties of menippean satire, and the diversity of generic analyses, see Kirk.

10.   Shakespeare uses "empty" comic forms in several places. The final reconciliation scene is another empty comic form in which conventional

actions can be used to generate unanswerable questions: in *Measure for Measure*, the final scene, the marriage dance in effect, leaves it completely unclear how Angelo and Mariana can be happy together, why (more deeply experienced) Duke Vincentio chooses Isabella for his wife and why she says nothing at this moment of "happiness." *Love's Labour's Lost* ends with deferral and impatience even while preserving the comic form of love, devotion, and marriage. In *Troilus*, Thersites holds the apex position in a hierarchy of knowledge, the master of the discrepant awareness, but the knowledge, which only the audience shares, is biting, cynical, and profoundly undercutting.

11. If anything, *Timon of Athens* is more disenchanted than *Troilus and Cressida*, and more disillusioned. If *Troilus* is dated c. 1601-02, and *Timon* c. 1603-04, it is possible Shakespeare was seeking a new genre (which, if one accepts Stephen Greenblatt's argument [*Negotiations*] concerning the communal and collusive nature of Elizabethan creation, could not be invented by a single originary genius in any event), but was forced to return to tragedy. If this is the case, it is not necessarily unfortunate since *Lear* was written around this time.

12. It has been noted that, contrary to the chivalric honour held so close in the ante-bellum American South, the merchants of the North transformed honour to serve business and commerce: one kept one's word and delivered the goods. See Wyatt-Brown.

13. Parry has indicated that Achilles lacks the language to define (or redefine!) the honour he perceives is due him. Vance has written on the "objectivity" of the epic world. See also, Southern 243-44.

14. Both the *Iliad* and *Beowulf* close with the major action, the fall of a people, just ahead. The first part of the *Song of Roland* also closes tragically but, apparently, its author desired to see epic reciprocity (as the convention of structural balance might be called) in his work, since the second part recalls Charlemagne's vengeance. Nonetheless, Part Two also closes with much unfinished business, and the Emperor deep in *Weltschmertz*. The structure of the *Odyssey* is more akin to romance than epic, with its many episodes ending favourably for the hero, if not for his companions. Still, the romance design is subordinated to epic structure: virtually all of Odysseus's (romance-like) adventures in the epic are related to the Phaiacians, not to the Homeric audience (which already knows the story anyway). The Phaiacians then return Odysseus to Ithaca for his final, epic adventure. Even so, the *Odyssey* does employ a large number of romance conventions. Virgil, in following the

structure of the *Odyssey*, also steers his epic close to the Charybdis of romance. The satisfying closure and powerful providential presence throughout the *Aeneid* suggest the rhetoric of romance, not of epic.

15. Gayle Greene observes that the scholarly audience of *Troilus* has normally taken its cues from the male characters in the play and has judged Cressida in a "overwhelmingly negative" manner (134-35). There has been a significant reaction to this prejudice in criticism over the past twenty years. More than thirty years ago, indeed, Robert Ornstein identified her dilemma as being a "daughter of the game" which men wish her to play and for which they despise her (245). The "wanton of tradition" may have been forced into wantonness, but that is all, a weak exculpation, that scholarship has been able to make of her situation until recently. This line of argument, finding the deficiencies of Cressida's character in the male society in which she must live, has dominated recent criticism. See Asp; Donaldson; Greene, *Light in Troy*; and Yoder. It is not a wrong argument, but it is essentially contextual (even narrowly sociological) and limited to the analysis of a single character in one play. Shakespeare emphasizes Cressida's vulnerability, but he does so as a convention of characterization that he uses elsewhere.

16. Ovid seems to have developed, though not codified, split awareness as a convention of characterization. One might argue that the convention was already in use in Euripides and that some evidence for it exists elsewhere in classical literature, but Ovid, in making split awareness a flexible convention, is the originary master. See Milowicki and Wilson.

17 Many of Shakespeare's characters, such as Falstaff, create self-conscious discursive zones. Ajax is important in this regard only because he is a minor character and, in being made self-conscious, so very different from his epic exemplars. The concept of a discursive zone is Bakhtin's. Because language is entangled, its most potent affects are experienced only as functions of close proximity. Language constantly beckons, invoking its users into a circle together, and always draws its overhearers up close, into its secrets. (Once one has read Bakhtin, it may seem that language is inherently a close-up phenomenon such that keeping one's distance, standing at the normal analytic remove, requires an acquired discipline: the discipline of rejection and renunciation.) The distinction between epic and novel, to which Bakhtin often recurs, is not simply the difference between the monologic epic and the (potentially) dialogic voice of the novel, but one of distance and proximity. The epic, a stand-offish genre, keeps its readers at bay. A discursive zone comes

into existence as a projection of a character's private world of values, concepts, and ideology. The public discursive zone that surrounds a character manifests the hidden world of the subject's intentionality. For Bakhtin, Dostoevsky was the writer who had best created self-conscious discursive zones. In every voice Dostoevsky could hear "two contending voices, in every expression a crack, and the readiness to go over immediately to another contradictory expression," and in every gesture he could detect "confidence and lack of confidence simultaneously" (*Problems of Dostoevsky's Poetics* 30). In the "cross-section of a given moment," many ideas and beliefs, not always in complete agreement, flow together in coexistence. And only in "the category of coexistence" could Dostoevsky "see and represent the world" (29). Characters can (and *do* in Dostoevsky's novels) both speak out of the coexistence of their own "contradictions and bifurcations," but also interact with other characters. For this reason, Bakhtin reiterates the importance of bearing in mind the existential realities out of which a character speaks, out of which its voice is heard: "*who* precisely is speaking, and under *what* concrete circumstances" (*Dialogic Imagination* 340). Bakhtin's analysis, though he limits it to Dostoevsky, can be extended widely since self-consciousness is a recurring dimension of literature. On Bakhtin's analysis of worlds, voice, and discursive zones, see Wilson, "Character-Worlds in *Pale Fire*."

18.   A division in values, often involving self-consciousness and leading to ironic reduction, has frequently been observed under other rubrics than split awareness. It can be called "perspectivism" (Spitzer), or it can be seen as an interior boundary between romance and realism (Ortega y Gasset, Martínez-Bonati) in which a permeable frontier between textual values allows romance and realistic conventions to co-exist in the novel. The argument in this essay is that these quite evident divisions may be seen as a convention of characterization, that they have a definite provenance in classical and medieval literature and that they are fully developed, at once flexible and extremely wide-ranging, in Shakespeare. *Troilus* is a preeminent instance. For a recent discussion of perspectivism, see Kyndrup.

19.   There are a great many questions in *Troilus*. According to Thomas, there are 400 or so questions and only a single scene (5.8) without questions. Thomas also locates more than 200 instances of characters analysing the attributes of other characters (1987, 102). The sheer number of questions is quite staggering and contributes to the overall

impression of voices intersecting and intercutting one another. However, as Harry Levin long ago pointed out, *Hamlet* is saturated with questions. *Hamlet* is, as Mack remarks, a play in the "interrogative mood." Levin observes that in the 322 lines of the Graveyard Scene (5.1), there are "seventy question marks" (*Question of* Hamlet 19). (The empirical counting of question marks is uncertain since editions vary. Harold Jenkins's Arden edition of *Hamlet* has 295 lines for the Graveyard Scene and fifty-eight question marks, though there are several passages of multiple questions [47-101 (5 questions), 183-5 (4), 270-1 (6)].) There are *more* than four hundred grammatical questions in the play, and this number does not include the several integrated series of questions that are governed by single question marks, such as Marcellus's five queries (1.1.73-82) or Polonius's three-part question to Claudius which he reiterates three times (2.2.131-9). There is also the by-play on "inquire" between Polonius and Reynaldo that is followed by seven questions, but which are grammatically governed by the question mark belonging to an eighth question (2.1.4-15). All of these questions Polonius collectively, but very explicitly, describes as this "drift of question" (10). Questions are like a current that flows, sweeping and piling onwards, through his speech, and through the play itself. The extraordinary number of questions does not suggest the intricacy of Hamlet's use of "question" in his third soliloquy (3.1.56). The word, which, Levin notes, occurs "no less than seventeen times, much more frequently than in any of Shakespeare's other plays" and concludes "Hamlet's most famous line," may well be "the key-word of the play" (20). Questions are tools for finding answers. They seek out paths across boundaries. In both *Troilus* and *Hamlet* questions propose, and inescapably *are*, quests.

20. Ulysses's speech concerns itself with a hierarchical, and hence essentially spatial, disposition of society, whereas Hector's argument is directed at moral imperatives, at correct behaviour in time. The one vision is vertical; the other, horizontal. But both perspectives are needed to describe the just society (obviously not even remotely present in the play).

21. Curtius has traced the topos in *European Literature and the Latin Middle Ages*. The twin ideals of *Fortitudo et Sapientia* were to be manifested in council and in battle, respectively.

22. Bakhtin, whose spirit permeates this essay, thinks that dramatic literature is "alien to genuine polyphony, permitting only one, not

multiple worlds (*Problems of Dostoevsky's Poetics* 34). Clearly, we do not agree with this. Shakespeare's plays contain complex, often bifurcated characters who, typically, bear with them their hidden private worlds. More than in most novels, characters in Shakespeare's plays are worlds, dialogic both internally and in their external relationships, always an "unclosed whole" (63). In this sense more than in any other, *Troilus* strikes us as a "matchless forerunner text" (Freund 34-35). It looks ahead to the immense complexities of characterization that Bakhtin found in the tradition of the novel.

Notes to "Two Tents on Bosworth Field" by *Harry Levin*

1.   All citations and quotations from Shakespeare's plays come from *The Riverside Shakespeare*, ed. G. Blakemore Evans (Boston: Houghton Mifflin, 1974).

Notes to "As They Did in the Golden World" by *Keir Elam*

1.   An earlier version of this paper was read at the conference *Shakespeare: la nostalgia dell'essere,* Taormina, August 1984, and published in the conference proceedings. References to *As You Like It* are to the Arden edition. In *Shakespeare's Universe of Discourse* I have argued that discourse is central to Shakespearean comedy as it is to Elizabethan culture, that it is both a privileged semiotic means and a direct dramatic and comic topic. Language, for the Elizabethans, becomes a primary channel and primary target for enthusiasms, suspicions, wars, and the dramatic and theatrical potential of words themselves. In Shakespeare's comedies (as in those of Lyly and Jonson) we can observe the identity of verbal form with the dramatic concerns of the play (*Shakespeare's Universe* 2). The relation between narrative and drama, which is expressed in discourse, plays with these implications and also implies the relation between the dramatic and theatrical texts, written and performed texts, that I discussed in *The Semiotics of Theatre and Drama* and in *Shakespeare's Universe of Discourse* (33-34).

2.   As I say in *Shakespeare's Universe of Discourse*, the drama, as Aristotle states, creates its fictional world by the direct representation of events "within" the dramatic world (*mimesis*) and not by narration from

"without" (*diegesis*). Narrative information is normally provided to the audience through the interactions of the persons who comprise the fictional world. The dramatic world defines itself as it proceeds, which represents the particular reflexivity of dramatic discourse. This kind of discourse has to convey expository content regarding the characters who supposedly issue and receive it (for instance, Shylock and Portia), the circumstances in which it is supposedly issued (for example, Venice and the courtroom), and the action that its issuing constitutes (the demanding, for instance, of a pound of flesh). But in the comedies, the dialogue's world-creating reflexivity is much more than a conventional narrative short cut (or way of expelling the story-teller from the story-telling). In itself it becomes a primary source of rhetorical vitality (*Shakespeare's Universe* 72). In my book on Shakespeare, I refer briefly to two directly related worlds, *As You Like It* and its main source, Lodge's *Rosalynde*. I refer you to that discussion (73-77) but want to emphasize here a few of its aspects. Shakespeare follows — at the levels both of *fabula* (underlying story) and actual plot — the inherited narrative pattern with an unusual degree of fidelity. Any parallel episode, such as the wrestling match, will, however, reveal the radical divergences in the elaboration of narrative material and, in particular, the disposition of discourse along the three axes of discursive orientation: objects of discourse (an orientation to the dramatic universe itself and its individuals), context of utterance (the I-you and here-now of the speech exchange of dialogue), and the co-text (the verbal context of the discourse with its internal semantic and syntactic structure [see Petöfi]). Lodge presents the event (the wrestling match) through classical narration — a mixture of straightforward diegesis, direct character portrayal, *oratio obliqua*, and quoted direct speech. The only elements indicating a distinct narrative voice — a collective proverbial voice — are the parenthetic and moralistic Latin tags that punctuate the account. By nearly eliminating the indices of the context of utterance (at most, dimly implied in the narrative point of view), Lodge places all the weight of his narration on the orientation, from without, towards its objects of discourse (the individuals and events described). The co-text remains self-effacingly outward-and backward-looking because references are always to the past fictional world and never to the discourse in progress. Shakespeare's dramatization of this incident (the wrestling match) is set, as is typical of his comedy, within an apparently rambling series of more or less playful colloquies, which the ladies' resolutions to defeat despondency through verbal pastimes introduces. The preliminary information regarding the scene's central event is introduced only after a long warm-up in the guise of a wit contest with Touchstone. Shakespeare resorts to the conventional solution of the messenger, interrupting the ladies' recreation with the "real" topic of the day, clearly signalled as a piece of tellable, listenable, and gossipy intelligence. Le Beau appears to represent an internal or introjected version of Lodge's narrator, ready to impart equivalent details with similar diegetic earnestness. But he is never permitted to fulfil so innocent an information-bearing role. From the outset, his attempts to orient his and the ladies' discourse to the other scene in that episode is exemplary in the referential poetics of Shakespeare's comedy. Direct narrativity of the kind that Le Beau originally intended (he is a delegate of the source romance) is refused in favour of a dialogue telling that privileges the current communicative context, and even more so the brilliantly self-propagating co-text, over the proposed objects of discourse. The absent other-place — the scene of the wrestling — soon becomes the here and now of the dialogue because it is brought to them, in order to be subjected to the ladies' commentary. As the emblematic scene of frustrated narration from *As You Like It* amply illustrates, the context of utterance is the first and main point of dialogue orientation. For a definition of context or micro-analysis, see Lyons (*Semantics* 572), and for a close analysis of role, status, province, degree of formality, pragmatic supposition, topic, elocutionary intentions, and propositional attitude in this scene, see Elam (*Shakespeare's Universe* 75-76).

3. In *Shakespeare's Universe of Discourse*, I discuss in detail the most explicitly pastoral scene in Shakespeare — 2 i of *As You Like It* (see 136-40). In this scene, Shakespeare introduces us to the quasi-Arcadian Arden. Duke Senior's opening oration and Amiens's eulogistic commentary rehearse two moments of the landscape — language relationship in pastoral. First, the Duke equates the natural scene and human discourse of which he is a direct receiver. Second, Amiens praises these linguistic metaphors ("tongues in trees, books in the running brooks / Sermons in stores") as a felicitous verbal rendering of the present circumstances of the foresters. The idea that nature manifests itself to the initiated observer as a language belongs to the philosophical Platonism of Ficino, Pico, or Paracelsus and to a literary tradition — the pastoral drama of Politan, Tasso, Ariosto, Guarini, and their continental

and English imitators — that is closely associated in origin with that philosophical movement. As Richard Cody has shown, Tasso's *Aminta* (1573) relates directly to Italian Platonic syncreticism. The *Aminta* establishes the model for an intimate communion between the "natural" poetry of the Arcadian shepherd and the poetry of nature in Arcadia itself. Shakespeare's Orlando, the self-elected poet of Arden, acts out the Duke's conventional figures, particularly his "bibliographical" trope, in the most literal fashion, further textualizing the forest through his amorous versions (3.2.5-6). The trees become doubly "readable," books containing books. But Orlando's romantic gesture is another game of good Ariostan and Tassonian stock, and specifically an allusion to the Angelica and Medora episode in *Orlando Furioso*, duly varied in Tasso's *Aminta* ("Lo scrisse in mille piante"). The reference to a lover writing on trees, which Lee has called an "already-overworked topos in European literature" (*Names on Trees* 7), is also pregnant with more or less automatic iconographic associations relating to a long and eminent series of sixteenth-century illustrations of the *Orlando* episode (for instance, the "Angelica and Medora," an engraving by Giorgio Ghisi after Teodoro Ghisi). Orlando's semi-serious conceit becomes an oblique mode of the pseudo-painterly "iconism" that is essential to the pastoral style. It is tempting to see in Shakespeare's debts to Ariosto, Tasso and their imitators some allegiance also to the syncretist (Platonic-Orphic-Hermetic) matrix from which the language of *Orlando Furioso* and *Aminta* springs (see Cody 13, 76ff.; Wind, *Pagan Mysteries* 1967, 236ff.).

4. I have somewhat abused the quoted passage, which in fact refers to Thomas Hardy and not to Shakespeare. It might be noted that David Lodge's own novel, *Small World*, is subtitled "An Academic Romance."

Notes to "Noble Deeds and the Secret Singularity" by *Paul Morrison*

1. There are, for example, two patronymic sons in *Hamlet*, Fortinbras and Hamlet; the latter, of course, shares his name with the play. For a reading of *Hamlet* as a drama of nomination, to which my own paper is indebted, see Calderwood *passim*.

2. The corporeal is also the order of the maternal and the feminine in terms of the sexual politics of the play. That is, the subjectivity that Hamlet claims for himself is gender specific. "Now mother, what's the

matter" (11.2222) Hamlet asks at the beginning of the closet scene, which, as Margaret Ferguson has suggested, makes explicit the association of ideas in another of his remarks: "[b]ut to the matter, my mother you say" (9.2040). Cf. Ferguson 295.

3. My essay owes a great deal to Barker, although I ultimately disagree with him. He argues, for example, that "Hamlet's promised but unfilled interiority ... is unacceptable to bourgeois ideology because it is not sufficiently fixated" (39). I argue, on the contrary, that *Hamlet* finds Hamlet's protobourgeois ideology of interiority unacceptable, despite the fact that this same ideology has claimed Hamlet for its own.

4. See *The Stage* 13 Jan. 11 1845 (qtd. in Spencer 192-93). Hamlet is placed in the company of Goethe's *Die Leiden des jungen Werthers* (1774), Byron's *Lara* (1814), Étienne de Senancour's *Obermann* (1804), and Chateaubriand's *René* (1802).

5. Stephen Greenblatt argues that in Renaissance drama "the traditional linkages between body, property, and name are called into question ... One can glimpse the early stages of the slow, momentous transformation of the middle term from 'property' to 'psyche.' But that transformation had by no means already occurred; it was on the contrary the result (not yet perfectly realized in our own time) of a prolonged series of actions and transformations" ("Psychoanalysis and Renaissance Culture" 221).

6. Paul H. Fry argues that Johnson overthrows Aristotle on character by realigning Aristotelian terms: "Whereas for Aristotle the mere accidents of a character reside in his idiosyncratic nature, for Johnson they are constituted by his role or office — by his assigned place, in short, in the plot. Thus Shakespeare willingly flouts the Aristotelian *muthos*: 'His story requires Romans or kings, but he thinks only on men'" (27). Historically, challenges to the Aristotelian subordination of character to plot tended to be allied to the study of Shakespeare; it is by no means certain, however, that Shakespeare, or at least the Shakespeare of *Hamlet*, can be claimed for the anti-Aristotelian party.

7. On this theme, see Murray (95-96 and *passim*).

8. The lines beginning "That monster custome" (2.2366-71) do not appear in F1, which is the copy text for Wells's and Taylor's *Hamlet*. For reasons that I trust my essay makes clear, I am not concerned with the integrity of any given play-text. I therefore feel free to raid Q2 to suit my own purposes (Wells and Taylor give Q2 readings that are rejected by F1 in an appendix). I chose not to use an edition that follows Q2 for the simple reason that all such editions modernize spelling and

punctuation. Shakespeare, for reasons that I trust my essay also makes clear, is not our contemporary.

9. The critical ingenuity that has gone into denying what seems to me the obvious meaning of the word is worthy of a paper in itself. Unfortunately, only two strategies can detain me here; one because it might have been developed by Hamlet himself; the other, because it is still very much with us. Of the first, Steevens's conjecture, which is based on Roberts's contention (1729) that the same actor who played Henry VIII played Hamlet, is representative: "fat" refers to the actor playing Hamlet, not Hamlet "himself." Later critics advance various candidates for the original Hamlet — Collier, in his *Memoirs of the Principal Actors in the Plays of Shakespeare* argues for Burbage — but the point itself remains constant. The play-text, the ideal *Hamlet* and Hamlet, is thus rescued from the accidents and aberrations of performance and performers. Hamlet's advice to the players has apparently not gone unheeded (see the note on "fat" in Furness 446). The second strategy, the one that is still very much with us, could not be simpler: "fat," we are told, does not mean fat. The editor of the Arden edition, for example, glosses the word as "sweaty," as does the editor of the Riverside; the editor of the Signet gives it as both "sweaty" and "out of shape." These glosses are not, of course, totally arbitrary, as the *OED* does give "charged with moisture or odors" as a possible meaning for "fat," although never in relation to a person or character, which none of the above editions notes. And while this in no way argues against Shakespeare so using it, it does raise the possibility that the word may mean what an "untutored" audience invariably takes it to mean: Hamlet is fat.

10. See Else's note on the term *zoion* (Aristotle 152).

11. This portion of my argument takes a great deal from Fry's chapter on the *Poetics*, "Aristotle as Oedipus" (11-46).

12. For a reading of the play based on the interchangeability of *dessein* and *dessin*, see Phillips 411-20.

13. On the figure of the monster in classical French aesthetic theory, see Merlin 179-93. On the specific connection between *le monstre* and *montrer* in *Phèdre*, and Hippolyte's status as *le monstre qui se montre*, see Czerniecki 1012-30.

14. I am more or less paraphrasing Jean Starobinski (*L'Oeil vivant* 71) here.

Notes to "Narrative and Theatre" by *Richard A. Young*

1. I am thinking of developments that have led to explorations along the same vein followed by Patrice Pavis.

2. In this respect our approach to the text differs from that of Anne Ubersfeld where the focus is on the relation between reading and performance.

3. The notion of polyphony in narrative is drawn, of course, from Mikhail Bakhtin, *Problems of Dostoevsky's Poetics.*

4. The notion of simultaneous narrative is taken from Genette's typology derived from a comparison between the time of narration and the time of the narrated (229).

5. They are, for example, told in the present tense, as if the narrative were a commentary on the image projected onto the movie screen.

6. See "Egloga" II and IX (Encina 31-41, 127-38); "Egloga o farsa del nascimiento" and "Auto o farsa del nascimiento" (Fernández 121-37, 139-56); "Auto pastoril castellano," "Auto de los reyes magos," "Auto de la Sibila Casandra" (Vicente 7-24, 25-38, 43-68).

7. See Torres Naharro, Vol. 2.

8. The two scenes in question deal with the satisfaction felt by characters with their social station, honesty, and the existence of true love. In some respects, they are comic interludes based on verbal jousting, but they serve the important function of airing questions of social and natural order. The numbering of the scenes here and in subsequent references follows that adopted in the edition cited.

WORKS CITED

Alberti, Leon Battista. *On Painting*. Trans. J.R. Spencer. New Haven: Yale UP, 1956.

Alberti, Leon Battista. *The Albertis of Florence: Leon Battista Alberti's "Della Famiglia."* Trans. Guido Guarino. Lewisburg: Bucknell UP, 1971.

Alighieri, Dante. *Purgatorio*. Ed. and trans. Charles S. Singleton. Princeton: Princeton UP, 1973.

Althusser, Louis. "Ideology and Ideological State Apparatuses." *Lenin and Philosophy and Other Essays*. New York: Monthly Review, 1971. 127-86.

Angerman, Arina *et al.*, ed. *Current Issues in Women's History*. London: Routledge, 1989.

Ariès, Philippe. *The Hour of Our Death*. Trans. H. Weaver. New York: Knopf, 1981: 10-13

Ariosto, Ludovico. *Orlando furioso*. Trans. B. Reynolds. Harmondsworth: Penguin, 1975.

Aristotle. *Poetics*. Trans. Gerald F. Else. Ann Arbor: U of Michigan P, 1967.

Asp, Carolyn. "In Defense of Cressida." *Studies in Philology* 74 (1977): 406-17.

Auerbach, Erich. *Mimesis: The Representation of Reality in Western Literature*. Trans. Willard R. Trask. Princeton: Princeton UP, 1953.

Bakhtin, Mikhail M. *Rabelais and His World*. Trans. Hélène Iswolsky. Cambridge, MA: MIT P, 1968.

Bakhtin, Mikhail M. *The Dialogic Imagination: Four Essays by M. M. Bakhtin*. Ed. Michael Holquist. Trans. Caryl Emerson. Austin: U of Texas P, 1981.

Bakhtin, Mikhail M. *Problems of Dostoevsky's Poetics*. Trans. Caryl Emerson. Minneapolis: U Minnesota P, 1984.

Bal, Mieke. *Narratology: Introduction to the Theory of Narrative*. Trans Christine van Boheemen. Toronto: U of Toronto P, 1985.

Barbaro, Francesco. "De re uxoria." *Prosatori latini del quattrocento*. Ed. Eugenio Garin. Milan: Riccardi, 1952. 105-37.

Barbaro, Francesco. "Concerning Wifely Matters." Kohl *et al*. 179-88.

Barber, C. L. *Shakespeare's Festive Comedy*. Princeton: Princeton UP, 1959.

Barish, Jonas. *The Antitheatrical Prejudice*. Berkeley: U of California P, 1981.

Barker, Francis. *The Tremulous Private Body: Essays on Subjection.* London: Methuen, 1984.

Barnet, Sylvan. "'Strange Events': Improbability in *As You Like It.*" *Shakespeare Studies* 4 (1968): 119-31.

Barthes, Roland. *Sur Racine.* Paris: Seuil, 1963.

Barton, Anne. "Introduction: *As You Like It.*" *The Riverside Shakespeare.* Ed. G. Blakemore Evans. Boston: Houghton Mifflin, 1974. 365-68.

Bauschatz, Cathleen. "Montaigne's Conception of Reading in the Context of Renaissance Poetics and Modern Criticism." *The Reader in the Text: Essays on Audience and Interpretation.* Ed. Susan R. Suleiman and Inge Crosman. Princeton: Princeton UP, 1980. 264-91.

Beaty, Nancy Lee. *The Craft of Dying: The Literary Tradition of the Ars Moriendi in England.* New Haven: Yale UP, 1970.

Bellay, Joachim du. *The Colloquies of Erasmus.* Trans. Craig R. Thompson. Chicago: U of Chicago P, 1965.

Bellay, Joachim du. *Les Regrets et autres oeuvres poétiques.* Eds. J. Jolliffe and M. Screech. Geneva: Droz, 1966.

Belsey, Catherine. "Disrupting Sexual Difference: Meaning and Gender in the Comedies." *Alternative Shakespeares.* Ed. John Drakakis. London: Methuen, 1985. 166-90.

Ben Jonson. Ed. Ian Donaldson. Oxford: Oxford UP, 1985.

Benjamin, Walter. "Der Erzhler." *Gesammelte Schriften Band* II.2. Frankfurt am Main: Suhrkamp, 1980. 438-65.

Benjamin, Walter. "The Storyteller." *Illuminations.* Trans. Harry Zohn. New York: Shocken, 1969. 83-109.

Benson, Pamela. *The Invention of the Renaissance Woman: The Challenge of Female Independence in the Literature and Thought of Italy and England.* University Park: Pennsylvania State UP, 1992.

Bloom, Harold. *Ruin the Sacred Truths: Poetry and Belief from the Bible to the Present.* Cambridge, MA: Harvard UP, 1989.

Blum, Claude "La mort des hommes et la mort des bestes dans les *Essais* de Montaigne: Sur les fonctions paradigmatiques des deux exemples." *French Forum* 5 (1980): 3-13.

Boccaccio, Giovanni. *Filocolo.* Bari: Gius, Laterza & figli, 1938.

Boccaccio, Giovanni. *Decameron.* Ed. Vittore Branca. Firenze: Le Monnier, 1965.

Bocock, Robert. *Hegemony.* London: Tavistock, 1986.

Boileau-Despréaux, Nicolas. "L'Art poétique." *Oeuvres.* Ed. Georges Mongrédien. Paris: Garnier, 1961.

Boon, Jean-Pierre. "La pensée de Montaigne sur la mort a-t-elle évolué?" *MLN* 80 (1965): 307-17.

Boon, Jean-Pierre. *Montaigne, Gentilhomme et Essayiste.* Paris: PUF, 1971.

Bornstein, Diane, ed. *The Feminist Controversy of the Renaissance.* Delmar, NY: Scholars' Facsimiles and Reprints, 1980.

Bowen, Barbara. *The Age of Bluff: Paradox and Ambiguity in Rabelais and Montaigne.* Urbana: U of Illinois P, 1972. 129-36.

Boyarin, Jonathan, ed. *The Ethnography of Reading.* Berkeley: U of California P, 1992.

Brady, Frank and W.K. Wimsatt, eds. *Samuel Johnson: Selected Poetry and Prose.* Berkeley: U of California P, 1977.

Breisach, Ernst. *Historiography: Ancient, Medieval & Modern.* Chicago: U of Chicago P, 1983.

Bremond, Claude. *Logigue du récit.* Paris: Seuil, 1973.

Brody, Jules. *Lectures de Montaigne.* Kentucky: French Forum, 1982.

Bruner, Jerome. *Actual Minds / Possible Worlds.* Cambridge: Harvard UP, 1986.

Buchet, Luc, ed. *La femme pendant le moyen age et l'époque moderne.* Paris: CNRS, 1994.

Buero Vallejo, Antonio. *El sueño de la razón.* Madrid: Espasa Calpe, 1970.

Buero Vallejo, Antonio. *La doble historia del Dr. Valmy.* Madrid: Espasa Calpe, 1976.

Burton, Robert. *Anatomy of Melancholy.* 3 vols. London: York: Dutton, 1932.

Burton, Robert. *The Anatomy of Melancholy.* Eds. F. Dell and Paul Jordan-Smith. New York: Tudor, 1948.

Butor, Michel *Essais sur les* Essais. Paris: Gallimard, 1968.

Calderon de la Barca, Pedro. *La Vida Es Sueño: Comedias.* Vol. 1. Madrid: M. Rivadeneyra, 1872.

Calderón de la Barca, Pedro. *No hay burlas con el amor [Love is No Laughing Matter].* Ed. Don Cruickshank and Seán Page. Warminster: Aris & Phillips, 1986.

Calderwood, James L. *To Be And Not To Be: Negation and Metadrama in Hamlet.* New York: Columbia UP, 1983.

Casa, Giovanni della and Baldassare Castiglione. *Opere.* Ed. G. Prezzolini. Milano: Rizzoli, 1937.

Cave, Terence. *The Cornucopian Text: Problems of Writing in the French Renaissance.* Oxford: Oxford UP, 1979.

Cave, Terence. "The Mimesis of Reading in the Renaissance." *Mimesis: From Mirror to Method, Augustine to Descartes.* Ed. John D. Lyons and Stephen G. Nichols, Jr. Hanover: UP of New England, 1982. 149-65.

Cave, Terence. "Problems of Reading in the *Essais*." *Montaigne, Essays in Memory of Richard Sayce*. Ed. I.D. McFarlane and Ian Maclean. Oxford: Oxford UP, 1982: 133-66.

Cave, Terence. *Recognitions: A Study in Poetics*. Oxford: Clarendon, 1988.

Cavell, Stanley. "Hamlet's Burden of Proof." *Disowning Knowledge in Six Plays of Shakespeare*. New York: Cambridge UP, 1987. 179-91.

Cervantes de Saavedra, Miguel de. *El Ingenioso Hidalgo Don Quijote de la Mancha*. Ed. Vicente Gaos. Madrid: Gredos, 1987.

Cervantes de Saavedra, Miguel de. "El cerco de Numancia." *Obras completas*. Ed. Angel Valbuena Prat. Madrid: Espasa Calpe, 1965.

Chambers, Ross. *Room for Maneuver: Reading (the) Oppositional (in) Narrative*. Chicago: U of Chicago P, 1991.

Charpentier, Françoise. "La Poétique de Pontus de Tyard entre Scève et la Pléiade." *Intellectual Life in Lyon*. Eds. Philip Ford and Gillian Jondorf. Cambridge: Cambridge French Colloquia, 1993. 173-91.

Chartier, Roger. "Les Arts de mourir, 1450-1600." *Annales* 31 (1976): 51-75.

Chartier, Roger. "The Practical Impact of Writing." *A History of Private Life: The Passions of the Renaissance*. Ed. R. Chartier. Trans. A. Goldhammer. Cambridge, MA: Harvard UP, 1989. 111-59.

Cicero. *De amicitia*. Trans. S. Armistead Falconer. Cambridge: Harvard UP, 1953.

Cody, Richard. *The Landscape of the Mind: Pastoralism and Platonic Theory in Tasso's Aminta and Shakespeare's Early Comedies*. Oxford: Clarendon, 1969.

Cohen, Walter. *Drama of a Nation: Public Theater in Renaissance England and Spain*. Ithaca: Cornell UP, 1985.

Compagnon, Antoine. *La Seconde Main ou le travail de la citation*. Paris: Seuil, 1979.

Compagnon, Antoine. *Nous, Michel de Montaigne*. Paris: Seuil, 1980.

Cooper, Richard. "Humanism and Politics in Lyon in 1533." *Intellectual Life in Lyon*. Eds. Philip Ford and Gillian Jondorf. Cambridge: Cambridge French Colloquia, 1993. 1-31.

Cope, Jackson I. *The Theater and the Dream: From Metaphor to Form in Renaissance Drama*. Boston: Johns Hopkins UP, 1973.

Cornford, Francis. *The Origin of Attic Comedy*. 1914. Cambridge: Cambridge UP, 1934.

Cotgrave, Randle. *A Dictionarie of the French and English Tongues*. 1611; rpt. Columbia, SC: U of South Carolina P, 1950.

Cruickshank, Don and Seán Page. "Introduction." *Calderón de la Barca* vii-xxxvii.

Cueva, Juan de la. *El infamador, Los siete infantes de Lara y el Ejemplar poético.* Ed. Francisco A. de Icaza. Madrid: Espasa Calpe, 1965.

Culler, Jonathan. "Comparative Literature and the Pieties." *Profession 86.* New York: MLA, 1986. 30-32.

Curtius, Ernst R. *European Literature and the Latin Middle Ages.* Trans. Willard R. Trask. New York: Harper, 1963.

Czerniecki, Krystian. "Déracination: *Phèdre's* Monstrous Pedagogy." *Modern Language Notes* (1986): 1012-30.

Daniélou, Jean. *Bible et liturgie.* Paris: Cerf, 1958.

Daston, Lorraine and Katharine Park. "The Hermaphrodite and the Orders of Nature: Sexual Ambiguity in Early Modern France. *Premodern Sexualities in Europe.* Eds. Louise Fradenburg and Carla Freccero. Special issue of *GLQ* 4 (1994): 49-68.

Davis, Natalie Zemon. *Society and Culture in Early Modern France.* Stanford: Stanford UP, 1975.

Davis, Natalie Zemon. "'Women's History' in Transition: The European Case." *Feminist Review* 3-4, 1975-76.

Davis, Natalie Zemon. "Women on Top: Symbolic Sexual Inversion and Political Disorder in Early Modern Europe." *The Reversible World: Symbolic Inversion in Art and Society.* Ed. Barbara Babcock. Ithaca: Cornell UP, 1978. 147-90.

Davis, Natalie Zemon. "Boundaries and the Sense of Self in Sixteenth-Century France." *Reconstructing Individualism: Autonomy, Individuality, and the Self in Western Thought.* Eds. T. Heller, M. Sosna, and D. Wellbery. Stanford: Stanford UP, 1986. 53-63.

Davis, Natalie Zemon and Arlette Farge, eds. *A History of Women: Renaissance and Enlightenment Paradoxes.* Cambridge, MA: Harvard UP, 1993.

Defaux, Gérard. *Marot, Rabelais, Montaigne: L'écriture comme présence.* Paris: Champion-Slatkine, 1987.

Dekker, Rudolf M. and Lotte van de Pol. *The Tradition of Female Transvestism in Early Modern Europe.* London: Macmillan, 1989.

Dekker, Thomas and Thomas Middleton. *The Roaring Girl.* Manchester: Manchester UP, 1987.

Desaive, Jean-Paul. "The Ambiguities of Literature." Davis and Farge 261-94.

Desan, Philippe. *Les Commerces de Montaigne: Le discours économique des Essais.* Paris: Nizet, 1992.

Dimić, M.V. "Opening a Dialogue with Thomas Greene's Literariness." *Canadian Review of Comparative Literature / Revue Canadienne de Littérature Comparée* 13.2 (1986): 225-29.

Donaldson, E. Talbot. *The Swan at the Well: Shakespeare Reading Chaucer.* New Haven: Yale UP, 1985.

Donne, John. "Sermon Preached at Lincoln's Inn." *Poetry and Prose.* Ed. Frank J. Warnke. New York: Modern Library, 1967.

Dulong, Claude. "From Conversation to Creation." Davis and Farge 395-419.

Ekstein, Nina. *Dramatic Narrative: Racine's Récits.* New York: Peter Lang, 1986.

Elam, Keir. *The Semiotics of Theatre and Drama.* London: Methuen, 1980.

Elam, Keir. *Shakespeare's Universe of Discourse: Language-Games in the Comedies.* Cambridge: Cambridge UP, 1984.

Elms, A.C. "Freud as Leonardo: Why the First Psychobiography Went Wrong." *Journal of Personality* 56 (1988): 19-40.

Emck, Katy. "Female Transvestism and Male Self-Fashioning in *As You Like It* and *La vida es sueño.*" *Reading the Renaissance.* Ed. Jonathan Hart. New York: Garland, 1996. 75-88.

Empson, William. *Some Versions of Pastoral.* London: Chatto and Windus, 1935.

Encina, Juan del. *Eglogas de Juan del Enzina.* Ed. Humberto López Morales. New York: Las Americas, 1963.

Epstein, Julia and Kristina Straub, eds. *Body Guards: The Cultural Politics of Gender Ambiguity.* New York: Routledge, 1991.

Erasmus, Desiderius. *Apophthegmes.* Colonial: Gymnius, 1538.

Erasmus, Desiderius. *Cinq Banquets.* Trad. B. Boudou. Paris: J. Vrin, 1981.

Febvre, Lucien. *Autour de l'Heptaméron: Amour sacré, amour profane.* Paris: Gallimard, 1944.

Ferguson, Margaret W. "*Hamlet*: Letters and Spirits," *Shakespeare and the Question of Theory.* Patricia Parker and Geoffrey Hartman, eds. New York and London: Methuen, 1985. 292-309.

Ferguson, Margaret, Maureen Quilligan, and Nancy J. Vickers. "Introduction." Ferguson, Quilligan, and Vickers xv-xxxi.

Ferguson, Margaret, Maureen Quilligan, and Nancy J. Vickers, eds. *Rewriting the Renaissance: The Discourses of Sexual Difference in Early Modern Europe.* Chicago: U of Chicago P, 1986.

Fernández, Lucas. *Farsas y églogas.* Ed. John Lihani. New York: Las Americas, 1969.

Fletcher, Antony and John Stevenson. *Order and Disorder in Early Modern England.* Cambridge: Cambridge UP, 1985.

Ford, Philip. "The *Basia* of Joannes Secundus and Lyon Poetry." *Intellectual Life in Lyon.* Eds. Philip Ford and Gillian Jondorf. Cambridge: Cambridge French Colloquia, 1993. 113-33.

Foucault, Michel. *Surveiller et punir: Naissance de la prison.* Paris: Gallimard, 1975.

Foucault, Michel. *The History of Sexuality, Volume 1: An Introduction.* Trans. Robert Hurley. New York: Random House, 1978.

Foucault, Michel. "What Is an Author?" *Textual Strategies: Perspectives in Post-Structuralist Criticism.* Ed. Josué Harari. Ithaca: Cornell UP, 1979. 141-60.

Fradenburg, Louise Olga. *City, Marriage, Tournament: Arts of Rule in Late Medieval Scotland.* Madison: U of Wisconsin P, 1991.

Fradenburg, Louise and Carla Freccero, eds. *Premodern Sexualities in Europe.* Special issue of *GLQ* 4 (1994).

Freccero, Carla. "The Other and the Same: The Image of the Hermaphrodite in Rabelais." Ferguson, Quilligan, and Vickers 145-58.

Freccero, Carla. "1527: Margaret of Navarre." *A New Literary History of French Literature.* Ed. Dennis Hollier. Cambridge, MA: Harvard UP, 1989. 145-48.

Freccero, Carla. *Father Figures: Genealogy and Narrative Structure in Rabelais.* Ithaca: Cornell UP, 1991.

Freccero, Carla. "Economy, Woman, and Renaissance Discourse." Migiel and Schiesari 192-208.

Freccero, Carla. "Politics and Aesthetics in Castiglione's *Il Cortegiano*: Book III and the Discourse on Women." *Creative Imitation: New Essays on Renaissance Literature in Honor of Thomas M. Greene.* Eds. David Quint, Margaret Ferguson, G.W. Pigman III, and Wayne A. Rebhorn. Binghamton: MRTS, 1992. 259-79.

Freccero, Carla. "Marguerite de Navarre and the Politics of Maternal Sovereignty." *Women and Sovereignty.* Ed. Louise Fradenburg. Special issue of *Cosmos* 7 (1992): 132-49.

Freccero, John. "The Fig Tree and the Laurel: Petrarch's Poetics." *Diacritics* 5.1 (1975): 34-40.

Freccero, John. "Medusa and the Madonna of Forlì: Political Sexuality in Machiavelli." *Machiavelli and the Discourse of Literature.* Eds. Albert Ascoli and Victoria Kahn. Ithaca: Cornell UP, 1993. 161-78.

Freund, Elizabeth. "'Ariachne's Broken Woof': The Rhetoric of Citation." Parker and Hartman 19-36.

Friedrich, Hugo. *Montaigne.* Trans. R. Rovini. Paris: Gallimard, 1968.

Frye, Northrop. "The Argument of Comedy." *Shakespeare: Modern Essays in Criticism.* Revised Edition. Ed. Leonard F. Dean. 1957, rev. 1967. London: Oxford UP, 1975. 79-89.

Frye, Northrop. *A Natural Perspective: The Development of Shakespearean Comedy and Romance.* New York: Harcourt Brace and World, 1965.

Frye, Northrop. *Fools of Time: Studies in Shakespearean Tragedy.* Toronto: U of Toronto P, 1967.

Frye, Northrop. *Anatomy of Criticism: Four Essays.* 1957. Princeton: Princeton UP, 1973.

Frye, Northrop. *The Secular Scripture: A Study of the Structure of Romance.* Cambridge, MA: Harvard UP, 1976.

Fry, Paul H. *The Reach of Criticism: Method and Perception in Literary Theory.* New Haven: Yale UP, 1983.

Furness, Horace Howard, ed. *Hamlet.* New York: Dover, 1963.

Gabe, Dorothy. "Maurice Scève: A Person Honoured by Lyon." *Intellectual Life in Renaissance Lyon.* Eds. Philip Ford and Gillian Jondorf. Cambridge: Cambridge French Colloquia, 1993. 193-203.

Garber, Marjorie. *Vested Interests: Cross-Dressing and Cultural Anxiety.* New York: Routledge, 1992.

Gardner, Helen. "Let the Forest Judge." *More Talking of Shakespeare.* Ed. John Garrett. London: Longman, 1959. 17-32.

Gay, Peter, ed. *The Freud Reader.* New York: 1989.

Gay, Peter. "Introduction." Gay xiii-xxix.

Genette, Gérard. "Discours du récit": *Figures III.* Paris: Seuil, 1972.

Goethe, Johann Wolfgang von. *Wilhelm Meisters Lehrjahre.* Ed. Ernst Beutler. *Gedenkausgabe der Werke, Briefe und Gespräche.* Zürich: Artemis, 1948-60.

Goldberg, Jonathan. *Voice Terminal Echo: Postmodernism and English Renaissance Texts.* New York: Methuen, 1986.

Gombrich, E. H. *Art, Perception, and Reality.* Baltimore: Johns Hopkins UP, 1972.

Gray, Floyd. "Montaigne's Friends." *French Studies* 15 (1961): 203-17.

Gray, Floyd. "The Unity of Montaigne in the *Essais.*" *Modern Language Quarterly* 22 (1961): 79-86.

Gray, Floyd. *La Balance de Montaigne:* Exagium / Essai. Paris: Nizet, 1982.

Green, D.H. *Medieval Listening and Reading: The Primary Reception of German Literature, 800-1300.* Cambridge: Cambridge UP, 1994.

Greenblatt, Stephen. *Renaissance Self-Fashioning.* Chicago, London: Chicago UP, 1980.

Greenblatt, Stephen. "Psychoanalysis and Renaissance Culture." *Literary Theory / Renaissance Texts*. Eds. Patricia Parker and David Quint. Baltimore: Johns Hopkins UP, 1986. 210-24.

Greenblatt, Stephen. *Shakespearean Negotiations: The Circulation of Social Energy in Renaissance England*. Berkeley: U California P, 1988.

Greenblatt, Stephen. "Fiction and Friction." *Shakespearian Negotiations* 66-93.

Greenblatt, Stephen. *Marvelous Possessions: The Wonder of the New World*. Chicago: U of Chicago P, 1991.

Greene, Gayle. "Shakespeare's Cressida: 'A Kind of Self.'" *The Woman's Part: Feminist Criticism of Shakespeare*. Ed. Carolyn Ruth Swift Lenz *et al*. Chicago: U Illinois P, 1980. 133-49.

Greene, Thomas M. *The Light in Troy: Imitation and Discovery in Renaissance Poetry*. New Haven: Yale UP, 1982.

Greene, Thomas M. "On the Category of the Literary." *Canadian Review of Comparative Literature / Revue Canadienne de Littérature Comparée* 13.2 (1986): 217-24.

Greene, Thomas M. "Closing Remarks." *Canadian Review of Comparative Literature / Revue Canadienne de Littérature Comparée* 13.2 (1986): 236-37.

Greene, Thomas M. "Ceremonial Play and Parody in the Renaissance." *Urban Life in the Renaissance*. Ed. Adele Seeff. Delaware: U of Delaware P, 1989. 281-93.

Greimas, Algirdas. *Sémantique structurale*. Paris: Larousse, 1966.

Grene, Nicholas *Shakespeare, Jonson, Molière: The Comic Contract*. London: Macmillan, 1980.

Grimm, Reinhold. "Identity and Difference: On Comparative Studies Within a Single Language." *Profession 86*. New York: MLA, 1986. 28-29.

Guarini, Battista. *Il Pastor Fido [The Faithful Shepherd]*. Ed. J.H. Whitfield. Edinburgh: Edinburgh UP, 1976.

Guillot, G. *Un table synoptique de la vie et des oeuvres de Louise Labé*. Paris, 1962.

Gutwirth, Marcel. *Montaigne ou le pari d'Exemplarité*. Montréal: PU de Montréal, 1977.

Hamilton, A.C. *et al.*, eds. *The Spenser Encyclopedia*. Toronto: U Toronto P, 1990.

Hampton, Timothy. *Writing from History: the Rhetoric of Exemplarity in Tasso, Montaigne and Cervantes*. Ithaca: Cornell UP, 1990.

Harrison, Jane. *Themis*. Cambridge: Cambridge UP, 1912.

Hart, Jonathan. "A Comparative Pluralism: The Heterogeneity of Methods and the Case of Fictional Worlds." *Canadian Review of Comparative Literature / Revue Canadienne de Littérature Comparée* 15.3-4 (1988): 320-45.

Hart, Jonathan. "Introduction: Narrative, Narrative Theory, Drama: the Renaissance." *Renaissance Narrative and Drama / Récit et Théâtre à la Renaissance.* Ed. Jonathan Hart. Special issue of *Canadian Review of Comparative Literature / Revue Canadienne de Littérature Comparée* 18.2-3 (1991): 117-65.

Hart, Jonathan. *Theater and World: The Problematics of Shakespeare's History.* Boston: Northeastern UP, 1992.

Hart, Jonathan. "Conclusion." *Theater and World* 203-16.

Hart, Jonathan. "The Ever-Changing Configurations of Comparative Literature." *Canadian Review of Comparative Literature / Revue Canadienne de Littérature Comparée* (1992): 1-20.

Hart, Jonathan. *Northrop Frye: The Theoretical Imagination.* London: Routledge, 1994.

Hart, Jonathan. "Images of the Native in Renaissance Encounter Narratives." *ARIEL* 25 (1994): 55-76.

Hendricks, Margo and Patricia Parker, eds. *Women, "Race," and Writing in the Early Modern Period.* London: Routledge, 1994.

Henry, Patrick. *Montaigne in Dialogue: Censorship and Defensive Writing, Architecture and Friendship, the Self and the Other.* Saratoga, CA: Anma Libri, 1987.

Hernadi, Paul. "What Isn't Comparative Literature?" *Profession 86.* New York: MLA, 1986. 22-24.

Herrick, Marvin T. *Comic Theory in the Sixteenth Century.* Urbana: U of Illinois P, 1964.

Hertz, Neil. "Medusa's Head: Male Hysteria under Political Pressure." *The End of the Line: Essays on Psychoanalysis and the Sublime.* New York: Columbia UP, 1985. 161-96.

Howard, Jean. "Cross-Dressing, the Theatre and Gender Struggle in Early Modern England." *Shakespeare Quarterly* 39 (1988): 418-40.

Howe, Nicholas. "The Cultural Construction of Reading." Boyarin 58-79.

Hughes, Philip. *A History of the Church.* New York: Sheed and Ward, 1947.

Hume, Peter. *Colonial Encounters: Europe and the Native Caribbean 1492-1797.* 1986. London: Routledge, 1992.

Ingarden, Roman. *The Literary Work of Art: An Investigation on the Borderlines of Ontology, Logic, and Theory of Literature.* 1973. Trans. George G. Grabowicz. Evanston: Northwestern UP, 1980.

Insdorf, Cecile. *Montaigne and Feminism*. Chapel Hill: U of North Carolina Dept. of Romance Languages, 1977.

Jagendorf, Z.J. *The Happy End of Comedy: Shakespeare, Jonson, Molière*. Newark: U of Delaware P, 1984.

Jakobson, Roman. "Linguistique et poetique." *Essais de linguistique générale*. Paris: Minuit, 1963.

James I. *The Basilicon Doron of King James VI*. Ed. James Craigie. Edinburgh: Blackwood, 1944.

Jardine, Lisa. *Still Harping on Daughters: Women and Drama in the Age of Shakespeare*. Sussex: Harvester, 1983.

Jed, Stephanie. "Chastity on the Page: A Feminist Use of Paleography." Migiel and Schiesari 1991, 114-130.

Jones, Ann Rosalind. "Surprising Fame: Renaissance Gender Ideologies and Women's Lyric." *The Poetics of Gender*. Ed. Nancy Miller. New York: Columbia UP, 1986. 74-95.

Jones, Ann Rosalind. "City Women and Their Audiences: Louise Labé and Veronica Franco." Ferguson, Quilligan, and Vickers 299-316.

Jones, Ann Rosalind. "Nets and Bridles: Early Modern Conduct Books and Sixteenth-Century Women's Lyrics." *The Ideology of Conduct: Essays in Literature and the History of Sexuality*. Eds. Nancy Armstrong and Leonard Tennenhouse. New York: Methuen, 1987. 39-72.

Jones, Ann Rosalind. *The Currency of Eros: Women's Love Lyric in Europe, 1540-1620*. Bloomington: Indiana UP, 1990.

Jones, Ann and Peter Stallybrass. "Fetishizing Gender: Constructing the Hermaphrodite in Renaissance Europe." Epstein and Straub 80-111.

Jordan, Constance. *Renaissance Feminism: Literary Texts and Political Methods*. Ithaca: Cornell UP, 1990.

Jourda, Pierre. *Marguerite d'Angoulême, duchesse d'Alençon, reine de Navarre: Etude biographique et littéraire*. 2 vols. Paris: Honoré Champion, 1930. Repr. Paris: Slatkine, 1978.

Kantorowicz, Ernst H. *The King's Two Bodies: A Study in Mediaeval Political Theology*. Princeton: Princeton UP, 1957.

Kelly, Joan. *Women, History and Theory: The Essays of Joan Kelly*. Chicago: U of Chicago P, 1984.

Kelso, Ruth. *Doctrine for the Lady of the Renaissance*. Urbana: U of Illinois P, 1956.

Kirk, Eugene P. *Menippean Satire: An Annotated Catalogue of Texts and Criticism*. New York: Garland, 1980.

Klapisch-Zuber, Christiane. *Women, Family, and Ritual in Renaissance Italy.* Trans. Lydia Cochrane. Chicago: U of Chicago P, 1985.

Knight, Stephen. *Geoffrey Chaucer.* Oxford: Blackwell, 1986.

Knights, L.C. "*Troilus and Cressida* Again." *Scrutiny* 18, 1951-52.

Kohl, Benjamin *et al.*, eds., *The Earthly Republic: Italian Humanists on Government and Society.* Philadelphia: U of Pennsylvania P, 1978.

Kuehn, Thomas. *Law, Family, and Women: Toward a Legal Anthropology of Renaissance Italy.* Chicago: U of Chicago P, 1991.

Kyndrup, Morten. *Framing and Fiction: Studies in the Rhetoric of Novel, Interpretation, and History.* Aarhus: Aarhus UP, 1992.

Labé, Louise. *Oeuvres complètes.* Genève: Droz, 1981.

Lacan, Jacques. *Ecrits: A Selection.* Trans. Alan Sheridan. New York: W.W. Norton, 1977.

Langer, Ullrich. *Perfect Friendship: Studies in Literature and Moral Philosophy from Boccaccio to Corneille.* Geneva: Droz, 1994.

Lanser, Susan Sniader. *The Narrative Act: Point of View in Prose Fiction.* Princeton: Princeton UP, 1981.

Laqueur, Thomas. "Orgasm, Generation, and the Politics of Reproductive Biology." *Representations* 14 (1986): 1-41.

Laqueur, Thomas. *Making Sex: Body and Gender from the Greeks to Freud.* Cambridge, MA: Harvard UP, 1990.

Lawall, Sarah. "The Canon's Mouth: Comparative Literature and the World Masterpieces Anthology." *Profession 86.* New York: MLA, 1986. 25-27.

Le Goff, Jacques. *La Naissance du purgatoire.* Paris: Gallimard, 1981.

Lee, Rensselaer W. *Ut pictura poesis: The Humanistic Theory of Painting.* New York: Norton, 1967.

Lee, Rensselaer W. *Names on Trees: Ariosto in Art.* Princeton: Princeton UP, 1977.

Levin, Harry. *The Question of Hamlet.* New York: St. Martin's, 1959.

Levin, Harry. *Grounds for Comparison.* Cambridge: Harvard UP, 1972.

Levin, Harry. *Playboys and Killjoys: An Essay on the Theory and Practice of Comedy.* Oxford: Oxford UP, 1987.

Levine, Laura. "Men in Women's Clothing: Anti-Theatricality and Effeminisation from 1579-1642." *Criticism* 28 (1986): 121-43.

Lodge, David. *Small World: An Academic Romance.* London: Secker & Warburg, 1984.

Lodge, Thomas. "*Rosalynde: Eupheus Golden Legacie* (1590)." *Narrative and Dramatic Sources of Shakespeare.* Vol. 2. Ed. Geoffrey Bullough. London: Routledge, 1958. 158-256.

Lomperis, Linda and Sarah Stanbury, eds. *Feminist Approaches to the Body in Medieval Literature*. Philadelphia: U of Pennsylvania P, 1993.

Long, Elizabeth. "Textual Interpretation as Collective Action." Boyarin 180-211.

Lope de Vega Carpio, Félix. *Obras escogidas*. 3 vols. Madrid: Aguilar, 1964.

Lope de Vega Carpio, Félix. *Arte nuevo de hacer comedias en este tiempo [The New Art of Writing Plays in this Age]*. 1609. *European Theories of Drama*. Ed. Barrett H. Clark. Rev. Henry Popkin. 1918. New York: Crown, 1947, rev. 1965. 63-67.

Lyons, John. *Semantics*. Cambridge: Cambridge UP, 1977.

Lyons, John. *The Rhetoric of Example in Early Modern France and Italy*. Princeton: Princeton UP, 1989.

Lyotard, Jean-François. *The Postmodern Explained: Correspondence 1982-1985*. Eds. J. Pefanis and M. Thomas. Trans. Don Barry *et al*. Minneapolis: U of Minnesota P, 1992.

Machiavelli, Niccolò. *The Prince and the Discourses*. Ed. Max Lerner. New York: Modern Library, 1950.

Macksey, Richard. "Last Words: the Artes Moriendi as a Transtextual Genre." *Genre* 16 (1983): 493-516.

Maclean, Ian. *The Renaissance Notion of Woman: A Study in the Fortunes of Scholasticism and Medical Science in European Intellectual Life*. Cambridge: Cambridge UP, 1980.

MacPhail, Eric. "Friendship as a Political Ideal in Montaigne's *Essais*." *Montaigne Studies* 1 (1989): 177-87.

Maitre, Doreen. *Literature and Possible Worlds*. London: Middlesex Polytechnic P, 1983.

McAlindon, Thomas. *English Renaissance Tragedy*. Vancouver: U of British Columbia P, 1986.

McHale, Brian. *Postmodernist Fiction*. New York: Methuen, 1987.

Mehlman, Jeffrey. "La Boétie's Montaigne." *Oxford Literary Review* 4 (1979): 45-61.

Menéndez y Pelayo, Marcelino. *Estudios sobre el teatro de Lope de Vega*. 6 vols. Madrid: Consejo Superior de Investigaciones Científicas, 1949.

Merlin, Helen. "Où est le monstre?: Remarques sur l'esthétique de l'âge classique." *Revue des sciences humaines* 49 (1982): 179-93.

Micha, Alexandre. *Le Singulier Montaigne*. Paris: Nizet, 1968.

Migiel, Marilyn and Juliana Schiesari, eds. *Refiguring Woman: Perspectives on Gender and the Italian Renaissance*. Ithaca: Cornell UP, 1991.

Milowicki, Edward and Rawdon Wilson. "Ovid Through Shakespeare: The Divided Self." *Poetics Today*, forthcoming.

Molière, Jean Baptiste. *Théâtre complet.* 2 vols. Ed. Robert Jouanny. Paris: Garnier, 1962.

Montaigne, Michel de. *Essais.* 3 vols. Ed. M. Rat. Paris: Garnier, 1962.

Montaigne, Michel de. *Oeuvres complètes.* Eds. A. Thibaudet et M. Rat. Paris: Gallimard, Bibliothèque de la Pléiade, 1962.

Montaigne, Michel de. *Les Essais de Michel de Montaigne.* Ed. P. Villey and V.L. Saulnier. Paris: PU de France, 1965.

Montrose, Louis. "'The Place of a Brother' in *As You Like It*: Social Process and Comic Form." *Shakespeare Quarterly* 32 (1981): 28-54.

Murray, Timothy. *Theatrical Legitimization: Allegories of Genius in Seventeenth-Century England and France.* New York: Oxford UP, 1987.

Nakam, Géralde. *Montaigne et son temps: Les événements et les Essais.* Paris: Gallimard, 1993.

Navarre, Marguerite de. *L'Heptaméron.* Ed. Michel François. Paris: Garnier, 1943.

Navarre, Marguerite de. *The Heptameron.* Trans. P.A. Chilton London: Penguin, 1984.

Nelson, William. "From 'Listen, Lordings' to 'Dear Reader.'" *University of Toronto Quarterly* 46 (1976-77): 110-24.

Nochlin, Linda. *Women, Art, and Power and Other Essays.* New York: Harper and Rowe, 1988.

Norberg, Kathryn. "Prostitues." Davis and Farge 458-74.

Norbrook, David. Preface. *The Penguin Book of Renaissance Verse: 1509-1659.* Ed. H.R. Woudhuysen. London: Penguin / Allen Lane, 1992. xxi-xli.

O'Connor, Mary C. *The Art of Dying Well: The Development of the Ars moriendi.* New York: Columbia UP, 1942.

O'Malley, John W. *Giles of Viterbo on Church and Reform.* Leyden: Brill, 1968.

O'Malley, John W. *Praise and Blame in Renaissance Rome: Rhetoric, Doctrine and Reform in the Sacred Orators of the Papal Court.* Durham: Duke UP, 1979.

Orgel, Stephen. "Nobody's Perfect: Or Why did the English Stage Take Boys for Women?" *South Atlantic Quarterly* 88.1 (1989): 7-30.

Ornstein, Robert. *The Moral Vision of Jacobean Tragedy.* Madison: U Wisconsin P, 1960.

Ovid, Publius Naso. *Metamorphoses.* Trans. Mary M. Innes. 1955. London: Penguin, 1988.

Ovid, Publius Naso. *Metamorphoses.* Trans. Frank J. Miller. Loeb Classical Library. Cambridge, MA: Harvard UP, n.d.

Pacteau, Francette. "The Impossible Referent: Representations of the Androgyne." *Formations of Fantasy*. Eds. Victor Burgin, James Donald, and Cora Kaplan. New York: Methuen, 1986. 62-84.

Pagden, Anthony. *European Encounters with the New World: From Renaissance to Romanticism*. New Haven: Yale UP, 1993.

Panofsky, Erwin. *Idea: A Concept in Art Theory*. Trans. J. Peake. New York: Harper and Row, 1968.

Parker, Patricia A. *Inescapable Romance: Studies in the Poetics of a Mode*. Princeton: Princeton UP, 1979.

Parker, Patricia A. *Literary Fat Ladies: Rhetoric, Gender, Property*. New York: Methuen, 1987.

Parker, Patricia A. "Gender Ideology, Gender Change: The Case of Marie Germain." *Critical Inquiry* 19.2 (1993): 337-64.

Parker, Patricia A. "Romance." *The Spenser Encyclopedia* 609-18.

Parker, Patricia and Geoffrey Hartman, eds. *Shakespeare and The Question of Theory*. New York: Methuen, 1985.

Parry, Adam. "The Language of Achilles." *The Language and Background of Homer*. Ed. G.S. Kirk. Cambridge: W. Heffer, 1964. 48-54.

Pavel, Thomas. *Fictional Worlds*. Cambridge: Harvard UP, 1986.

Pavis, Patrice. *Problèmes de sémiologie théâtrale*. Montréal: PU du Québec, 1976.

Petöfi, János S. *Vers une théorie partielle du texte*. Hamburg: Buske, 1975.

Petrarca, Francesco. *Secretum*. Roma: Guido Izzi, 1993.

Phillips, K.J. "Enclosing Designs in Racine's *Phèdre*." *Romantic Review* 73 (1982): 411-20.

Poggioli, Renato. "The Oaten Flute." *Harvard Library Bulletin* 11 (1957): 159.

Pratt, Mary Louise. "Comparative Literature as a Cultural Practice." *Profession 86*. New York: MLA, 1986. 33-35.

Pratt, Mary Louise. *Imperial Eyes: Travel Writing and Transculturation*. London: Routledge, 1992.

Propp, Vladimir. *Morphologie du conte*. Paris: Seuil, 1965.

Puig, Manuel. *El beso de la mujer araña*. Barcelona: Seiz Barral, 1958.

Puig, Manuel. *La traición de Rita Hayworth*. Barcelona: Seiz Barral, 1968.

Puig, Manuel. *Maldición eterna a quien lea estas páginas*. Barcelona: Seix Barral, 1980.

Puttenham, George. *The Arte of English Poesie* (1589). Eds. Gladys Doidge Willcock and Alice Walker. Cambridge: Cambridge UP, 1936.

Rabelais, François. *Oeuvres complètes*. 2 vols. Ed. Pierre Jourda. Paris: Garnier, 1962.

Racine, Jean Baptiste. *Oevres complètes II*. Paris: Gallimard, 1950.

Rackin, Phyllis. "Androgyny, Mimesis, and the Marriage of the Boy Heroine on the English Renaissance Stage." *PMLA* 102 (1987): 29-41.

Rappaport, Roy. *Ecology: Meaning, and Religion*. Richmond: North Atlantic Books, 1979.

Regosin, Richard. *The Matter of my Book: Montaigne's Essays as the Book of the Self*. Berkeley: U of California P, 1977.

Regosin, Richard. "Le mirouer vague: Reflections on the Example in Montaigne's *Essais*." *Oeuvres et Critiques* 8 (1983): 73-86.

Rendall, Steven. "Fontenelle and His Public." *MLN* 86 (1971): 496-508.

Rendall, Steven. "*Mus in pice*: Montaigne and Interpretation." *MLN* 94 (1979): 1056-71.

Rendall, Steven. "In Disjointed Parts / Par Articles decousus." *Fragments: Incompletion and Discontinuity*. Ed. L.D. Kritzman. New York: New York Literary Forum, 1980. 71-83.

Rendall, Steven. "Reading Montaigne." *Diacritics* 15.1 (1985): 44-53.

Rendall, Steven. *Distinguo: Reading Montaigne Differently*. Oxford: Oxford UP, 1992.

Rendall, Steven. "Introduction." D'Urfé.

Rigolot, François. "La Loi de l'essai et la loi du père: Socrates, Erasme, Luther et Montaigne." *Etudes Montaignistes en hommage à Pierre Michel*. Ed. Claude Blum and François Mouret. Geneva: Slatkine, 1982. 223-31.

Rigolot, François. "Montaigne's Purloined Letters." *Yale French Studies* 64 (1983): 145-66.

Rigolot, François. "L'amitié intertextuelle: Gournay, La Boétie, et Montaigne." *L'esprit et la lettre: Mélanges offerts à Jules Brody*. Tübingen: Gunter Narr, 1991: 57-68.

Roelker, Nancy. *Queen of Navarre: Jeanne d'Albret*. Cambridge, MA: Harvard UP, 1968.

Rojas, Fernando de. *La Celestina*. Ed. Julio Cejador y Frauca. Madrid: Espasa Calpe, 1963.

Romera-Navarro, Miguel. "Las disfrazadas de varón en la comedia." *Hispanic Review* 2.4 (1932): 269-286.

Ronsard, Pierre de. *Oeuvres complètes*. Ed. Paul Laumonier. Paris: Nizet, 1968.

Rosenthal, Margaret. *The Honest Courtesan: Veronica Franco, Citizen and Writer in Sixteenth-Century Venice*. Chicago: U of Chicago P, 1992.

Saenger, Paul. "Silent Reading: Its Impact on Late Medieval Script and Society." *Viator* 13 (1982): 367-414.

Sarolli, Gian Roberto. "Noterella Biblica sui sette P." *Studi Danteschi* 34 (1957): 217-22.

Saslow, James M. *Ganymede in the Renaissance: Homosexuality in Art and Society*. New Haven: Yale UP, 1986.

Schaber, Bennet. "The Aesthetics of Deception: Giotto in the Text of Boccaccio." *Postmodernism Across the Ages: Essays for a Postmodernity That Wasn't Born Yesterday*. Eds. Bill Readings and Bennet Schaber. Syracuse: Syracuse UP, 1993. 47-62.

Schapiro, Meyer. "Leonardo and Freud: An Art-Historical Study." *Journal of the History of Ideas* 7 (1956): 147-78.

Schiesari, Juliana. "In Praise of Virtuous Women? For a Genealogy of Gender Morals in Renaissance Italy." *Women's Voices in Italian Literature*. Eds. Rebecca West and Dino Cervigni. Special issue of *Annali d'Italianistica* 7 (1989): 66-87.

Schiesari, Juliana. *The Gendering of Melancholia: Feminism, Psychoanalysis, and the Symbolics of Loss in Renaissance Literature*. Ithaca: Cornell UP, 1992.

Schlossman, Beryl. "From La Boétie to Montaigne: The Place of the Text." *MLN* 98 (1983): 891-908.

Schochet, Gordon. "Patriarchalism, Politics and Mass Attitudes in Stuart England." *The Historical Journal* 12.3 (1969): 413-41.

Schochet, Gordon. *Patriarchalism and Political Thought*. Oxford: Basil Blackwell, 1975.

Scott, Joan. *Gender and the Politics of History*. New York: Columbia University Press, 1988.

Screech, M.A. *Ecstasy and the Praise of Folly*. London: Duckworth, 1980.

Serpieri, Allessandro, ed. *Shakespeare: la nostalgia dell'essere*. Parmi: Pratiche, 1985.

Shakespeare, William. *The Riverside Shakespeare*. Ed. G. Blakemore Evans. Boston: Houghton Mifflin, 1974.

Shakespeare, William. *As You Like It*. Arden edition. Ed. Agnes Latham. London: Methuen, 1975.

Shakespeare, William. *The Complete Works: Original-Spelling Edition*. Eds. Stanley Wells and Gary Taylor. Oxford: Clarendon, 1986.

Shakespeare, William. *Troilus and Cressida*. Ed. Kenneth Muir. Oxford: Oxford UP, 1984.

Sharrett, Peter. "The Imaginary City of Bernard Salomon." *Intellectual Life in Renaissance Lyon*. Eds. Philip Ford and Gillian Jondorf. Cambridge: Cambridge French Colloquia, 1993. 33-48.

Shemek, Deanna. *Ladies Errant: Gender and Politcal Order in the Age of Ariosto*. Durham: Duke UP, forthcoming.

Silverman, Kaja. "Liberty, Maternity, Commodification." *new formations* 5 (1988): 69-89.

Singleton, Charles S., ed. *Commentary. Purgatorio. Dante*. Princeton: Princeton UP, 1973.

Sofia, Zoe. "Exterminating Fetuses: Abortion, Disarmament, and the Sexo-Semiotics of Extraterrestrialism." *Diacritics* 14 (1984): 47-59.

Sophocles. *Ajax*. Ed. W.B. Stanford. London: Macmillan, 1963.

Southern, R.W. *The Making of The Middle Ages*. New Haven: Yale UP, 1953.

Spackman, Barbara. *"Inter musam et ursam moritur*: Folengo and the Gaping 'Other' Mouth." Migiel and Schiesari 1991, 19-34.

Spelman, Elizabeth. *Inessential Woman: Problems of Exclusion in Feminist Thought*. Boston: Beacon, 1988.

Spencer, T.J. "The Decline of Hamlet." *Hamlet: Stratford-Upon-Avon Studies 5*. New York: St. Martin's, 1964. 185-99.

Spenser, Edmund. *The Faerie Queene*. 2 vols. Ed. J.C. Smith. Oxford: Clarendon, 1909.

Stallybrass, Peter. "Patriarchal Territories: The Body Enclosed." Ferguson, Quilligan, and Vickers 123-42.

Stallybrass, Peter and Allon White. *The Politics and Poetics of Transgression*. Ithaca: Cornell UP, 1986.

Stanton, Domna, ed. *Discourses of Sexuality from Aristotle to AIDS*. Ann Arbor: U of Michigan P, 1992.

Starobinski, Jean. "Montaigne: Des morts exemplaires à la vie sans exemple." *Critique* 24 (1968): 923-35.

Starobinski, Jean. *L'Oeil vivant*. Paris: Gallimard, 1969.

Starobinski, Jean. *Montaigne en Mouvement*. Paris: Gallimard, 1982.

Stierle, Karlheinz. "L'histoire comme Exemple, l'exemple comme Histoire." *Poétique* 3 (1972): 176-98.

Stock, Brian. *The Implications of Literacy: Written Language and Models of Interpretation in the Eleventh and Twelfth Centuries*. Princeton: Princeton UP, 1983.

Stock, Brian. *Listening for the Text: On the Uses of the Past*. Baltimore: Johns Hopkins UP, 1990.

Stone, Donald. "Death in the Third Book." *L'Esprit Créateur* 8 (1968): 185-93.

Stubbes, Phillip. *Anatomie of Abuses*. London, 1583.

The Tale of Gamelyn. Ed. Walter W. Skeat. Oxford: Clarendon, 1893.

Tasso, Torquato. *Aminta*. Milano: Rizzoli, 1976.

Tenenti, Alberto. *La Vie et la mort à travers l'art du XVIe siècle.* Paris: Armand Colin, 1952.

Tenenti, Alberto. *Il Senso della morte e l'amore della vita nel Rinascimento (Francia e Italia).* Turin: Einaudi, 1957.

Thomas, Keith. *Religion and the Decline of Magic.* New York: Scribner's, 1971.

Thomas, Vivian. *The Moral Universe of Shakespeare's Problem Plays.* London: Croom Helm, 1987.

Tillyard, E.M.W. *Shakespeare's History Plays.* London: Chatto and Windus, 1944.

Tillyard, E.M.W. *Shakespeare's Problem Plays.* 1950. London: Chatto and Windus, 1964.

Todorov, Tzvetan. *La Conquête de l'Amérique.* Paris: Editions du Seuil, 1982.

Torres Naharro, Bartolomé de. *Propaladia.* Madrid: Real Academia Española, 1936.

Turner, Graeme. *British Cultural Studies: An Introduction.* Boston: Unwin Hyman, 1990.

Turner, James G., ed. *Sexuality and Gender in Early Modern Europe: Institutions, Texts, Images.* Cambridge: Cambridge UP, 1993.

Turner, Victor. *The Forest of Symbols.* Ithaca: Cornell UP, 1967.

Ubersfeld, Anne. *Lire le théâtre.* Paris: Sociales, 1978.

d'Urfé, Honoré. *L'Astrée.* Tran. S. Rendall. Binghamton, NY: SUNY, 1995.

Vance, Eugene. *Reading* The Song of Roland. Engelwood Cliffs: Prentice-Hall, 1970.

Vicente, Gil. *Obras dramáticas castellanas.* Ed. Thomas R. Hart. Madrid: Espasa Calpe, 1962.

Vickers, Nancy. "Diana Described: Scattered Woman and Scattered Rhyme." *Critical Inquiry* 8 (1981): 265-79.

Vickers, Nancy. "'The Blazon of Sweet Beauty's Best': Shakespeare's *Lucrece.*" *Shakespeare and the Question of Theory.* Parker and Hartman 96-116.

Villey, Pierre. *Les Sources et l'évolution des Essais de Montaigne.* 2 vols. 1908. Paris: Hachette, 1933.

Vovelle, Michel. *Mourir autrefois.* Paris: Gallimard, 1974.

Waswo, Richard. *Language and Meaning in the Renaissance.* Princeton: Princeton UP, 1987.

Weller, Barry. "The Rhetoric of Friendship in Montaigne's *Essais.*" *New Literary History* 9 (1978): 503-23.

Whigham, Frank. *Ambition and Privilege: The Social Tropes of Elizabethan Courtesy Theory.* Berkeley: U of California P, 1984.

266 / Works Cited

Whitfield, J. H. Introduction. Battista Guarini. *Il Pastor Fido [The Faithful Shepherd]*. Edinburgh: Edinburgh UP, 1976. 1-43.

Wiesener, Mary. "Women's Defense of their Public Role." *Women in the Middle Ages and the Renaissance: Literary and Historical Perspectives*. Ed. Mary Beth Rose. Syracuse: Syracuse UP, 1986. 1-27.

Wilson, Katharina M., ed. *Women Writers of the Renaissance and Reformation*. Athens: U of Georgia P, 1987.

Wilson, R. Rawdon. "Narrative Reflexivity in Shakespeare." *Poetics Today* 10 (1989): 771-91.

Wilson, R. Rawdon. "Shakespeare's Narrative: The Craft of Bemazing Ears." *Shakespeare Jahrbuch* 125 (1989): 85-102.

Wilson, R. Rawdon. "Character-Worlds in *Pale Fire*." *Bakhtin and The Languages of The Novel: Evaluations, Reconsiderations*. Special issue of *Studies in The Literary Imagination* 23 (1990): 77-98.

Wilson, R. Rawdon. "Narrative Boundaries in Shakespeare's Plays." *Canadian Review of Comparative Literature / Revue Canadienne de Littérature Comparée* 18.2-3 (1991): 233-61.

Wind, Edgar. *Pagan Mysteries in the Renaissance*. London: Faber & Faber, 1958.

Wind, Edgar. *Pagan Mysteries in the Renaissance*. Harmondsworth: Penguin, 1967.

Wright, Thomas. *The Passions of the Minde*. London, 1601.

Wyatt-Brown, Bertram. *Southern Honor: Ethics and Behavior in the Old South*. New York: Oxford UP, 1982.

Yoder, R.A. "'Sons and Daughters of the Game': An Essay on Shakespeare's *Troilus and Cressida*." *Shakespeare Studies* 25 (1972): 11-25.

CONTRIBUTORS

Keir Elam, who has taught at the University of Florence, teaches at the University of Pisa. He has published widely in Renaissance studies and in drama. Among his books are *The Semiotics of Theatre and Drama* (1980) and *Shakespeare's Universe of Discourse: Language Games in the Comedies* (1984).

Katy Emck has studied at Oxford and Alberta and is a member of the Institute for Historical Research in London. In addition to having published several articles in Renaissance studies, she has written on theory. Her present research interest is in the relation between gender and genre among Renaissance women writers in Italy, France, and England.

Carla Freccero teaches at the University of California at Santa Cruz. She has contributed essays to important collections on the Renaissance and is the author of *Father Figures: Genealogy and Narrative Structure in Rabelais* (1991). In 1994, she edited (with Louise Fradenburg) *Premodern Sexualities in Europe*, a special issue of *GLQ*.

Thomas M. Greene, Yale University, has published many distinguished essays and books in Renaissance studies. Among these works are *Rabelais, A Study in Comic Courage* (1970), *The Light in Troy: Imitation and Discovery in the Renaissance* (1982), and *The Vulnerable Text: Essays on Renaissance Literature* (1986).

Jonathan Hart has been a Visiting Fellow or Visiting Scholar at Toronto, Harvard, and Cambridge. His books include *Theater and World: The Problematics of Shakespeare's History* (1992), *Northrop Frye: The Theoretical Imagination* (1994), and (edited with Richard Bauman) *Explorations in Difference: Law, Culture and Politics* (1995).

Harry Levin taught at Harvard for many years. He was an influential editor and critic and produced seminal works like *The Overreacher: A Study of Christopher Marlowe* (1952), *Shakespeare and the Revolution of the Times; Perspectives and Commentaries* (1976), *Playboys and Killjoys: An Essay on the Theory and Practice of Comedy* (1987).

Edward Milowicki is Professor of English Literature and Chair of the Department at Mills College. He has written on medieval mysticism, Chaucer, Ovid, Malory, and Chrétien de Troyes. He has published essays on the problem of "character" in early modern European literature. His co-authored essay, "Ovid Through Shakespeare: The Divided Self," will appear in *Poetics Today*. "Ovid's Shadow: Character and Characterization in Early Modern Literature" will appear in *Neohelicon*.

Paul Morrison teaches in the Department of English at Brandeis University in Boston. His critical and theoretical interests range widely from Shakespeare through Wallace Stevens to Paul de Man. His essays have appeared in distinguished journals like *Representations*.

Lisa Neal teaches French at the University of Puget Sound in Oregon. She writes on early modern women writers, first-person narrative, and problems of death and writing in the Renaissance. Her translation of Helisenne de Crenne's *Les Angoysses douloureuses qui procedent d'amours* is being published by the University of Minnesota Press. She is currently working on a book on "last words" in early modern culture.

Steven Rendall teaches French and Comparative Literature at the University of Oregon. He is also editor of *Comparative Literature*. His recent publications include a book on Montaigne (Oxford University Press) and a translation of Honoré d'Urfé's *L'Astrée*.

Robert Rawdon Wilson has been a Visiting Fellow or Visiting Professor in Australia, the United States, and Denmark. He has published many essays and books, such as *In Palamedes' Shadow: Explorations in Play, Game and Narrative Theory* (1990) and *Shakespearean Narrative* (1995).

Richard A. Young, Chair of Modern Languages and Comparative Studies at University of Alberta, has published widely on Spanish literature. His *Ocxtaedro en cuartro Tiempos: Texto y Tiempo en un Libro de Cortázar* appeared in 1993.

INDEX